ONE ~,,... --

Alex Christou is a writer, freelance journalist, and communications consultant. He has had articles published by The Scotsman and on www.evo.co.uk.

Alex has a BA (Hons) in Corporate Communication from Aberdeen Business School, at the Robert Gordon University, and an MSc in Cultural Studies from University of Edinburgh. After 15 years in Scotland he is now based in London.

You can follow Alex at www.twitter.com/alchristou and see photos and videos from his adventures behind the wheel at www.irresponsiblecitizen.com.

ALEX CHRISTOU

ONE CAREFUL OWNER

A journey from daydreamer to car enthusiast

This book is dedicated to Rita, Kathy and Alasdair.

Without you it wouldn't have been written.

Acknowledgements

I would like to thank all those people that directly or in-directly supported the writing of this book. In particular Charles Morgan, Gildo Pastor, Lord Mexborough, Russ Malkin and Juergen Obermann for taking the time to speak with me about their love for cars and driving, and Eamonn Vincent and Hannah Shakespeare for taking time to provide constructive feedback.

Finally, thank you to the many car enthusiasts that I have connected with through Twitter. You have shown me what it really means to be a petrolhead.

"The fundamental symbolism of the car is both complex and inescapable. It conjures up images of speed, excitement and vitality. At the same time it communicates a sense of cosy seclusion – a womb-like refuge. Its potential deadliness gives it an air of aggression while its power and shape endows it with a sense of sexual potency. It is precisely because the car can communicate such a variety of messages that it has captured our imagination. As if this were not enough, we have provided the automobile with the potential for communicating a second set of messages. These are to do with style and class, status, elegance and personal taste. This combination of both types of symbols makes the car the most psychologically expressive object that has so far been devised." (Marsh and Collett, *Driving Passion: the psychology of the car*)

Contents

Prologue

I think that every journey has a moment, however fleeting, during which you suddenly find yourself reflecting on how you got there and whether you had really thought things through properly in the first place.

I can't remember how many times I questioned my sanity over the 12 month period during which I sought to embrace a latent passion for cars and driving but one moment stands out quite vividly, even though it lasted for no more than a second or two.

Spencer was driving. He was pushing hard as the road cut and carved down the hillside, the look of concentration on his face masking considerable excitement. For years we had dreamt of taking an unforgettable road trip in an unforgettable car and now we were living that dream. The combination of challenging mountain passes and the raucous V8-engined Ferrari F355 Berlinetta meant that, so far, this trip was living up to our expectations. The car had been given a thorough workout already that day as we powered from Zurich towards the Italian border with the aim of experiencing some of Europe's greatest driving roads. Trees, rocks and sheer drops lined the ribbon of tarmac that we were following. An experienced driver and a good friend, Spencer had been the obvious choice for co-driver on this section of the journey.

He was someone that I could trust to make the most of the opportunity without putting our lives at risk. Or so I thought.

The Flüela Pass was behind us now. The snow-lined mountain roads had been temporarily replaced by lush green valleys as we made our way to the Italian border and a date with the renowned Stelvio Pass. It seemed as though we had the road to ourselves and Spencer was making the most of it. Every time the revs climbed the noise from the Ferrari's engine would smash the Alpine tranquillity; a screaming red dart flying across the landscape. By now the engine was hot and the brakes were squealing and slightly faded from numerous high-speed stops, one required each time we approached a corner and prepared to fling ourselves off towards the next. The speed and noise were addictive but the roads themselves would take no prisoners. Too much exuberance would be foolish up here.

We were about to be reminded of that as the road opened up in front of us, gently drifting right and downhill before what looked like a short, sweeping left-hand corner. Spencer was in good rhythm. He dabbed the brakes to take off some speed as we approached the turn but as the balance of the car shifted and we started pulling left, it became clear that the corner had a double apex and was both longer and tighter than it had first appeared. Realising that we were carrying too much speed, Spencer came off the throttle and touched the brakes again midway through the turn, something that had the potential to unbalance the mid-engined car and catapult us off the road. The waning brakes locked-up, just for a moment, wresting almost complete control of the car from Spencer as the tumbling hillside and evergreen trees loomed to our right. Spencer quickly shifted down a gear, the pitch of the engine rising sharply as he got back on the power, the superb mechanical grip of the car and its hot tyres pulling us back on line, around the corner and onto the next straight. Spencer and I glanced briefly at each other in recognition of the potentially deadly moment.

"Try not to do that again mate," I said, as we both tried to calm the brief hit of adrenaline that was coursing through our veins.

I settled back into my seat and looked out of the window as the scenery zipped by. I couldn't help but smile despite what had just happened. I was exhilarated by the whole experience and I knew that there was more to come.

If you are a car enthusiast then you probably need no explanation as to what I was doing on that mountain road in the first place. It's probably the kind of trip that you have already taken or are planning to take soon. For car enthusiasts there is something elemental about driving. It can be the feeling of the wind in your hair, the surge of acceleration, or simply the feeling of freedom that comes with being on the road. The relationship between man and machine is a complex one but the simple fact is that driving a great car on a great road feels really good.

The simple pleasure of driving aside, it was an innocuous question from my uncle that finally pushed me to live out my motoring dreams. We were catching up over lunch in north London and the topic had moved from family matters on to cars and driving, Eamonn being well aware that I had a propensity to change my cars on a regular basis.

"Is motoring as we know it dying?" Eamonn asked me, as he reached for another piece of calamari and I battled with wrapping some spaghetti around my fork. "Is the iconic image of a classic sports car being enjoyed out on the open road under threat?"

These were big questions and the truth was that I didn't have the answers, even if it was obvious that things were changing in the world of motoring. That much was clear to anyone. Rising petrol prices, rising insurance costs, poorly surfaced roads, and increasingly restrictive environmental and safety regulations were having a huge impact. Even those magazines dedicated to performance cars seemed to have admitted defeat, editors having come to realise that fuel efficiency had become just as important as top speed to even the most committed petrolhead.

We discussed some of these issues, finished lunch and then said our farewells but Eamonn's question stuck with me as I made my way home. Despite my reticence to keep cars for very long, mostly out of a desire to experience as many different cars as possible, I had never quite gotten around to embracing the latent petrolhead within. It always seemed too easy to put off doing motoring activities, particularly when very few of my close friends had any real interest in cars. I had always thought that there would be plenty of time to tick off my varied motoring ambitions but it suddenly occurred to me that that might not be the case. Was Eamonn onto something? Was time running out for people like me to really enjoy driving as we knew it? And what of that image of the classically-styled sports car, tearing along a mountain road in the sunshine, its raspy exhaust note bouncing off the hillside as the driver nails the perfect gear change, petrol fumes lingering in the air? The way things were going it seemed quite possible that this traditional driving experience might soon be consigned to motoring nostalgia, only to be enjoyed by enthusiasts at revival events and classic car shows. Future generations would come to know – and no doubt love – a different kind of motoring but today's car enthusiasts would be left reminiscing about the good old days, no longer able to enjoy driving as they had come to know it.

It might seem a little melodramatic but ongoing developments to the cars that we drive and limitations as to how we drive them really will have a lasting impact for all motorists, even if it will be the driving purists and motoring aesthetes that are most upset by this. Once you start to understand the reasons behind these changes it becomes clear that we are on a slippery slope towards greater regulation on the roads and increasing automation of most road vehicles. Take design, for example. There are some truly gorgeous modern cars out there but they rarely compare to their diminutive ancestors in the size stakes. Many supercars are now comically oversized and unsuitable for driving on all but the widest roads. There might be handling benefits associated with extra track width for the highest performing cars but safety legislation means that even humble family cars need to have crash zones to protect occupants and pedestrians. This means new cars are invariably much bigger and more unwieldy.

And what about that raspy exhaust note that is so characteristic of performance cars? For many enthusiasts, the unique sound of a Porsche flat-six or a Ferrari V8 engine is part of the appeal of the car. Sadly that will soon be replaced by bespoke engine sounds created in music studios and then piped through your car stereo speakers as you drive. The current BMW M5 does exactly that, while many other companies already tune the exhaust note to some degree. For some people that will be preferable to the relative silence associated with the growing number of electric cars on our roads but surely it is only a matter of time before they are offered with customisable soundtracks. Maybe it will one day be possible to have a Toyota Prius that sounds like a Lamborghini. I, for one, don't look forward to the day when cars are as annoying as novelty mobile phone ringtones.

More worrying are the numerous technological developments that are slowly taking control away from the driver. The most obvious of these is the demise of the manual gearbox. There is certainly a time and a place for an automatic, particularly in town and during motorway driving, but many sports car manufacturers seem to be making a more permanent shift away from even providing a manual option. It is true to say that those systems which allow drivers to change gear using paddles behind the steering wheel have improved significantly, providing at least some involvement in the gear-changing process and allowing relentless progress to be made while both hands are kept on the steering wheel. However, the effective manipulation of a good manual gearbox has long been one of driving's greatest pleasures and it is a worry to see that companies like Ferrari no longer offer the option, with many other manufacturers appearing to be following their lead.

It's not just the gearboxes that are being drawn into the digital age. There are now a number of cars on the market with options that would seem more at home in science fiction films. Cars can now parallel park themselves, monitor their position within motorway lanes, steer without driver input to maintain the appropriate line, and slow down and speed up according to whether there is traffic in front or not. This means that, in the most straightforward of driving situations, there are already cars out there that can pilot themselves without much need for human input. There are other cars in development that can use radars, sensors and GPS information to navigate once a destination has been set. These cars are already legal in some states in the US. This doesn't bode well. Aside from the fact that this will make journeys much more boring for those that enjoy the actual process of driving, consider the implications for insurance.

Some insurance companies are now insisting on the installation of so-called 'black boxes' in the cars of new drivers. These devices use GPS and G-force technology to monitor speed, braking behaviour, acceleration, cornering and other usage statistics. The idea is that insurance companies can provide bespoke policies based upon the way that each driver uses the car, penalising them for driving in a spirited manner or using the car during busier times of the day. How long will it be until all modern cars come with these black boxes fitted as standard and drivers are penalised by their insurers if they don't make full use of all the automated driving features of their car? The danger is that soon we might reach a point where many of us cannot afford *not* to let the car do the driving.

Before I start to sound like some kind of motoring doomsayer, I should point out that there are some positives to these developments. Thankfully, new construction technologies and a bigger drive towards weight-saving means that cars are actually starting to get lighter again. This is one result of the stricter emissions policies that are forcing manufacturers to make cars more efficient, thankfully providing some help in offsetting horrifically high fuel prices. Most importantly, improved construction and safety features mean that the roads are getting safer and that drivers, passengers and pedestrians have a much greater chance of survival should there be an accident.

Changes to car production and motoring legislation aside, we are constantly being bombarded with lists of things that we must do before we die. Car enthusiasts are not spared from this. In magazines, on television and on the internet, we are regularly told how exciting it is to drive certain cars or being fed ideas for 'must-do' driving experiences. "50 car things to do before you die." "The 10 roads you must drive before you die." Even on web forums you can regularly find car enthusiasts discussing which cars they most want to drive before they die (invariably the McLaren F1 or Ferrari F40). But what if we don't have a lifetime to enjoy these things?

It was during a quiet moment as I sat in my office back up in Aberdeen that I decided to make some changes in my life before mortgages, marriages and children got in the way, and before motoring had changed beyond recognition. I had known that the enviable exploits of motoring journalists might one day get the better of me and I would be forced to emulate some of their epic feature stories, but now I was pushed by a fear that time might not be on my side after all.

The plan was simple. I would leave my Corporate Communications job in the oil and gas industry. I would leave Aberdeen and move south to London. I would make time to take a pilgrimage of sorts, a personal journey that would finally allow me to stand proud as a *bona fide* petrolhead.

It is a journey that would take me thousands of miles around Europe and the UK to find some of the best driver's roads. It would allow me to drive on track for the first time and take on the legendary Nürburgring. It would also give me an opportunity to meet some true car enthusiasts and hear some untold stories from their lives. I would come to understand what it is like to live with a 90s supercar and catch a glimpse of the future of motoring. Most importantly, at least for the sake of my finances and the sanity of my loved ones, it is a journey that would allow me to understand just how important cars are to me.

The Frozen North

Goodbye Aberdeen

I looked through the blinds of my office window and out over the internal atrium for one last time. The skylight above showed the sky already to be pitch black, snow visible around the bottom edge of the glass and hinting at sub-zero temperatures outside.

My simple office had been packed up, all traces of my having inhabited it now removed, boxed up, or thrown away. I had said my farewells, even given my cafetière to a colleague with whom I used to enjoy mid-morning coffee and office gossip. Now it was time to put on my scarf and gloves and make my way out into the abrasive Aberdeen air, load up my car and head to the airport. A day earlier I wasn't even sure if I would be able to make it down to London for Christmas due to all the snow which was clogging up Aberdeen – the so-called Granite City. Flights and trains had been sporadically cancelled and so I had lined up three options, just in case. All was looking well for tonight's journey. If not, I would call on plans B and C and take another plane or train the next morning.

The car park was almost empty except for a few snow-dusted cars that sat scattered across the white surface and the vague outlines of industrial equipment just about visible on the edges of the darkness. It was for days like these that I had bought a Volkswagen Golf R32, the four-wheel drive hatchback replacing the Porsche Boxster S that had let me down the previous winter. That Christmas it had got stuck in the snow at my family home for six weeks and I was reliant upon my ex-girlfriend for lifts to work. With no girlfriend to rely on, this winter that was not an option. I felt pleased with myself for having predicted the hard winter and having made the decision to change cars in the autumn, my decision seemingly vindicated as I settled into the sculpted driver's seat which began gently warming up beneath me as the windscreen defrosted.

The journey across the city was dull but thankfully uneventful and I was soon being ushered onto the plane that was to carry me in comfort down to London, to my family and friends. A plane at night is a wonderful place for reflection, the hum of the engines and the dense blackness outside somehow cocooning you and providing sustenance for your thoughts. It had been 16 years since I had first moved to Scotland as a 13 year-old, fairly reluctantly it must be said. I had grown to love it in many ways. I had been to school there, studied there, worked there. Scotland, the place that seemed so foreign to me as a teenager, had come to act as the backdrop to all the significant experiences and opportunities of my life.

I thought about my job, my steady career as an in-house corporate communications professional that I had thrown away, for now at least. I might never have felt passionate about the oil and gas industry in the way that many of my colleagues did but I still wanted to make a difference within my realm of influence. I had come to respect many of the people I worked with and would miss seeing them on a regular basis. I was particularly touched by the kind words of support and encouragement that many had given me when they discovered I was leaving. It was the first time that they had shared something real, something non-work-related about their views on life and it seemed a shame that it was only to come at the end.

I thought about Rita and the date that we had made for the following evening. Thankfully I was going to make it and with Aberdeen rapidly fading from view it felt as though she and I might have a chance of starting a real relationship. The first time I had asked her out some years earlier there was no chance. As soon as she had agreed to go out with me I had to return to my life in Scotland and by the time I saw her again we had both found ourselves involved with other people. This time would be different, even if I would have to mask that I was just as excited about spending time with her as I was about my new start in London.

I thought about my friends and the many activities and get-togethers that I had missed over the years, opportunities that I would be *in situ* for from now on. It seemed to be a time when everyone was getting married or scattering to far flung corners of the globe. It felt like the days of getting together with mates for drinks and meals, conversation and laughter, were under threat. I wanted a piece of the action before it was too late and I wanted to be nearby in case any random last minute trips to the Alps or the Balearics came up. Maybe next time there was a photo of some grinning idiots posing in vintage ski gear I would be leading the charge.

Finally, as the plane pitched downwards and we closed in on the millions of twinkling lights that make up London at night, I began to think about cars. Years of marvelling at magazine articles about Lamborghinis tearing across the snow-lined Alps, tales of Ferraris being driven to or from the factory at Maranello in Italy, and stories about Porsches tackling the Nürburgring had taken their toll on my motoring ambitions. I loved the way that the best journalists were always able to put me in the driver's seat through their words. What are the interior materials like? Does it have a starter button or do you simply turn the key? What does it *feel* like to drive the car? That's what I wanted to know. The stories that stuck in my mind were always reinforced by impossibly vivid images that conveyed perfectly the movement and dynamism of the world's most desirable cars driven on roads that I could only dream of. Even stories that originated closer to home, such as those about supercars taking on the TT course on the Isle of Man with its derestricted speed limits or enjoying the near-deserted roads of the Scottish Highlands, seemed epic and glamorous. The more I read, the more I wanted to emulate these journeys but I rarely made any effort to organise anything. In truth, I was nothing more than a daydreamer and I wanted to change that, especially as I came to realise that others out there were making the effort to live out their motoring fantasies. I only had to pick up a magazine or log-on to a web forum to see people writing about their road trips and the track days and rallies they were taking part in. These were the real car enthusiasts, the petrolheads that were proactively engaging with the wonderful world of motoring. By contrast I had become an armchair enthusiast; a car lover able to recite what I had picked up in magazines but with little first-hand experience. I had never driven on a track, I had never visited the Ferrari factory and I had never owned a classic car.

Now I was going to grab the bull by the horns and change all that. I had given myself a year out to focus on some freelance communication projects, so as long as I was sensible with time and money I could theoretically take a day here and there to do 'car things'. I would have the chance to drive the roads I had always wanted to drive, drive some of my dream cars and engage with some real petrolheads. I would even get to see a little more of the world. I didn't want to be the kind of person who ignored their interests anymore, the kind of person that would always play it safe. I just needed to come up with an action plan and convince my family and friends, who had all been supportive of my decision to leave Aberdeen, that I wasn't wasting my time and money as part of an early mid-life crisis. In fact, I probably needed to convince myself of that first and then rope one or two of them into some of these adventures.

The Influence of Location

A meeting with Gildo Pastor

It was mid-April by the time that any of my plans came together. I had been getting a little carried away with London life. Professional and motoring ambitions were slowed as a result of excessive socialising and the simple challenges of finding my feet in a city I only knew in parts. Thankfully my 'networking' paid off and I found myself heading to Monaco to meet local businessman Gildo Pastor. It had been explained to me that Gildo was a car enthusiast and former racing driver who had bought French car company Venturi Automobiles and turned it into a manufacturer of electric vehicles. I was intrigued to find out more about the shift in his passion for motoring.

The plans for my weekend in Monaco had come together nicely. Not only would I be meeting Gildo but I had also lined up a meeting with Juergen Obermann, the founder of a new car club which was due to launch at the Top Marques car show. I had also arranged to drive a Bentley Continental GTC along the Col de Vence, a road that wriggles up and over the hills that overlook Nice and one that had played a supporting role in a good number of feature articles I had read in car magazines over the years. I had even lured Spencer out for a couple of days with the promise of beautiful cars, good food and sunshine. All in all it promised to be a good trip.

People have very mixed opinions of Monaco. They either love it or hate it. They love the weather, the glamour, the buzz. They hate the prices, find it ostentatious, think it devoid of culture. Like everything, it is a matter of taste but the time of year that you visit can affect your perception wildly. Visit for the first time in the summer months and hang around the casinos and it can feel like a tourist trap; it becomes a voyeuristic environment where day visitors come to look at how 'the other half' live, to be awestruck by wealth. You might look at the 'touristy' things to do and find them to be limited to the exotic gardens or oceanographic museum. Dig a little deeper, spend some time there living like a resident and you will find greater depth. I love it.

Aside from the fact that Monaco is clean, easy to get around and also quite friendly, it is also a petrolhead's paradise. It is a place where there are a great many car lovers with the means to live their motoring dreams. You can find yourself gawping at the latest Ferrari only for the driver to give an appreciative pump of the throttle pedal before blasting off down the road. You will see cars parked up outside hotels that you will never see again in your life due to their rarity. Many of the best examples vie for one of the few parking spaces around the hotels and casinos that line the iconic Place du Casino – the Hotel de Paris, the Hotel Metropole and the legendary Casino de Monte-Carlo. That is enough of a draw for many visitors to the principality, most choosing to sit at the ideally-placed Café de Paris to engage in some people and car watching.

The morning of the meeting I made an early start for the Gildo Pastor Centre. The sun was already glinting off the Mediterranean as I made my way along the deserted streets to the bus stop, flashes of bright blue appearing between the buildings. I arrived some 20 minutes early for my 8am meeting and explained to the security guard about the appointment. Apparently Monsieur Pastor had not yet arrived but yes, I could take a seat in the vast, marble-floored lobby. As I sat on one of the correspondingly vast grey, crescent-shaped sofas and watched the office workers make their way in, through the lobby, past the two fountains and off to their offices beyond, I glanced at my notebook and realised that I knew very little about Gildo Pallanca Pastor despite having undertaken some research back in the UK.

He was born in Monaco in 1967 and is described on the Venturi website as being a 'serial entrepreneur'. At the age of 19 he took over the project management for the construction of the Gildo Pastor Center; a building not named after him, as I had assumed, but after his grandfather who had started developing property in Monaco in the 1930s. The elder Gildo Pastor was responsible for developing key areas of the city, such as that around Avenue Princesse Grace which lines the seafront. The Pastor name has since become synonymous with construction and real estate in Monaco, something that you can't help but notice as you travel around the city; the signs, adverts and estate agencies are difficult to miss. In 1986 Gildo became involved in the management of his family's real estate assets and also began participating in numerous capital risk and investment ventures. He began racing cars at around the same time, something that continued for 12 years, and in 2001 he bought little-known French car maker Venturi Automobiles and turned it into a manufacturer of electric vehicles.

I looked up from my notes to see the security guard standing by an open door and gesturing for me to follow him. We left the lobby and made our way upstairs to a deserted hallway, the security guard explaining that I would have to wait while Gildo finished a phone call. It seemed as though we were the only people in this section of the building, the executive suite I guessed. At 8.00am exactly, the door flew open and Gildo Pastor appeared, dressed casually in jeans and shirt. He shook my hand and apologised for having kept me waiting, before ushering me into his office.

"To understand what is wrong with me, we have to start right here in Monaco," he began, pointing me to a chair and then picking up the phone to request coffee and some *pain au chocolats.*

From an early age Gildo fell under the spell of Monaco. As any young boy would be, he was drawn in by the beautiful cars that would cruise the streets and he was bowled over by the annual spectacle of the Formula 1 Grand Prix that would flood the town with sound, colour and excitement. Of course things were different back then; you could touch the F1 cars and even sit in them. In the days before such stringent health and safety rules it was possible for Gildo and his friends to climb the trees that lined the circuit and watch the cars whizz by like bullets below.

With this influence it is perhaps little surprise that Gildo grew up wanting to race cars, so that's exactly what he did. It was never a full-time profession for him but he raced in the Renault Cup and Porsche Supercup series, even driving the Monaco circuit on three different occasions. He raced in the Daytona 24 Hours and took on the Monte Carlo Rally, as well as racing the rare Bugatti

EB110 with friend and former Formula 1 driver Patrick Tambay. Despite having a full time job in the family business he even found time to break the world speed record for driving on ice. It was in March 1995, at a place called Oulu in northern Finland, that Gildo Pastor drove a Bugatti EB110 SS to an average speed of 184mph on the frozen seas of the Arctic Circle, enough to see the 28 year-old break the world record. The car ran on regular as opposed to spiked tyres, the only modification was some extra weighting to help with grip, and the record stood for 12 years until 2007 when former rally driving champion Juha Kankkunen reached 199.83mph in a Bentley Continental GT.

When he had stopped racing – and true to his 'no nonsense' approach – Gildo decided to buy his own car company. On the car enthusiasm spectrum (if there is such a thing), he seemed about as far away from me as it was possible to get. I hadn't even driven on track yet and this was a guy that had given up racing and graduated to car manufacturing. Thankfully he seemed very grounded and more than happy to share his experiences.

We talked for a while about the Grand Prix which he still attends each year. If his claimed two day recovery period is anything to go by, he parties pretty hard. He tells me how he drove Prince Albert around the circuit in a Venturi Fetish sports car just before the main race a couple of years back and you can sense how much that meant to him; the pride at being able to drive his envi-ronmentally-aware monarch in an electric car that he had built, and excitement at being part of the spectacle.

"It's hard to only watch the race on TV when you live in Monaco," he tells me. "The whole city is so intensely focused on the track. It vibrates. The scream of the first engine in the morning, it's like..." he tails off with a very expressive sigh and gesture that perfectly conveys the point.

If you have even a passing interest in cars it is impossible to think of Monaco without thinking about the Formula 1 Grand Prix. The first Grand Prix was run here in 1929 and it has since become one of the world's most famous races, an event which draws Monaco's inhabitants and visitors into a three day frenzy of noise, excitement and celebration. The Monte Carlo Rally is not to be forgotten though, another local event close to Gildo's heart. It has been running since 1911 and still draws admiring spectators from all over the world. Many of them come to witness cars being thrown around the numerous hairpins that make up the Col de Turini, a mountain road set back from the Riviera and often covered with snow and ice when the event takes place in January. These events have played a huge role in helping to glamorise Monaco, not only for tourists and motorsport fans but for generations of drivers and manufacturers that have come to make their mark on history.

I find myself a little taken aback by how friendly and relaxed Gildo seems. There are spells during which I can simply sit back and sip my coffee while he speaks passionately and intelligently about his relationship with cars, leaning back in his chair with his hands linked behind his head. What's clear is that his passion for cars and driving has evolved over the years, shifting from an interest that culminated in racing and breaking records to a focus on the technological development of electric vehicles. He refers to car enthusiasm as "a disease", something that might start through car ownership, through an interest in racing or through proximity to a race track, before developing from there. In many ways it was racing rather than road cars that had the biggest impact on him, the competition experience providing an opportunity to develop a strong understanding of the mechanical and technical aspects of the cars he was driving. This soon grew into a general "passion for technology", as he calls it. He began financing other technologically-innovative companies before the decision came to manufacture an electric vehicle himself, something which aligns nicely with the environmentally-conscious outlook Prince Albert has promoted in Monaco.

That is why he bought Venturi in 2001. It was a struggling, low-volume French manufacturer that seemed to have spent much of its recent history in and out of bankruptcy. Even so, it had still managed to build a decent following since the company's first car was unveiled at the 1984 Paris Motor Show with the intention of being the only French-manufactured sporting GT car. Within ten years Venturi had managed to produce the fastest French production car ever built – the 400GT – and by the time Gildo bought the company it had run its own 'arrive and drive' racing championship, had a brief foray into Formula 1, and produced a car that was seen as a good alternative to the Lotus Esprit in the Atlantique 300 Biturbo. It had a brief but rich history.

Venturi is a very different company today. It is focused completely on developing and promoting electric vehicle technology. This means that you are unlikely to see one on the road – though it is possible to buy one – but you might read about some of their achievements, such as the all-electric, Venturi-powered Citroen Berlingo that drove from Shanghai to Paris. It shows huge commitment to technology on Gildo's part and perfectly illustrates how far his passion for cars has developed.

"Cars, for me, are purely about business," Gildo tells me when I probe further. "For sure it started as a passion from childhood but I think with everything, if you want to achieve something, then you somehow have to make a business out of it. It's not that I wouldn't love to own a Ferrari F40 for instance but I have to have a car that is built by myself to develop the right level of interest."

Does that mean he doesn't collect cars in any way? His response is typically candid and he admits that part of his current attitude towards cars is a result of him being spoilt when he was younger and being able to get the cars he wanted. Today things are different.

"I have many vehicles. Some have great value and are part of the assets of the company and others have no real value but are very interesting technically-speaking. All of them have an intimate relationship with my work. So it's not really a collection and, in fact, they are parked everywhere in the building; they are not lined up in a garage somewhere as an indicator of wealth or success."

We talk for a little while longer about the cars of the moment and the popularity of kit cars in Britain but, before I go, I'm interested in finding out whether he believes car enthusiasts share any commonality. Afterall, his own interests have shifted a fairly long way since he sat ogling racing cars as a youngster.

"Car enthusiasts, whatever their financial status, are exactly the same. It is like entering a religion. You have your gods; you need to know the history; you need experience; and you need to be introduced to this world." But it is the Brits that have made the biggest impression on him as far as car enthusiasm goes and he proves his point with a story about the Ferrari 126 C2B Formula 1 car.

It was 1983 and Patrick Tambay found himself lined up in third position at the San Marino Grand Prix at Imola in a number 27 Ferrari. He had been drafted in to the team after his good friend and fellow racing driver Gilles Villeneuve had died almost a year earlier. San Marino had been Villeneuve's final race, also in a number 27 Ferrari and also starting in third position. Despite Villenueve holding the lead in that race, his team mate at Ferrari, Didier Pironi, disregarded team orders to slow down and hold formation, instead snatching victory from Villeneuve in the dying moments of the race. Any anger or disappointed was brutally put into perspective when Villeneuve died during qualifying for the Belgian Grand Prix two weeks later.

Emotions were running high for drivers and the fans alike on 1st May 1983. The Ferrari faithful were out in force on home soil and some fans had even painted a Canadian maple leaf on the track the night before the race in memory of Villeneuve. Patrick began to cry when he saw it. Memories of what happened during the race a year earlier and the shock at Villeneuve's death so soon afterwards were still fresh. It was a hard-fought race but Patrick won and later he spoke of feeling that his friend Gilles was with him throughout the race, somehow guiding him to victory and undoing the injustice of the previous year. Ferrari let Patrick keep the car at the end of the season but his wife ended up with it when the couple divorced some years later.

Patrick's former Ferrari 126 C2B would remain tucked away for many years until it came up for auction in Monaco in 1997. Gildo was there with his friend Patrick, the former having sold a car in the morning and the latter eager to see where his old race-winning car would end up. Gildo was taken aback by the price of the Formula 1 car. It was not as expensive as he had imagined and it occurred to him that he was in a position to buy it with the proceeds of the car he had just sold.

"So I buy the car," he tells me. "I find myself owning a Ferrari Formula 1. Great. Fantastic. But I had no desire to actually drive a Formula 1 car. I had never done so before and even though I was racing at the time I was not prepared to do that."

But Patrick was less reticent. It was agreed that he would drive it at a few choice historic events and the car was soon on its way to Ferrari's specialist engineers to be brought back to race-ready condition. The first chance he had to drive it was alongside a number of other classic racing cars at the 1999 Goodwood Festival of Speed. It had been raining all morning and Gildo stood tucked under an umbrella watching as his friend Patrick prepared to race his old Ferrari Formula 1 car once more. But just before the race was due to start the situation changed dramatically. It turned out that Patrick was under some kind of contract with Renault and was forbidden to drive a Ferrari Formula 1 car in public.

"Patrick was very pissed off," Gildo explains. "He hadn't driven his car for almost 20 years. He gets out of the car, looks to me and says, 'You drive it'. So I get in the car, not wearing a racing suit, without shoes but with his helmet and his gloves... and I went for it."

The 1983 Ferrari Formula 1 car was a notoriously powerful, turbocharged car. It was tricky enough to drive in dry conditions due to its spiky power delivery and Gildo was forced to call on his many years of racing experience to tame it. Thankfully he managed to complete the race safely and brought the Imola Grand Prix-winning car over the finish line unscathed.

After the race, as he made his way to the pitlane, Gildo removed his helmet to have a listen to the engine and to catch the lap times which were being announced over the PA system. He was buzzing from this unexpected experience but everyone else was still under the impression that Patrick had been driving, that was clear from the results announcement. Back in the paddock a number of British motorsport fans approached the car and asked Gildo for his autograph, forcing him to declare: "Guys, I'm not Patrick Tambay. I'm no one."

"We know you're not Patrick," one of them responded. "You're Gildo Pastor." It was his autograph that they wanted and looking back now Gildo is still surprised.

"They knew everything! I don't think that there are car enthusiasts like the British anywhere else on Earth."

It would have been nice to have a tour of Gildo's scattered collection of cars but he had to get back to work. I gathered my stuff and went out to feel the warmth of the spring sunshine. Heading back towards Place du Casino from the more business-orientated Fontvielle area of Monaco I reflected on my conversation with Gildo. It really did amaze me how far his interest in cars had shifted. He had enjoyed every opportunity to drive, own and race cars since he was young but now it was clear that his passion was for technology and engineering. The world of motoring might have been changing but the requirement and subsequent demand for more environmentally-friendly vehicles actually provided Gildo with an opportunity that perfectly fitted his evolved interest in cars.

As I sat on the bus gazing out at the changing scenery – luxury yachts, car showrooms, apartment blocks, cave-like tunnels – I couldn't help but think back to the last time I had visited Monaco over Grand Prix weekend. It had been five years earlier but the memories were still vivid in my mind. Looking back, it wasn't hard to understand how the young Gildo Pastor had been so enthralled by the riot of noise and colour, the smell of high octane petrol, and the feeling of excitement that pervaded his home town once a year.

Ear plugs and champagne

Memories of the Monaco Grand Prix

I managed to ignore the increasing regularity of the engine drone, along with my impending hangover, but I was fighting a losing battle on both fronts. It was Sunday 28th May 2006. Spencer and I were in Monaco for the Grand Prix and race day was here.

Spencer and I had originally met through a mutual friend shortly after leaving school and through the years we had become very close. His knowledge of and passion for cars was clear from the very earliest days of our friendship and it soon became a mutual interest. We both wanted to attend the Monaco Grand Prix one day and now, seven years after first meeting, that day had come.

Having arrived two days earlier we had begun to get a feel for the occasion. We had just missed the Friday practice sessions but had enjoyed the lively atmosphere that continued long into the evening. Things begin to escalate on the Saturday, it being qualifying day and many more people flooding into town. There was a build up in tension and apprehension that seemed to engulf the whole principality, a kind of cultural foreplay before the big race. The geography of the town even took on a different shape as the streets were carved up and blocked off around the outline of the racetrack. The streets themselves were abuzz with throngs of people, wealthy and less so, mixing amongst the backdrop of supercars and stunning women. Monaco being Monaco, they say the only way to *really* experience the Grand Prix is from a boat and that was exactly what Spencer and I would be doing for the qualifying sessions and for the race itself. Spencer is not known for doing things half-heartedly but it still came as a huge surprise to me that he had managed to secure an invitation for us to watch the Grand Prix from a yacht. He warned me that the crowd might be quite corporate, most working in finance roles back in the City, but it would take more than that to put me off. My contact book might not have been as big as Spencer's but I had done my part and managed to call in a favour as well. Rather than commuting in each day we would be staying in an apartment directly over the tunnel that forms part of the Grand Prix circuit, running towards the harbour. We would be perfectly placed to enjoy any partying opportunities that might arise in the evenings and be right in the action when we woke up in the mornings. If we had known which boat we were due to be watching the race from, we could probably have spotted it from the balcony of the superbly-located apartment. The harbour is not that big and from the apartment it would only take about 15 minutes to walk to the boat. From there we would enjoy plentiful champagne and a front-row seat to watch the F1 cars hammering past.

Despite the buzz around town, there was still a little less intensity on qualification day than there would turn out to be on race day. People walked around casually in an attempt to get their bearings, not so constrained by the race start time and therefore less rushed. We too fell into this mentality, knowing that we had a big 24 hours ahead of us and choosing to have a slow start to the day.

A simple breakfast on the balcony gave us another chance to survey the scene which somehow appeared more cluttered than when we had arrived the day before. Boats, people and scaffold-based seating areas were scattered around the edges of the harbour where the race track ran, following streets that would normally be used by Renault Twingos and Mercedes SLKs. The engine noise from the tunnel below told us that we wouldn't be able to leave the apartment block from the ground floor. This would normally be the most direct route to the boat, allowing us to cross the road and drop down to the harbour a little further along. The other exit would take us upwards towards Casino Square and would probably add a few more minutes on to our journey.

Emerging in the bright sunshine, sunglasses already in place, it was immediately clear that it was going to be another stunning day. However, it soon occurred to us both that this might not be so straightforward. Our supposedly simple route to the boat was blocked by grandstands, barriers and crowds. Spencer and I stood silent for a second, like rats in some kind of maze-orientated laboratory experiment, before turning right, away from the boat, and trying to cut around the opposite side of Casino Square. The crowds seemed larger now and the surge of movement ebbed and flowed in accordance with the width of the streets. We squeezed through and approached a barrier where an official was stood with the sort of 'don't mess with me' attitude that he must have learnt from the local police.

"Excusez-moi. Parlez-vous Anglais?" I ventured.

"Oui." The response was delivered with expert nonchalance.

"We are trying to get down to the port. Is this the quickest way?" I said, pointing to the barrier he was guarding.

"May I see your tickets?"

Spencer and I looked at each other briefly before Spencer responded, "We are going to be watching from a yacht so we don't have tickets." We hadn't even considered that! Spencer's contact hadn't mentioned anything about getting to the boat, merely a rough location and its name.

The official looked at us properly for the first time. Power was his to be wielded. "Non. I have not the authorisation to allow you inside with no tickets."

Shit. This obviously wasn't going to be plain sailing afterall. The official's gaze now moved beyond us and it was clear that the conversation was over. We protested but it did no good and we were forced to set off again, back into the crowds, heading up hill and further away from the harbour. By now we were beginning to feel the heat as the air temperature rose, even in the shadows. Ten minutes later we still seemed to be moving away from the harbour, trapped on the outside of the race track with no way through. We pressed on, following the track around anticlockwise, buffered by barriers and F1 fans and realising now that we had no time to delve inwards in case our search for another way through was in vain. We were treated to the sight of the occasional beautiful woman of course but we assumed that most of them were bronzing themselves on boats and balconies by now, champagne in hand and a lot more relaxed than we were.

By the time that we reached the next barrier entry point the qualification laps were well under way, the noise from the cars a constant presence in the air around, seemingly urging us to press on as quickly as possible. We both knew now that we should have left much earlier but there was no time to dwell on that. It was Spencer's turn to kick things off this time, starting with the standard "parlez-vous Anglais" of course.

"Can you tell us how we get down to the port please? We are expected on a boat."

"May I see your tickets please?" This official seemed a bit more laid-back but was obviously following the same set of guidelines as his colleague.

We went through the motions again, explaining that we did not have tickets and needed to get down to the boat quickly. We were told that we needed to go to the next checkpoint and speak to them but the official there would probably not help us without a ticket. There was nothing to do but press on, Spencer trying and failing to contact anyone on the boat, their ringtones presumably masked by the engine drone and the sound of popping champagne corks. By now I was cursing my decision to wear flip-flops, footwear seemingly designed neither for comfort nor speed as we ploughed uphill through another crowd of people.

The conversation at the next checkpoint, once we finally got there, followed a familiar pattern though somehow we managed to convince the official that we were not just trying to blag our way in but really were expected on a boat. Just as we were congratulating ourselves and thinking about enjoying a well-earned beer, we found ourselves at yet another barrier. We tried to act cool, nodding and smiling at the guy guarding it and making to walk straight past him as though we belonged there. It seemed he had seen this approach before and stopped us, asking to see tickets. My turn...

"Parlez-vous Anglais?" I use our standard opening line and he nods in response.

"We have just been speaking to your colleague over there", I continue. "We are on our way to one of the boats so tickets are not required. We are expected and we are now late. He said that this is the quickest way. Is that correct?"

As I was hoping, I throw him slightly with the revelation that his colleague had said that we should proceed even though we had no tickets. There was a bit of back and forth and finally the guard let us through. Now, over 90 minutes after we left the apartment we found ourselves approaching the boat, tired, thirsty and sweating. As we got closer we realised that something wasn't quite right.

"Shit. The cars have stopped," I said, turning to Spencer. "No wonder he let us through. We've missed it!"

We clambered onto the back of the boat, did all the necessary introductions, grabbed a drink and proceeded to explain how we missed qualifying. It turned out that the best way to reach a yacht during the Grand Prix was by taking one of the taxi boats which left from some of the beachside hotels on the other side of town. After a couple of beers, refreshed, relaxed and confident with our travel plans for returning the next day, we decided to go back to the apartment and put our feet up before a Saturday night out on the town.

Things got a little messy that night, despite having started off in a sophisticated manner with canapés and cocktails on the balcony. One of Spencer's friends was involved in organising a VIP party and kindly said that we could come as her guests. We were told that it would be *the* place to be, that it would have an open bar, and that it would be flooded with celebrities.

We arrived, already in good spirits and looking suitably like international playboys, only to come across another moody Monegasque man that didn't want to let us pass without tickets, this time a bouncer. Thankfully Spencer's friend wasn't far away and we were soon inside enjoying the end of a small concert as we made our way to the bar, enjoying a bit of subtle celebrity spotting as we went – a Hollywood film star over here, a Brazilian supermodel over there. We got stuck in to the free drinks and tried to strike up conversations with our fellow party-goers, mostly unsuccessfully, though some of us had more luck than others. Just as I was settling into conversation with a nice Greek girl, Spencer and our hostess decided that it was time for us to go to Jimmy'z, a popular and absurdly expensive Monaco night club. Spencer and I had been with a group of friends once before but that must have been a quiet night as you could barely move for the amount of people wanting to be seen at Jimmy'z on Grand Prix weekend. I quickly managed to lose the others and thought I'd better get a drink and stay in one place so that they could find me. One horribly expensive drink later, strategically enjoyed over the period of half an hour, I decided to call it a night. I stumbled home slowly but attentively just in case I spotted Spencer somewhere. Instead I spotted a rare Maserati MC12 on the side of the road, the only time I have ever seen one. To his credit, it turned out Spencer had not only found his way home but had managed to convince the security guard to let him in. He was fast asleep when I arrived back.

I'm not sure what time the Porsche SuperCup races began on the Sunday morning but the engine drone had been reverberating upwards from the tunnel below us for some time before I admitted that I couldn't ignore it any more.

There was an overwhelming buzz engulfing Monaco now we had reached Grand Prix day. We could feel it as soon as we stepped out onto the balcony. The morning sun was beating down on the boats and grandstands. People were already scuttling around as far as the eye could see and the air was thick with the sound of the highly-tuned cars that were competing in the races leading up to the main event. The harbour appeared to have been expertly filled with luxury yachts, while numerous other boats hovered beyond the harbour wall in the distance like a flock of curious seabirds. The excitement on the streets was tangible and much more elevated than the previous day. Everyone seemed poised, ready and waiting for the first Formula 1 car to fire up. For some people this was going to be a once-in-a-lifetime visit to the Monaco Grand Prix and they were ready to witness motor racing history in the making. For some it was a chance to see the streets of their home town transformed beyond recognition and to enjoy the carnival that surrounds it. For others it was time to throw themselves into the socialising and networking that goes hand-in-hand with one of the most glamorous events on the sporting calendar.

Showered, sandwich and cup of tea consumed, we walked away from the crowds and back towards the beach, stopping short of Jimmy'z and heading into the Le Meridien hotel that sits near the waterfront. From here we joined a couple of other people in a small, elegant speed boat and set off towards the yachts that were crowded around the race track, eventually convincing our driver to take us all the way to our destination despite some concerns on his part that I never really understood. We clambered on to the boat, calm and cool unlike the previous day, and prepared to put up with the inevitable jokes about having made it in time before comparing notes on the Saturday night partying. The boat itself was one of the oldest in the harbour. It had a vast upper deck, spacious enough to allow a crowd of us to hang out and chat without the worry of toppling each other over the edge on the way downstairs to the lower decks. There must have been around 25 people on board, all dressed casually in swimsuits, polo shirts and shorts. Cool boxes were strategically placed around the boat, all overflowing with bottles of beer and champagne. Spencer and I didn't hesitate to get stuck in, this seeming like the perfect day to drink through our hangovers. It was a friendly crowd and we were soon engaged in an animated conversation with a group of people that had taken up residence in the small hot tub. Others were hiding from the sun's rays on the deck below us, occasionally appearing to have a ciga-rette or grab another bottle of beer. Everyone had an opinion on the race and I was pleased that there was genuine interest in the event we were about to witness.

The front of the boat pointed outwards, away from the track and towards the entrance to the harbour which re-mained hidden behind a small navy of luxury yachts. Huge TV screens had been mounted at various points around the harbour. These would provide a useful insight into what was actually going on once the race finally began. As close to the track as we were, there would be no way to work out what was happening when the cars were ripping past in full fury. Most of us made our way to the back of the boat to watch the cars snaking along during warm up, darting from side to side, then braking heavily as they tried to warm their tyres and brakes. Ear plugs were quickly handed around and then, as the race started with an eruption of noise from the other side of the track, conversations gradually stopped and everyone started trying to follow the progress of the race, occasionally signalling to each other to offer a beer or top-up of champagne.

Someone once told me that you can't go into the tunnel without ear protectors during the Grand Prix as the noise will burst your eardrums. I find that easy to believe. The almost monotonous drone of the Formula 1 cars that you might hear on television on a Sunday afternoon, the sound that I found so boring as a child, does no justice to the intensity of the sound you hear at a race. The first time you hear the sound of the F1 cars tearing around the track it will give you goose-bumps, no matter how much you care about the sport. There is something savage and ferocious about these machines, the sound and the speed seeming out of control and at odds with the degree to which they are engineered and honed. The noise seems to travel through the air in the form of intense sound waves that reverberate through your body in an almost sickening manner. Ear plugs are a must if you are anywhere near the circuit.

Spencer and I made our way back and forth between bow and stern. We were torn between enjoying the proximity to the cars at the back of the boat or the relative calm at the front of the boat. At the front we could get an update on race proceedings from those that had been watching the big screens. At the back you would catch a snapshot of the action and nothing more. No matter where you stood there was no hiding from the noise of the cars which seemed to permeate through everything, screeching and buzzing at different pitches, culminating in intensity as they passed the boat. It was incredible and I couldn't help but smile at the ferocity of these machines as they were piloted to their limits around the tight city streets.

Everything really did stop from a social perspective during the race, the noise somehow blanketing everything so that there was no expectation to engage and converse until it came to a conclusion. For many people on the boats this was a good opportunity to chill out, some even having a quick sleep despite the noise and much to the amusement of others. It was tough to keep track of what was actually happening and who was winning. You couldn't tell much from looking straight onto the track from the back of the boat. It wasn't much better straining to see the details on the big screen from the front, with my eyesight at least, and so I had to keep pestering others for updates. Then, suddenly, the race was over. The engine noise dropped, stopped and was quickly replaced with cheering followed by conversation and the clinking of glasses as everyone began to discuss the race. We stood and watched as the grandstands emptied and the town began to open up again.

In due course we headed onto the track ourselves and started walking back to the apartment, noting the huge quantity of rubber that had been left behind by the perishing tyres of the F1 cars. Crowds of spectators made their way straight for the train station or got on buses. Many others stayed to enjoy the post-race parties that night. Presumably good times would be had all the way down to Nice and beyond. You knew that people were already thinking about the night ahead, either by drinking more or, sensibly, having a siesta before dinner.

On the Monday morning we sat on the balcony and watched the boats flooding out of the harbour, moving on to whatever the next big thing was. This was an indication that things were already getting back to normal in the 'millionaire's playground'. We threw our clothes into bags and followed suit. Remarkably, the generosity of various hosts and friends meant that a weekend at the most glamorous of motorsport events was cheaper than a night out in London, though I feared it might never come together in quite the same way again.

Owner's Club

Top Marques and Type-41

The morning after my meeting with Gildo I wandered out into the early morning sunshine to visit the Top Marques car show. I used the network of stairs and elevators to make my way down towards the sea below as opposed to the buses that dance around the tangled road network. Spencer was due to arrive later that day but I wanted to take the opportunity of attending the press preview on my own before all the crowds rolled in.

The Grimaldi Forum sits on Avenue Princesse Grace at the edge of the Mediterranean. It is a large modern building made of glass and concrete, somehow looking much more comfortable in its surroundings than it should do. The main entrance is primarily constructed of glass. It means that the entrance is filled with natural light, bright and airy. Around the corner are a number of large concrete bays that face the road, presumably for loading and unloading exhibition items into the main hall. During Top Marques these are the so-called 'pit lanes' – areas for potential buyers to come for test drives, a key differentiator for the show and reason for the unofficial tagline of "see it, drive it, buy it". Coffee was being served outside as I arrived and passes were being handed out at a small stand just inside the main doors. I found a seat and waited alongside numerous other people – mostly journalists and local officials I assumed – until Prince Albert had officially opened Top Marques and we could filter inside. I quickly passed by the stands selling high-end furniture and Persian rugs, ignored the signs for the watch exhibition upstairs, and headed onwards into the main exhibition hall. This is the concrete-roofed section of the building and is reliant upon bright ceiling lights that reflect off all the highly polished cars.

Top Marques is not your normal car show. It is clearly seen as a platform from which to reach potential customers, customers that have a lot of money at their disposal and might be tempted into buying an obscure or customised car so that they can stand out from the crowd. The previous year, total sales at Top Marques had reached a staggering €200 million. While that included watches and other luxury toys – such as the small, James Bond-style 'water scooters' that are popular with divers and luxury yacht owners – a majority of the figure was made up of car sales. As a result it felt like a giant showroom.

There was a strange contrast between the mainstream supercars and luxury saloons that could easily be spotted in showrooms around the world, and the niche brands that were exhibiting unheard of cars to the public for the first time. Somewhere in between those two extremes were the dream cars, the super supercars. These are the Paganis, Nobles and Koenigseggs – cars that cost hundreds of thousands of pounds and are rarely seen outside of the pages of motoring magazines. It was a great opportunity to get up close to some of today's motoring icons, the friendly brand representatives always happy to talk about specific details and figures. There were some pretty outlandish cars there as well. The Knight XV stands out in my memory simply for being the biggest car that I've ever seen. It is bomb-proof and bullet-proof as standard so I can only assume it is designed with drug dealers, arms dealers and Third World dictators in mind.

I enjoyed looking at the cars, especially some of the crazier ones, but I think sometimes you can have a bit too much of a good thing. After all, cars are made to be driven first and foremost, no matter how good they look. That's presumably why Top Marques has two 'pit lanes' from which potential customers can test drive a selection of the cars on display. It means the manufacturers can say, "Oh, you like the look of it? I've got one right outside if you fancy a quick spin." Even if you don't manage to blag yourself a test drive it is worth hanging around outside the Grimaldi Forum near the pit lanes so that you can see and hear some of the cars flying by, though for the full-on aural experience it's worth making your way to the famous tunnel that heads towards the harbour. The tunnel is normally the first place any potential customer would want to take a supercar in Monaco.

I wasn't there to just drool over the latest cars. I had been invited to meet with Juergen Obermann, a German businessman that was using the car show to launch a new invitation-only supercar club for the Riviera. Type-41 was conceived to offer members access to some of the world's most exclusive and desirable cars, with a focus on limited edition and rare models. I was astounded that something like that wasn't already in place considering the type of people that visit this region each year. I understood that Juergen was an entrepreneur with roots in IT and technology but wanted to start something that embraced his love of supercars. Quite the enthusiast then. I liked the fact that he was building a business to fuel his own passion for cars and driving; it made perfect sense to me and aligned with some of the things Gildo had expressed about needing to make your passions profitable for them to be sustainable.

I found the Type-41 section in the exhibition hall easily enough and waited while some photos were being taken of people next to a white Lamborghini Gallardo LP 570-4 Spyder Performante – one of the clubs rare but not limited edition cars and the first one in the south of France. It was as striking as anything else at the Grimaldi Forum. I have always loved the Gallardo and this latest model looked better than ever, all angles and attitude.

Juergen himself seemed very relaxed and was clearly enjoying the moment. He was dressed in jeans, shirt and jacket and seemed friendly from the off. We had some banter about the girls in Union Jack dresses that were helping promote the Keating supercar next to us before I tried to find out a little more about his love of cars.

The origin of his passion for cars can be traced back to two key moments in his life. The first was when he was only ten years old and saw a Porsche 911 2.7RS for the first time. He loved the shape of the car and the design of the now iconic Fuchs wheels. Juergen told himself that one day he would have a similar car. The second moment came when he was much older and working for the technology company Cisco who sponsored the McLaren Formula 1 team. Juergen was invited to attend the Monaco Grand Prix and immediately became a fan of the sport. He also began to develop a taste for fast road cars.

It was in 1997 that he finally bought his first Porsche – a Boxster which he had tuned from 205bhp to 360bhp. "It was faster than the Ferrari F355 at the time," he tells me with a triumphant smile. In 2000 he bought his first Ferrari – a 360 Modena. From that point on he was hooked. He owned various high-end cars and began to take part in what he calls "gentlemen's track events" where he learned to drive better and more safely at speed.

The idea for Type-41 came when Juergen went to take his limited edition Mercedes CLK DTM cabriolet out for a drive after it had been parked up and unused for a while. He found the battery to be dead and, when he had finally started it using jump leads, found the electronics weren't working properly and the roof wouldn't go down. Juergen realised that there must be others like him, international businessmen that want to enjoy driving a supercar when they arrive in Monaco but don't want the associated hassles of ownership. There are similar clubs in the UK. You pay an annual fee and have a certain amount of points that allow you to use the different cars over the course of a year. The most special cars require more points and a weekend would demand more points than a weekday. So if the model isn't new why hasn't it been done in the south of France before and how does Type-41 differ?

Juergen explained to me that there had been attempts before but the wrong approach was used. He didn't want to emulate the "high end rental company" model that he felt reflected the service offered by supercar clubs in the UK. Instead Type-41 would focus almost exclusively on limited edition cars, membership would be limited to a maximum of 111 people, and a significant focus would be placed on the social aspect of the club.

"You can rent a normal Ferrari F430 or 599 in Cannes or Monaco but Type-41 is more about having really special cars and a really enthusiastic group of people with it," he explained. "My first client is a Premium Client. He has 20 cars in his garage but he still joins because he wants to drive these cars, cars that you can't get very easily. He also wants to meet other like-minded people."

I understood what he was talking about, even if I felt that the proposition was more akin to existing clubs than he did. Reading magazines and digging online had already shown me that there was huge demand for the events-orientated, social side of motoring. This had already become a central feature of all the leading supercar clubs in the UK. Other clubs, such as the Gentleman Drivers Club, were launched with the sole aim of bringing existing performance car owners together. People have always wanted to share their passions and it is no different for petrolheads.

The fact still stood that this was the only serious proposition on the Cote d'Azur and the events that Type-41 members would enjoy certainly sounded special. I was a little envious to hear that special track days would be organised during which there would be opportunities to drive old Formula 1 cars. On the topic of track events, I was keen to discover what Juergen thought of the Nürburgring and it turned out that he was a big fan. After urging that I build a visit into my own plans, Juergen told me about one of his visits to the 'Ring when Formula 1 legend Michael Schumacher had been lined up to provide training and passenger experiences.

"It was one of those experiences that you didn't want to miss."

To make sure he didn't miss it, Juergen and a friend drove through the night to Germany. They left from Monaco at 10pm and just managed to reach the Nürburgring in time for the 11am safety briefing the next day, a required part of the programme at all track events. He had taken his Ferrari 430 Scuderia – a track-focused, electronics-laden derivative of the already seriously-capable F430. Having completed the track sessions, finishing second fastest, it was soon Juergen's turn to do some passenger laps with Michael. He described to me how Michael was driving in cowboy boots, one hand on the wheel and chatting casually, though still remaining devastatingly quick on the circuit.

"He was a really nice guy but I made a bit of a *faux pas*," Juergen tells me. "Michael asked what my favourite car was and I told him that it was the Ferrari 360 Challenge Stradale I once owned. 'The Challenge Stradale, for me, was one of the best Ferrari's ever made', I said. 'The Scuderia is nice but it's not you driving, it's the computer. The car is always correcting you. It means that you can go much faster but it's not the real thing'."

Michael was apparently unmoved and simply nodded knowingly. "Yes. Yes I can see that."

"It was at that moment that I remembered that Michael had been an integral part of the Ferrari development team for the 430 Scuderia," Juergen continues. "He was one of the guys that designed the car to be like that!"

Michael was characteristically cool in the face of this accidental criticism and continued to scythe his way around the Nürburgring at high speed whilst chatting about cars and racing. It was only later that Michael explained, to Juergen's considerable relief, that he too prefers a pure driving experience from his cars.

Before I let Juergen get back to whatever schmoozing was required, I tried to find out a little more about potential clients. To my surprise, he told me that local cultural issues were one reason why there is demand for something like Type-41. He used the example of one potential client from Brazil who finds it both socially unacceptable and dangerous to drive supercars at home, preferring to come to the south of France where he can spend a few days touring in something special.

"He's an absolute car nut but he wouldn't dare to drive even a Ferrari F430 in Brazil," he explains. "He once had a Porsche and almost got shot at, so he drives whatever local car is acceptable there and he comes here to drive whatever he pleases without any hassle."

It's an issue that I had never considered before, particularly having spent much of my time in countries where supercars are more or less celebrated as opposed to countries where social inequality means they are targeted for what they represent. I had not yet met a persecuted petrolhead but the fact is that many of the most desirable cars also carry very clear connotations of wealth and inequality. In those parts of the world where wealth is seen to be the result of corruption at the expense of the masses, driving a prestige car, particularly in the wrong area, would almost certainly invite abuse and maybe even violence. Even closer to home, in the aftermath of the banking crisis and the furore around excessive bonuses, the latest high-end cars are looked at with some derision. Quite simply, someone who can afford to go out and buy a brand new £150,000 car is in the minority. At the very least they are likely to receive some fairly disgusted glances from passers-by at some point, even if many are awestruck by their car. Many people love cars. It is a passion that can often provide common ground for connection between strangers but only a fool would assume that driving the latest Lamborghini somehow gives you social and cultural *carte blanche*.

He might have built his business to focus on the motoring desires of the super rich but, like Gildo Pastor, Juergen was well aware that you do not have to be wealthy to be a petrolhead.

"The French are not known to be great car lovers but if you have a car enthusiast in France, they are real thing," he tells me. "They will go out of their way, maybe not eating lunch, just so that they can buy a Porsche. So if you go to a normal French track event you will find the hardcore car fanatics, the guys that are willing to jeopardise other things in their lives for their passion. It gives you a real feeling for what being a car enthusiast is all about. It's not like people that have 20 cars in the garage that they never drive. These guys drive their cars every weekend and if they crash the car they will sit and fix it themselves."

I returned to the UK with renewed vigour. I was inspired by my conversations with Gildo and Juergen. They were both very wealthy and this had allowed them to explore their passion for cars and driving without limitation. They raced at exclusive events, drove the world's most exclusive cars and rubbed shoulders with motorsport legends. Gildo had even set a world record. Even so, neither of them had lost sight of the fact that being a petrolhead is nothing to do with wealth but simply about passion for motoring, about making an effort to bring a love for cars into your life. Gildo and Juergen had both done that, albeit in very different ways. Now I was ready to do the same.

Taking the Plunge

Finding a car fit for a petrolhead

Back in London I jotted down a list of all the things that I wanted to do over the coming months and all the people I would like to meet. It was ambitious and unrealistic. I simply couldn't afford to make it work so I began to simplify it and my plans shifted from being global to European. Even so, if I achieved half of what I had listed it would surely turn out to be one of the most memorable years of my life.

With no suitable tours to join or the tyre tracks of a motoring great to follow, it became clear that I would have to plan my own trip if I wanted to tick off more than a couple of the things I had in mind. There was stuff that I could do at home in the UK, and that would be easy to arrange. It was the things that I wanted to experience and the places I wanted to see in Europe that would pose more of a challenge. In London I began to look at maps and distances to work out some kind of plan. I cross-referenced with diaries of European motoring events on the off-chance I could add them to my itinerary. I checked when the public sessions were for the Nürburgring and flicked back through old magazines to help identify the best driving roads. Google Maps became my best friend as I dragged lines around Germany and Italy, regularly recalculating section travel times as to ascertain how much driving would be involved, reluctantly acknowledging that some of it would have to be on generic stretches of motorway. As far as I was concerned, the most fun and most economical way of doing it would be to piece together one serious road trip, a motoring pilgrimage around Western Europe that would link together as many roads and attractions as possible. I didn't mind that I might have to break up the journey and take a few bites of the apple to make it work.

Part of the problem was the issue of finding a co-driver. Understandably, none of my friends could afford to take long periods away from work to swan around in a car with me – even if I would have jumped at the chance had the tables been turned. This meant that I would have to tailor my trip around my co-drivers to some degree. I simply didn't fancy doing it alone. I wanted to share the experience and the memories with someone. Besides, I didn't fancy facing European toll booths in a right-hand drive car on my own. And then there was the choice of car...

In the months leading up to my departure from Aberdeen I had developed a habit of spending hours browsing the car classifieds online even though I didn't need a new car. Arguably I didn't even need a *different* car. I had a car that was barely three-years-old, a car which did everything that I could possibly require and which I had only owned for six months. Nevertheless, I would sit there at my desk trying to work out the highest performance, rarest, most reliable, best looking, not-too-impractical car that I could buy. It became an obsession for me.

There were specific factors that guided my search. You need rules, even when daydreaming. For example, my target price was set based upon an assumption of the current value of my car on trade-in, plus a little extra money that I could feasibly 'liberate' from my bank account. To ensure that it would be a straightforward purchase it would have to be bought from a reputable dealer. Upkeep was a consideration too. What would be the point in buying a car that required thousands of pounds spent on maintenance and servicing costs? Therefore, sadly, any aging supercar was out of the question. It would also have to be something that could live on the street and handle a week or more without being driven. That ruled-out anything pre-90s, maybe even pre-00s in some cases. This new car would have to be sporty, fun to drive and appealing to members of the opposite sex. It would also have to endow me with enough 'car cred' in the eyes of members of the same sex. Ideally it would go one step further and be something a bit unique, something that others like me would recognise with a knowing nod of approval. Most importantly it would be a perfect companion for the mythical moment when I found myself on the perfect driving road which, I was pretty sure, was nowhere near London but probably back in Scotland or somewhere in mainland Europe.

The strict criteria I developed meant that a shortlist would begin to emerge quickly. Lotus, Porsche, Nissan, Mercedes, Honda... I had no allegiance to a particular brand or country of origin. Once I discovered a potential inclusion to this list, something that might tick most if not all of the boxes, I would refer to any nearby car magazines and check its rating. Four or five stars would earn it a mental note of approval, though trying to ignore the merits and high rating of my existing car was a challenge in itself. I originally bought it because it ticked so many boxes and perfectly blended convenience and performance. Now it seemed a little too safe and a little too boring, especially when I no longer had to worry about commuting to work on snowy roads.

As my plans for a trip around western Europe began to fall into place, the time came to put my car searching skills to the test. If I was going to take a motoring pilgrimage then I needed to do it properly and if I wanted people to take me seriously as any kind of enthusiast then I needed to demonstrate that I actually was. It just wouldn't feel as though I was truly embracing this journey and what it represented if I didn't go and buy something iconic. Besides, if I was doing all this driving I might as well enjoy it and I had already spent hours and hours searching online for my next car.

Having convinced myself of the requirement for a special car I threw myself into the process of finding something suitable and soon found myself attracted to the idea of a Honda NSX. It seemed to be just what I was looking for and I loved the fact that you rarely see one on the road.

The NSX is an iconic car for a number of reasons. Firstly, it will always be remembered for Ayrton Senna's role in helping develop the handling characteristics of the car, giving it a benign balance that is still respected today. Secondly, the NSX made a huge impact on the more established supercar elite by showing that a supercar could have Japanese levels of reliability and be easy but rewarding to drive. It is often put forward as one of the reasons that Ferrari worked so hard to up the game of its entry-level V8 supercar, moving from the widely unloved

348 to the universally adored F355. Despite a reasonable production run of fifteen years from 1990, there are never that many cars available to buy at a given time and I believed that an early, high mileage example would not cost me much – if anything – in terms of depreciation. Lack of depreciation was very important to me in choosing a car for this trip. I was spending money that I shouldn't have been and I couldn't afford to get something that was going to be constantly losing value. As the obsession with depreciation grew – something partly based upon a realisation of how much money I had lost on more modern cars in recent years – it occurred to me that I could feasibly buy something more expensive than an NSX, a modern classic of some sort, and run it for a year and only have to pay for upkeep and insurance before selling it on. Arguably the NSX is a modern classic but this approach could mean that I could buy one of my personal dream cars and find out what it was like to run it for a year.

I convinced myself of all this quite easily and decided to look at the car I really wanted – the Ferrari F355 Berlinetta.

Ferrari launched the 3.5 litre V8-engined F355 to great fanfare in 1994. The much improved aerodynamics and damping over its predecessor, the 348, meant superb handling and the manic engine revved to an intoxicating 8,800rpm, higher than any other supercar in production at that time. The 380bhp car was capable of 0-60mph in 4.6 seconds and had a top speed of around 180mph; not big figures for a supercar by today's standards but very significant in the mid-90s and still faster than a majority of cars that you see on the road. Its open-gate manual gearbox was a thing of beauty but that didn't stop Ferrari launching its paddle-shift F1 gearbox in 1997, something that was seen as a game-changer at the time even if it is a common sight today. Customers also had a choice of the fixed roof Berlinetta, the convertible Spider, or the targa-styled GTS which had a removable roof panel that could be tucked behind the seats. There were around 11,000 of these cars produced during the 5 year production run which means that there are plenty around, even though it is something that you would never consider to be common.

I remember vividly the first time that I *really* noticed one, the first time I said to myself "one day I will have one of those". I was heading to see a specialist at a small private hospital in Aberdeen after a skiing accident that had left me needing an operation. There was a grey F355 parked right outside, very subtle against the granite building behind it and under the grey skies which are a regular feature of the north-east of Scotland. The car looked so good, the proportions so right. I had seen them many times before, and in more exotic locations, but this car had been brought into my day-to-day reality and stood out against the cold functionality of the medical institution I was approaching. It brought its own little piece of Italian car culture to the car park. It was exotic and alluring.

It was five or six years later that I found myself sitting on the train heading westwards out of London to test drive my first F355, my first Ferrari of any kind in fact.

I had read more and more about the car and it seemed that depreciation had more or less stopped, commentators feeling that the car would start going the other way over the coming years. Cars were available from a low of £35,000 up to £50,000 and beyond, depending on age, mileage and specifications. My budget would allow me to buy nearer the lower end of the scale but that would hopefully mean less room for losing money. Despite this I still had some concerns, not least around the issue of parking and storage as the practicalities of owning a supercar in London started to creep into my mind.

The block of flats that I was living in had underground parking spaces but the car park was being renovated over a period of about three months and it wasn't clear when things would be back to normal. In the meantime they would be shifting other people around the available spaces to avoid the works and no spare spaces were available, even if it looked like there were plenty whenever I looked. I don't think my anger at not having been informed of this impending development would have given the staff much inclination to help me out even if they could do, so I began to consider the possibilities of hiring a space in another underground car park. I was quickly warned by Spencer that he had significant troubles with his Audi R8 due to the front of the car being so low. It would often scrape and sometimes he had to give up and reverse out. His advice was to check any potential garage properly before committing. If the bottom of the ramp levelled out with too acute an angle then it might be impossible to get the car inside without serious damage to the bodywork. Street parking didn't seem tempting, even with a car cover.

I had these things in my mind as I trundled along on the train, plunging deeper into the countryside that leads to the Cotswolds, the sun thankfully shining in a clear blue sky. I would at least have the chance to drive my first Ferrari on dry roads rather than battling with it in the wet.

The dealership itself was not a Ferrari specialist, rather more of a general sports and race car specialist. Having looked at some of their available stock on the website they seemed pretty serious players and so it felt like a good place to begin. I had been warned in advance that another potential customer was seeing the car just before me. I assumed it was a just sales tactic but, sure enough, a middle-aged man and his wife were having a final walk around the car just as I arrived. The car was making a gentle ticking noise as it cooled down after his test drive. It looked good in Rosso Corsa red with cream leather interior – arguably *the* classic combination for a Ferrari – and appeared to be in relatively good condition. As I chatted with the sales manager, I realised that the car was perhaps showing its age more than I had anticipated it would, or should. The interior was a bit dated, the plastics scratched and the leather looking a little tired in places, even if the stone chips at the front of the car didn't put me off. I was keen to get it outside as I couldn't help but feel that the light in their showroom didn't do the car justice.

I sat in the passenger seat first as we rolled backwards out of the showroom and made our way up to the main road, the sales manager at the wheel of the car. He clearly felt at ease with it and was as relaxed as I was nervous. I was struck by how serene the car felt at these speeds, the damping feeling firm but not as bone-crushingly harsh as many modern cars, and the engine not too overwhelmingly powerful. Where were the fireworks that you expect from a Ferrari? I was about to find out.

Once we got on to the open road he put his foot down and, as the revs climbed, I witnessed the Jeckell and Hyde character of the F355 for the first time as it shot forwards ferociously, the sound from behind matching the movement. At low revs it was refined and could trundle along in traffic if required and at high revs it felt like a snarling race car ready to pummel the road into submission. It seemed to corner hard, feeling flat and stable but responsive, almost up on its toes. The interior felt a bit dated, particularly compared with the more bespoke-feeling and grander interiors of modern Aston Martins and Bentleys, and even when compared with its successor the 360. It didn't put me off as such but I think I was expecting it to feel a little more special.

My test drive was brief. It was also tentative as I had no intention of crashing. Looking back, I don't think I got the car above around 5,000rpm but it still made rapid progress along the road as I tried to finesse the gearstick through the open gate without looking down too often. The traffic wasn't on my side. I didn't know these roads and any overtaking did not appeal in this unfamiliar car. I could hold back a bit and then play catch up and that was enough to tell me that the car provided a pure and unfiltered driving experience compared to what I was used to. As is often the way, the experience was a bit of a blur and I didn't really get a feel for the car, soon finding myself back at the showroom where I spent some time going over the history file. I walked around the car a few more times, looking at it closely. I was very disappointed but the fact was that I didn't love it as I had hoped I would. I went back to London feeling a bit underwhelmed by the whole experience, though I couldn't put my finger on the problem.

Rather than heading straight home, I had a pre-arranged meeting to attend and it felt like perfect timing. To get a better feel for the world of classic cars, I had been put into contact with Adam Reynolds by Spencer a week earlier.

"You've got to speak to Adam," he insisted. "He's got a Ferrari F40 which he claims is one of the best in the country. And he's doing up an E-type Jag at the moment."

I took him up on his offer of an introduction and was immediately glad that I had. We met at his office which was tucked away at the end of a cobbled mews in Belgravia and, because the meeting room was unavailable, moved immediately to the pub round the corner.

It seems as though there are all sorts of car enthusiasts out there but my favourites are the ones that like to talk, no matter what their precise interests might be. As we sat sipping ice cold Cokes on the bench outside, enjoying the excuse for making the most of the good weather though falling short of ordering up some beers, it became clear that Adam was one such person.

It was true that he had a concours-winning Ferrari F40 and was in the process of doing up an old E-type Jaguar but the conversation seemed to focus more on the business of buying and selling classic cars, of which he knew quite a lot. In fact, he was in the process of putting together a classic car fund as an investment vehicle, if you'll excuse the pun. He tried to explain to me some of the considerations that are necessary when buying a classic car. He simplified things for me a bit but the crux of it was as follows...

If you've got two identical classic cars but one has been restored in the past and is in great condition at

£300,000 and one is in need of lots of attention at £200,000, the experienced buyer will probably end up going for the more expensive option. The inexperienced buyer will think that the cheaper car is a bargain, even considering the work required to bring the car up to scratch. However, they are unlikely to have considered that things might have changed since the more expensive car was restored. Today's labour rates might be higher, parts costs might be higher, VAT might be higher. Without detailed research it might cost well in excess of £300,000 to bring the cheaper car up to the standard of the more expensive car at today's rates. The problem is that many people think with the heart rather than the head when buying cars.

"If you're spending £40,000 on shares you are likely to undertake an appropriate level of due diligence to assure that your investment is as safe as possible," Adam explained. "But people don't always do their due diligence on cars and that can be risky. You need to be careful to avoid the piranhas that look to take advantage of weakness in a sales situation," he insisted.

As if to prove his credentials as someone that was 'in' with the classic car scene, a stunning vintage Aston Martin rolled up next to us mid-conversation, roof down and chrome glistening, an acquaintance of Adam's jumping out and chatting for a while about his car and the apparent demand for classic, left-hand drive Aston Martins on the international market. The conversation moved on to China, being seen as a market with the potential to impact the global classic car market once its many millionaires and billionaires got bored with the latest Rolls Royce and caught on to the desirability and investment potential of classic cars.

I sat by and listened to the conversation, all of us muttering general appreciation of the cleanliness of the Aston Martin before Adam's friend drove off. Adam shouted after him to make sure he would be the first to know if it ever came up for sale and then we moved back to the discussion of buying and selling, Adam giving me some examples of things not always being as they seem. In one case a dealer was selling an E-type Jaguar as a right-hand drive, manual, soft-top example even though some research subsequently showed that it had started life as a left-hand drive, automatic, coupe. It was wildly overpriced once you knew this. Another dealer was selling a "chairs and flares" Ferrari Dino at the time we spoke but were not disclosing in their advert that the car had been modified with extended wheel arches and Daytona seats sometime after purchase, rather than being one of the rare, expensive originals they were claiming it was. I wondered if I might come across some piranhas over the months ahead.

I talked about my intentions to buy an F355 to sounds of approval from Adam. I had more or less set my mind on a manual Berlinetta, believing it to be the purest of the breed and Adam had confirmed that it was "the one to have" from his perspective.

I walked away with a clear impression that you should always buy the best car that you can afford and that buying from a respected dealer counts for something when it comes to selling on. It was also reassuring to hear from someone in the know that the F355 was indeed a sensible and fun choice so two days later I found myself on a train again, this time heading south out of London on an equally sunny day and with another car to see.

I was picked up at the station by Tony, the friendly sales manager from Foskers in Kent. We made our way through the tight, winding roads that make up the Kent countryside, passing village pubs and avoiding numerous trucks whose drivers had decided it was a good idea to squeeze themselves down these tiny lanes, before eventually reaching our destination.

The premises were simple but sizeable and, more importantly, literally overflowing with Ferraris of different varieties. Inside I spotted three F40s, numerous Dinos and cars I didn't even recognise. At that moment I knew that coming to a dedicated Ferrari specialist had been a good idea. Of course many of the cars were not for sale but I saw that as a good thing – anyone trusted to look after these kinds of cars must be highly rated by picky owners. As I pottered around and admired all the cars inside I heard a feral bark from one of the cars outside as it sprang to life, revs rising and falling as someone prodded the throttle pedal. One of the dealership's Ferrari 456 Challenge cars was in the process of being tweaked, the bottomed-out 456 prices and potential for weight reduction having inspired them to create these race cars.

The car that I was here to see was almost identical to the car I had driven a couple of days earlier, with Rosso Corsa paint and cream leather interior. The only differences were that this car had been specified with carbonfibre-backed sports seats and a fire extinguisher, the latter of which I hoped not to need, the former certainly looking the part.

The test drive took the standard formula, with Tony taking the wheel to start with and keeping things at low revs until the car had warmed through. I almost burst out laughing when he leaned through the window at a petrol station and asked me if I wanted any sweets, remembering the warnings I had been given regarding cars and strangers when I was a child. Then we launched off onto the road again, this time with great vigour. A very high speed blast down a dual carriageway and some hard cornering quickly showed me what this car was all about. I was hugely impressed at the speed and ferocity of the car. As we pulled onto a small, gravelly offshoot from the road and switched seats, I promised myself that I would drive the Ferrari harder than I had last time to really try to get a feel for the car from the driver's seat. I took a couple of minutes to get comfortable, the sports seats in this car feeling a little deeper and more sculpted than the standard items but no worse for it.

True to my intentions, I pulled back onto the road and extended my foot further towards the floor, now certain that I had only used 50% of the power before. I tried to hold out until nearer the red line in each gear, the noise and speed seeming relentless. When the chance came to corner hard around a roundabout I made an effort to emulate what I had just witnessed from the passenger seat, knowing that I would have enough grip if I didn't push any harder than Tony. It cornered hard, the grip levels greater than anything I had driven before, then slingshotted us up the road and back towards the workshop.

It was all over too soon and I was hooked.

"Thanks for taking me out and driving it hard so I could see what it can do," I said.

"You didn't do too badly yourself," came the response from Tony. I couldn't help but feel a little smug for having given a good account of my driving skills and got out still buzzing from the experience of my first proper drive in a Ferrari.

I took my time to check out a similar but slightly cheaper car that they had for sale, this one with black leather interior and standard seats. I knew there and then that I wanted the car I had just experienced and bonded with and I felt much more comfortable with the idea of buying from a respected specialist even if I hadn't quite made my peace with spending the profits of my Aberdeen flat sale which should have been safely tucked away for my next home.

That night I ended up going for a boozy dinner with a few mates. If I wasn't sure about buying the car before, I certainly was after a few beers and some encouragement. The next day I called up, slightly hungover, and put a deposit down on the F355 I had driven. The first step to buying my first Ferrari, my first classic, my first supercar had been taken.

I was excited but also a little apprehensive. I was spending big money and no matter how many times I have bought or sold a car I am always scared of somehow making a huge financial mistake. You always know that the dealer is going to make some money on the sale, that's a given, but I had never owned a Ferrari before and didn't know if there was something vital that I should have checked on or asked about. I'd obviously done some research beforehand but had I done enough? I had gone to a reputable dealer for peace of mind and all I had could now was wait for them to do an MOT, give it a good clean and a final look over. Hopefully I had chosen well.

Rita came with me on the day of the pick-up. I was like a cat on a hot tin roof but my nerves subsided as soon as I saw the car again. I paid for the car and Tony showed me around it in detail and gave a few bits of advice – "Don't floor it in first gear when the tyres are cold or you'll end up facing the other way" being my favourite – and then we were on the road and off back to London. I was quickly shown how low the front of the car was as we pulled in to get some petrol, slowing down before the ramp to the forecourt with Spencer's warning in mind. Clearly it wasn't slow enough and I was both angry and upset at myself for causing the scraping of the underside of my new car, Rita having to put up with my continuing emotional volatility. I had a look and no damage was done. In a way it was good to get this first scraping experience out of the way. As I would come to learn it is unavoidable from time to time in these cars. You simply learn to avoid it where possible and keep calm when it happens.

Just as I was about to pull off, someone leaned out of their car and, with a nod at the Ferrari, said, "Nice car mate". That really set the tone for the journey and I couldn't help but smile every time I saw someone admiring the car, more often than not children in the back seat of their parents' car clambering to see out of the window. The M25 on a sunny Saturday afternoon turned out to be a bit of a baptism of fire in terms of building familiarity with my new car. I may have been nervous but I was thoroughly enjoying the experience and was already dreaming of piloting it down the autobahn, along Alpine mountain passes, and to its birth place in Italy.

Sunday Breakfast Club

Supercars and bacon and eggs at Goodwood

I had a few short drives over the following days to get a feel for the Ferrari but nothing memorable. Even so, the fact that I now owned such a car was beyond surreal and filled me with a concoction of feelings, from pride and excitement through to guilt at my being so irresponsible. I was temporarily storing the car in the garage beneath my parents' London flat. Alasdair, my step-father, had spoken to Arthur, the caretaker, who had allowed me to use an absent resident's space for a short period of time. From what I could tell he had grown surprisingly protective of my car and would check with my parents if it had been away for any length of time. The first time I drove it in to the garage Rita and Arthur acted as lookouts, me coasting slowly down the ramp on the brakes as we all assessed whether it was going to be possible without damaging the front of the car. Thankfully it was possible. With the parking sorted, the car signed up for automatic Congestion Charge payments, and a TomTom satnav system stuck unstylishly to the windscreen I felt ready for life with a Ferrari in London.

Of course London living meant that traffic jams, roadworks and restrictive speed limits were all conspiring to get in the way of any real fun I might be able to have on the road. I needed an excuse to get out of town and I wanted to see another aspect of car culture. Thankfully I had read that a series of Breakfast Club events took place at Goodwood on Sunday mornings throughout the year and there was one coming up. It was the perfect opportunity to take the Ferrari out for a proper drive down to the south coast and to see what the breakfast event was like on the way back. It was also a perfect excuse for another excursion with Rita. She was always happy to go somewhere new or to be doing something different and even the idea of looking at lots of cars didn't put her off. Besides, having lived through the dilemmas and emotional fireworks of the Ferrari purchasing process, she was as keen to get out and about in the car as I was.

Setting off in an F355 is always an event, starting with the simple task of getting inside. The first few times that you open the door you find yourself grasping around inside the air scoop that makes up much of the door, trying to find the handle on the upper side of the panel. It opens cleanly and swings out without drama leaving you to find the best approach to seating yourself in the low-slung sports seats. There are numerous possibilities here but it will depend on your height as to what works for you, though unless you can open the door fully you will undoubtedly find yourself pulling muscles and twisting joints as you navigate the wide ledge, high seat bolster and the steering wheel. I tend to put one foot in and then use the ledge to help lower my backside into the seat before swinging the second leg in and pulling the light-weight door, which shuts with a surprisingly solid sounding 'clunk'. The seat itself only has limited adjustability but it is comfortable and everything is well positioned around you. Visibility is excellent, with no obvious blindspots, meaning that the main challenge with driving it is getting over the aura of being in a Ferrari and getting used to its dimensions. If you haven't used an open-gated manual gearshift before then your eye will be drawn to the splash of aluminium that sits between the two seats, standing out against the cream and black leather that makes up the rest of the cabin and somehow adding to its credentials as a serious driver's machine.

Of course a car like this is all about the engine and starting it up in an underground car park quickly became one of life's pleasures for me. As you turn the key everything lights-up on the dashboard as though taunting you and daring you to take the next step. There's no fancy starter button here, just a simple black key that needs turning a little further. It should catch the first time that you try to start it, the whole car seemingly wheezing like an asthmatic smoker for a moment if you give up too soon. It barks in to life with a fierce flare of revs before settling down into a slightly lumpy idle that will continue until the engine and fluids have warmed through properly. You wait as it warms through in stages. First a high-pitched whine, that you may not have initially noticed, drops out. You might lightly prod the throttle pedal in an effort to speed up the rate at which the oil temperature rises. As you do, you notice the oil pressure gauge rising in direct correlation to the pressure of your foot. It's a good lesson in understanding the stresses that driving with cold oil can put on an engine, so you wait a bit longer.

Eventually you are ready to roll and you toy with the handbrake that sits to the right of the driver's seat, pulling it up all the way before holding the button in and depressing it all the way down. The controls feel light and the car is easy to manoeuvre, though the steering requires a little more force at lower speeds than it does once it's on the move. If you find yourself in an underground car park the first issue is edging onto the ramp that leads you to ground level, the front of the car catching and making a sickening noise all too often if you're not careful. Speed bumps are the same when you're on the move. Less is more in these situations. Besides, edging along feathering the clutch and throttle pedals gives you more opportunity to enjoy the bassy blare of the engine at low revs as it echoes around you.

Rolling out into the daylight quickly reminds you that a red F355 Berlinetta is not a subtle car. People look, they point and they take photographs. I often wonder if the general public are more approving of a classic car – or modern classic in this case – than they are of the current equivalent. Do people associate the newest models with overpaid footballers or bankers and older models as the choice of more discerning buyers? Some do. For many others the sight of a rare car, even a new one, can be quite exciting, aspirational even.

Driving through town isn't difficult in this car. Like their hatchback or SUV equivalents, modern supercars are much larger than their ancestors and this means that older cars are often much better suited to the tight streets and multi-lane roads of somewhere like London. Of course there are times when you find yourself wincing as a truck blasts past you as though the driver wants your wing mirror for a trophy but that happens no matter what you drive. Of course, a real petrolhead doesn't buy a Ferrari simply to drive it around a city. To this day I am horribly frustrated by the amount of time it takes to reach a decent driving road from central London. Say what you like about Aberdeen but it is surrounded by superb driving roads. If only you could still put your car on the train and take it to Scotland...

In London you endure the traffic until, at last, the road opens up in front of you. Then you put your foot down and only then can you enjoy the aural fireworks that accompany the developing speed, starting low and gruff and rising in volume and pitch. It warbles but has a metallic edge that fits perfectly with the incessant, linear building of speed.

The route through Surrey was never going to allow for particularly high speeds or traffic-free driving but would allow us to stop for lunch at Chiddingfold to check out The Mulberry Inn, a pub owned by media powerhouse and renowned Ferrari collector Chris Evans. I secretly hoped that Chris would turn up, spot my car outside and seek me out to chat about cars. This didn't happen but, frustratingly, some months later Spencer did send me a photograph of him and Chris standing in front of a couple of Ferraris having met at a hotel. Lack of celebrity Ferrari collectors aside, Rita and I did have a lovely lunch and shortly afterwards I had an opportunity to drive the F355 a bit more vigorously for the first time. It was not anywhere near the best drive I had in the course of the year but a four-car overtaking move stuck in my mind for demonstrating how quickly and easily this car can pile on speed. Funnily enough, access to that speed gives you a feeling of security at times rather than danger, knowing that you can overtake quickly and safely when required. I couldn't claim that Rita felt quite the same about the speed though. For my part, as much as I was enjoying it, I kept thinking to myself how amazing the car would be once I got it to the Alps. It would certainly prove to be in due course.

I was up at the crack of dawn to wash my car on the Sunday. I stood alone in a public car park in the coastal resort town of Littlehampton as the morning sun hung low in the sky and the noise of some all night party people still enjoying themselves could be heard somewhere nearby. I had been advised to get to the circuit in good time on the Sunday morning and having pre-registered there was a chance that I'd be able to park my car on the grid with some of the other supercars that would be in attendance. I had never really understood the Sunday morning car washing mentality before but there I was, sponge in hand, trying to make my car look as good as possible before anyone else saw it, removing all the grime and dead flies that had accumulated on the drive down the day before.

I had absolutely no idea what to expect as Rita and I made our way to the Goodwood circuit. The weather deteriorated as we pressed on and the country roads and brief sections of dual carriageway were more or less deserted. I thought I spotted a Porsche in the rear-view mirror in the distance but it wasn't until we neared the Goodwood entrance that other supercars suddenly materialised in front and behind us. We were soon to realise how popular these events were as we set eyes on a vast line of supercars queuing to get inside the gate. Having approached from the wrong side, we were filtered slowly around the roundabout and to the back of the queue. There was plenty of mutual appreciation going on between drivers as we all checked out each other's cars in the slow moving traffic. I seem to remember providing a running commentary of what we were seeing to Rita, drawing on my years of reading car magazines and probably boring her in the process. There was a constant hum of engine noise, occasionally shattered by a roar from one of the more outlandish cars. As we approached the stewards at the entrance an argument was going on. A BMW M3 driver was seemingly trying to put the case forward for parking his car on the grid and the steward presumably feeling that it didn't fit with the supercar theme. We were directed to the right-hand side whilst the discussion continued, me not knowing the layout of the grounds and more than happy to go with the flow. I was quickly disappointed to discover that we had been pointed to an overflow car park rather than a spot on the grid. My car obviously wasn't special enough in their eyes but at least that implied there would be some very special cars on the grid.

As things would turn out, parking away from the grid was actually a blessing in disguise as it meant that we could get in and out easily without having to battle through crowds of people. For now it meant that we were conveniently parked alongside lots of other interesting cars a stone's throw from the grid and certainly a lot closer than the public parking. Having parked up next to another Ferrari we set off on foot, checking out the many cars around us as we went. It was mostly British marques such as TVR and Lotus, as well as the odd Ferrari or Honda NSX. I was flattered to turn around and see two young guys photographing my car but I imagine that they hadn't made their way to the grid area yet as this is where the serious cars were to be found. Jaguar XJ220s were lined up alongside Koenigseggs, American muscle cars were vying for attention alongside the finest Italian exotica. Cars were still flooding through the gates and would continue to do so until after we left later that morning. Rita pottered around, diligently taking photos whenever people would get out of the way as I explained the significance of various cars. She had her favourites and I had mine but there was no doubting that all tastes were well catered for.

It was quite quiet at this time, us having arrived just before 8am and many people still to arrive. Most people at the early stages of the event appeared to be owners of the cars on the grid or the surrounding display areas. There were clearly some good conversations, connections and re-connections going on. We ducked off to get our bacon and egg rolls and cups of tea. With the weather now cold and grey, fuel and warmth were required and we hid from the wind behind the food caravan with some other car enthu-siasts. From there we went on to explore the other display areas which seemed to be dominated by Ferraris and Por-sches, clearly the cars of choice for many people. Lambor-ghinis, TVRs, Ford GTs and GT40s, Audi R8s, Mercedes SLSs, even DeLoreans and some kit cars. They were all lined up and being pored over by the keen enthusiasts. There were a few companies handing out fliers but what-ever they were promoting was clearly taking a back seat, the cars rightly taking centre stage and the sheer number of supercars in one place pulling most people around in swirling patterns as they tried to find their favourites.

Back on the grid and the line up of the rarest cars continued. A steward stood directing the latecomers to the ends of the rows as we looked on. Every now and then he would have to ask the noisier drivers to stop showing off, no matter how much the crowds liked hearing as well as seeing the cars. And there were certainly crowds now. It seemed to be getting busier by the minute as families arrived for a Sunday excursion, all flooding in from the distant car parks and creating big problems for the drivers still trying to get in and display their cars. Each time another car would arrive the crowds would part like the Red Sea, occasionally an enthusiastic boy running after a Ferrari Enzo or similar, camera held out in front of him as he tried to capture the shapes and sounds for enjoyment later.

We made our way back up the grid towards my car. Rita had given up on taking photos as people swarmed around the cars. It had certainly been enjoyable up until this point. I had never before seen so many supercars in one place at one time and I loved the fact that this in turn brought together so many people with a shared passion for cars, people that were willing to give up their Sunday morning to go and display their cars or simply to gawp at others' and take photos and videos to enjoy later.

We pulled out of the gates and past the waiting enthusiasts who were lined up with their cameras. They took the opportunity to get some pictures of another Ferrari for their collection, me giving some appreciatory revs as I sped off up the damp, tree-lined roads. Driving along we would see other supercar drivers heading to the event, fellow Ferrari owners waving or flashing their lights in a show of camaraderie, something I've never really experienced in any of my previous cars. For much of the way we were closely followed by a Porsche 996 GT3, overtaking almost in unison at times and enjoying a little fun but safe cat-and-mouse driving until he launched ahead on the motorway at speeds I wasn't willing to emulate.

It was good to have a proper run in the F355, to get a true feel for the speed and cornering ability of the car. Overtaking had never felt so easy knowing that the car would simply keep accelerating until you ran out of road. However, the journey also exposed a few problems and it soon needed to go back to Foskers for a bit of attention. In particular, the right-hand indicator light was only working sporadically which was clearly dangerous, motorway lane-changing in particular requiring good planning and awareness. The visit would also allow me the chance to have a more modern stereo fitted so that an iPod could be hooked up – a must for the duller moments of an epic road trip around Europe.

Local Hero

A morning with Lord Mexborough

As my own journey to becoming a car enthusiast progressed, I became increasingly interested in understanding other people's love for cars. There were a number of people that I would have loved to talk to about the origins and extent of their passion. It would have been fascinating to hear a few untold stories and adventures from some iconic petrolheads but I wasn't surprised when those I approached were apparently unavailable or simply didn't respond. By contrast, I was pleasantly surprised when a few of them agreed to speak with me.

It was while I was finalising plans for my pilgrimage around Europe and trying to pin down a suitable co-driver that the opportunity arose to travel to Yorkshire to meet with Lord Mexborough, one of the people whose name I had jotted down on the way back from Monaco. I was aware of Lord Mexborough by name only. Over the years he had lent some of his rare cars to various magazines so that they could do comparative tests. As far as I was concerned, if this was the guy that my favourite magazines went to for a favour then he would almost certainly be someone worth talking to. I had been warned in advance that his collection was not as large as it once was but that didn't put me off. I wasn't going there to inspect his cars, even if I was quite interested to know the extent of the collection; I was going to find out about Lord Mexborough as a car enthusiast.

I had to get there first and even if the journey to Yorkshire wouldn't be the most exciting, I did have the Ferrari to do it in. As the meeting was at 10am on a weekday morning, I had arranged to stay with the parents of my friend Tom the night before. Tom was one of my best friends from school and I knew Neil and Carol very well having spent a lot of time with the family when they lived in Scotland. Although I didn't know Yorkshire very well I had been to their house once before and remembered it being in a lovely, picturesque location. My memory hadn't tricked me. After the monotony of the motorway, peeling off onto the country roads that took me to their house was a welcome relief and a chance to finally enjoy the process of driving. This area – between York and Scarborough and to the south of the North York Moors – is comprised of small towns and villages and rolling agricultural land. It is beautiful in parts and the small village of Hutton Buscel is no exception. The tight roads are lined with low stone walls, lush green gardens and cottages, all looking like they belong in a Constable painting. Neil and Carol's home fits this imagery perfectly and I was soon enjoying some tea, scones and homemade jam in the summer house at the end of the garden. They were hugely interested in the car and I was quickly reminded where Tom gets his infectious enthusiasm for things. I excused myself from the conversation and spent half an hour washing the car before taking each of them for a spin. They both loved it, Carol particularly keen on the inertia-free feeling of travelling in a Ferrari at speed.

"This must be the closest thing to flying!" she exclaimed after I had put my foot down on an arrow-straight section of road that seemed to pull upwards towards the horizon. I had to agree.

The next morning I was denied such an experience until turning off the main road – which was clogged with commuter traffic – and heading towards the moors. I felt an immediate sense of calmness as the traffic vanished and the roads began to wind and undulate. They would shift regularly from double to single-tracked roads, all lined with stone walls bordering green fields that seemed to roll off into eternity. Eventually I found myself crawling along a broken, rutted road, the sat nav no longer any use. I had to forego any sense of male pride as I stopped to ask for directions. It turned out that I was just a couple of hundred metres away. I knew that I was in the right place when I turned and dipped down a driveway beneath overhanging trees I saw a grand estate house with an Audi, a Porsche and a Mercedes sat on the gravel ahead. Barely three minutes later and I was following Lord Mexborough through the house and out the other side, he having decided to show me the two garages before we sat down to talk.

The first garage wasn't quite what I had expected. It felt more like a workshop in many respects. It was spacious and airy and the walls decorated with old motoring posters such as the eternally popular vintage Monaco Grand Prix prints. There were a number of Porsche 911s in here, some waiting for MOTs to be carried out and one covered in mud. Not that I had a problem with a muddy car. It actually looked good that way, as though someone had been for a good hack in it. I discovered it to be the preferred vehicle for the family time trials which are held on a grass track somewhere on the estate, something that had been going on for 12 or so years. Lord Mexborough explained that the grass circuit provides an excellent environment to learn about oversteer, especially when damp, though he confessed to having been usurped at the top of the rankings by one of his sons now.

In another section of the garage an Audi Quattro sat forlornly in the corner. It needed significant restoration work but the cost of doing so would far outweigh the value of the car, so it waits, for nothing in particular. A deep green vintage Ace-Bristol sat nearby, its red leather uncomfortably contrasting with the paintwork but doing nothing to take away from the good looks of the car. Unlike the Audi, the Ace-Bristol was in the process of restoration.

As Lord Mexborough started switching off lights and setting the alarm, he explained that there used to be many more cars in that garage but he had been paring his collection back for some years. He later told me that he had 36 cars at the peak of his collecting days, including 7 or 8 Ferraris and numerous Porsches. His allegiance to these brands became clear when he showed me garage number two. This was obviously where the special stuff was kept, the wooden floors and white walls creating a slightly more welcoming environment. To the left, in the red corner, a Ferrari 288 GTO sat nose to tail with a Ferrari Daytona, also known as the 365 GTB/4. I was immediately drawn to the 288, one of the most handsome designs ever in my opinion. I was struck by the design cues that had clearly been carried forward from this car and were now evident on my own. By contrast the Daytona was a car that I had never found to be particularly beautiful but, looking at it closely, I became intrigued. To me, in the metal, its dimensions looked reminiscent of an E-Type Jaguar or a Corvette Stingray, the long bonnet swooping off toward the distant front wheels as to accommodate the V12 engine. Of the four cars in the garage this is apparently the most physically-demanding to drive.

On the right, and in the white corner, was Stuttgart's riposte; a Porsche 911 2.7RS Lightweight sitting closely behind a Porsche 959. Both these cars were stunning in their own right but both offered very different interpretations of the same basic formula. I loved the simplicity and compact nature of the old 911. It is something that I have come to appreciate more as I have got older, not really finding classic Porsches aesthetically pleasing in my youth. This particular example was driven in the Porsche Production Car Championship back in 1973; a concessionaires car driven by British racing driver Nick Faure. He won 14 of the 15 races, won the championship and earned the right to keep the car. Some years later it would be bought by Lord Mexborough. By contrast the 959 looked like a 911 on steroids, more of a race car for the road, and that's essentially what it was. There were only 292 of these cars made, designed with Group B racing in mind. In contrast to the Daytona, Lord Mexborough reckons that this car is almost too easy to drive, its complex electronics and four-wheel drive system taking the edge off the raw power.

These are not museum pieces and Lord Mexborough explained that he does drive them when he can. He would consider having more cars if he had time to enjoy them all but it seemed like this might be the limit of his collection for the foreseeable future. Like me, he believes that these kinds of cars were made to be driven and enjoyed. He must be one of the only people in the world to own both the Ferrari 288 and the Porsche 959 from new, having picked them both up from the respective factories. There were only 12 examples of each made available to the UK market at launch which gives an idea of the rarity of these vehicles. Lord Mexborough went on to tell me how he enjoyed both experiences and the factory tours but that, if anything, Porsche made a little more fuss over the clients. Production of the 959 was running late and so Porsche also arranged a few private track events and demonstrations to appease the eager customers.

As in the other garage there were pictures on the walls but these were neatly framed photos, many having been from magazine photo shoots. We spoke briefly about that and it's clear that he is happy to lend his cars to those publications and journalists that he trusts, those people that he knows will respect the cars and will review them seriously rather than abuse them in search of a sensationalist story that might appeal to the masses. There were other photos too, personal ones of previous cars such as the Ferrari 275GTB/4 he now regrets selling. It is apparently the one car he would buy back if he could. On the other side of the room there were some lovely old photos of a sky blue Ferrari Dino GTS, Lord Mexborough's young daughter sitting on the front of the car.

"She dented the bonnet," he said, seeing me looking at it, and smiling at the memory.

Back in the house we sat down for coffee and biscuits and went back to the beginning. I was intrigued to know where Lord Mexborough's passion for cars originated.

"Partly hereditary," he tells me.

His grandfather had apparently been "a bit of a racing driver", once holding a speed record for breaching 100mph at the beginning of the last century. His mother was not an enthusiast as such but she did have a 1934 Bentley that he would eventually learn to drive in. It was such a difficult car to drive that anything afterwards turned out to be easy. His father had no interest in cars whatsoever, openly disapproving of his son's love of them. Even so, he gave him a Sunbeam Talbot as a 21st birthday present. Sadly Lord Mexborough not only crashed it the same day but twice more in the course of the year, realising now that he had been an inexperienced driver at the time. I can only assume that this did nothing to further endear his father to cars. Since then he's only had one accident, and that was in 1958. His father's indifference to cars was something that he would make the most of and he soon found that he could change cars as long as he kept the colour the same, his father never noticing anything different.

The beginning of the 1960s heralded what Lord Mexborough refers to as "the golden age of driving", a period he now looks back on fondly.

"If you had an E-type, which I did at the time, you were the king of the road. You were in a car that could do 140mph plus, when the average family car could only do 70 or 80mph flat out. No motorways. No speed limits. You could get to London as quick in an E-type Jaguar driving fast then as you can now on the motorway keeping to the speed limit. The problem with the E-type was, from here, you couldn't get to London without filling up once and then all the cars you had passed would get in front of you again."

Lord Mexborough explained to me that he gave up on cars for a little while and took up flying planes, sharing a Piper Comanche plane with his brother and travelling to Africa, the Middle East and anywhere else that took their fancy. At that point he had one car but was by no means a collector. That changed in 1979 when his father passed away leaving him some inheritance money. He decided to invest some of this money in his earlier passion. He bought a Ferrari Daytona, similar to the one now in his garage, and began to build a collection from there. The choices of car were simply based upon those that he liked and those that he wanted to drive. His decisions were never purely based upon speculation and the potential for profit though he sensibly didn't want cars that would lose money. Over the years he made money and lost money, particularly in the boom of 1988/89 and the bust of 1990/91 during which he "both gained and suffered". Despite reaching a peak of 7 or 8 Ferraris his interest in the marque began to diminish as he grew fonder of the Porsche 911, seeing them as "more fun to drive, easier to drive, and smaller". To many that know of him as a collector, Lord Mexborough is best known for his love of Porsches.

He has driven many other cars over the years too, from the McLaren F1 which left him wondering whether he could get a syndicate together to buy one, to battling with French rush hour traffic in the Bugatti Veyron. As a renowned collector, Lord Mexborough is often lent new cars by the manufacturers, presumably to see if they can tempt him to buy one. A month before we met he had been lent the latest Porsche 911 GT3 RS, then the purest and most focused Porsche on sale. Echoing the many positive reviews of that car he claims it was "perfect" for spirited driving on the Yorkshire moors due to its pace and the way that it deals with direction changes and broken surfaces. He went on to tell me a little bit about the Ferrari F40 he once owned and how it felt quicker than anything else, its undoubted speed combining with being noisy, low and wide. Apparently there were particular challenges with driving the Porsche 959 he had shown me on track and it took Le Mans legend Derek Bell to show him how to get over the inherent understeer to get the best out of the car. We briefly touched on the topic track driving, Lord Mexborough explaining that he used to be a fan before he got "too old", Donington being his favourite UK circuit.

With the two of us deep in conversation the morning flew by. Soon the coffee was cold and it was time for me to get my stuff together and drive back down to London. It was refreshing to speak with a man that has spent much of his lifetime embracing his passion for cars and driving, especially as I was only just starting to embrace mine. There was nothing complicated about it either. He had the opportunity to buy some nice cars and to drive them and that's exactly what he did. It was fascinating to me that Lord Mexborough placed the golden age of motoring so firmly in the past, never to return as a result of greater restrictions and the ever-increasing amount of traffic on our roads. It was equally interesting to hear how his preference for Porsches came from wanting performance cars that were not too wide or unwieldy for the road, as Ferraris had slowly become. The very changes to motoring that continue today began affecting Lord Mexborough's enjoyment of cars long before I was even born. Perhaps the changes we will see over the next 30 or 40 years will be even more dramatic.

Before I left and say goodbye I asked if there were any experiences that stood out in all his years of being a car enthusiast.

"Twelve supercars raced the Orient Express train from platform 11 at Victoria station, London to Venice," Lord Mexborough responded after a moment's thought, the memory causing a cheeky smile to emerge on his face. "That was quite fun."

The response stuck in my head as I drove back down the A1 to London. He had given me a few more details – one or two of the other participants, a couple of the other cars involved – but nothing to do justice to what sounded like one hell of a story. I did a little research and discovered that the event had been organised by Russ Malkin, best known for producing the *Long Way Down* and *Long Way Round* documentaries with Euan McGregor and Charley Boorman. This was one of his first high-profile projects. Russ was away filming *Extreme Frontiers* with Charley in Canada. I was eager to get the full story on his return but in the meantime I had my own trip to take.

On with the show

London–Calais–Spa

The planning for the European road trip had taken over my life in the weeks leading up to my departure, particularly as I needed to plan a suitable route and lock-down my co-drivers. I wanted to set the dates so that I could cram in as many car-related experiences as possible. I was looking at motorsport events, classic car events and introductory track sessions but trying to link these things together with some of Europe's best driving roads and visits to a few key places was getting quite complicated as they were scattered all over the place. Thankfully it all seemed to come together as we approached the departure date. I had three different co-drivers lined up to tackle different sections of the journey and I was already looking forward to the ways these different personalities might affect my own experiences. The car was all ready to go; high-vis vests, a large European map and other necessary odds and ends taking up some of the precious storage space. I had downloaded the "Alps and main European roads" map for my sat nav, written an itinerary, and arranged data bundles for my mobile phone so that I could keep up with emails on the road without incurring extortionate roaming charges. All the boring stuff was done.

My first co-driver, Ned, arrived in London from Norfolk the night before we were due to leave. Despite being cousins we really didn't know each other at all and I couldn't actually remember when we had last spoken until Mum suggested that I call him. I had heard that he was quite into cars and had been to Le Mans a number of times with his father, my uncle. I also knew that he used to do some motocross racing until an accident put a stop to it. We talked a few times and exchanged some emails. He claimed to be a confident driver and a keen photographer, which sounded like an ideal combination. As he was only 21 years-old I was concerned about insurance costs but it turned out to be fairly cheap to add him to my policy. We spent a bit of time chatting upon his arrival but there would be plenty of time to get to know each other and catch up on family news over the coming days. A train to France awaited and in less than 24 hours we would be at Spa-Francorchamps in Belgium, reportedly one of the world's greatest race circuits.

Departure day finally arrived and we made our way over to the garage first thing in the morning. I started by talking Ned around the car in much the same way as Tony had with me outside Foskers' premises a month earlier. We both appeared pretty relaxed on the outside but the excitement had been building for days now and I couldn't wait to hit European soil. It was about time.

I took the wheel to start with, guiding us out of central London just as the Monday morning rush hour traffic began to build. As we started the dull drive through south London and down to the south coast I continued explaining the intricacies of the F355 to Ned alongside the usual family small talk. It was my first time using the Channel Tunnel and I wasn't quite sure what to expect. Ned was a veteran from all the Le Mans trips he had been on and assured me that there was no way to go wrong. He was right. I couldn't help but smile when the ticket machine greeted me by name and produced the tag that we needed to hang from the rear-view mirror. After a little breakfast in the terminal we returned to the car and crawled along with the other traffic towards the train. I had an image of parking carriages interspersed with passenger carriages but it was clearly nothing like that, simply carriages lined with cars and the occasional lavatory. The attendant tried to find a space on one of the more spacious carriages with the lorries and buses but that wasn't to be.

"I'll just check for you," he politely said without prompt. "A lot of people with cars like that prefer a little more room."

I could see what he meant once I traversed the ramp onto the train with the other cars and motorbikes. Had my car been any wider I don't think we would have fitted between the ledges that run down the sides of each carriage. My car's wider successor, the Ferrari 360, would have been an even greater challenge. Luckily we were ok. I got out and went for a bit of a walk, passing estate cars with middle-aged couples snoozing and groups of motorcyclists having loud, animated conversations overlooking their vehicles like proud fathers.

On arrival into Calais we pulled slowly out of the train having patiently made our way through carriage after carriage until we reached the opening. From there we burst onto dull motorways again. Once we had got our bearings and the sat nav had decided to wake up we stopped for petrol and a change of driver. I had really hoped to give Ned a chance to drive the Ferrari for the first time back home on familiar roads but we simply ran out of time in the lead up to our departure date. I wasn't worried and neither should he have been, the car being surprisingly easy to drive and the roads being fairly quiet. He pulled back onto the motorway and we pressed onwards into the French countryside and over the border into Belgium, passing lines of trucks but very little else on the grey Monday morning. I asked Ned later about his impressions of driving the Ferrari for the first time and his answer was predictably enthusiastic.

"Amazing!" he told me. "It's smooth but it's not super smooth. It's got that rumble and burble behind you and you can feel that it's a powerful car. You put your foot down and it builds momentum and then just goes and goes and goes."

We stuck to the main roads initially, heading north towards Brugge, then westward past Gent and towards Brussels, laughing each time the voice from the sat nav failed to pronounce the names properly. One thing became clear pretty quickly; Ned and I had very similar taste in music. His interest in 90s and 00s hip hop would give me the chance to introduce him to a few classics along the way, though the music policy was far more eclectic than that might imply and dependent upon who was in the passenger seat and therefore on DJ duty. Despite having standard creature comforts such as air conditioning and a stereo, the F355 is never a car that lets you relax fully. Even as a passenger you feel involved in the driving process and unless you're a really heavy sleeper there's little chance of a nap. To alleviate the boredom of the motorway we decided to change the route slightly. Looking at the map it seemed as though we could head south from Brussels towards Namur and then wiggle across on some country roads towards Spa. Of course these were all simply names to us and had no meaning. We didn't know what these places were like or if the roads would be fun but we decided to have a go, all in the spirit of adventure.

The road to Namur was straightforward but things got a little more interesting from there on. The sat nav soon decided that we were no longer on a "major European road" and went blank as we turned off the motorway and cut into the Belgian countryside. I didn't care for the moment as I was finally having a chance to enjoy some proper driving on European soil. Ned was attempting to navigate with the large scale European map I had brought along but it didn't go into enough detail for us to work our way through this web of rural roads. I pressed on, pleased to be able to work through the gearbox once more and to enjoy a bit of scenery after a diet of trucks and tarmac. We started to go the direction we thought we should be heading in, skirting a small valley before ducking under trees, leaves glistening from the rain that had been dusting the landscape since we crossed the border. We pulled over in a small village to get our bearings and I decided to try to use the map function on my phone but the lack of signal scuppered those plans too. We set off again, none of the local villages and towns appearing on our map and no one around to ask. Time was becoming an issue now. We had to make it to the Spa-Francorchamps race circuit for 5pm for the start of the *baptême de piste* that I had booked us on to.

We crossed through another town just as some local school children were making their way home, them stopping and pointing open-mouthed as the gleaming red Italian rolled through, instantly bringing a splash of colour to the grey Belgian day. We then managed to delve deeper into agricultural country, blasting past wide, open fields. Often we would find progress marred by roads in desperate need of repair, some looking as though they hadn't been touched for decades. The truth was that they were probably only used on occasion by local farmers and the lack of traffic implied that it would be a little while before another Ferrari would be here.

Eventually we found a larger town that did appear on our map and decided to duck into a petrol station for some help, our combined male sense of direction no match for Belgium's road network. It turned out that we had added almost two hours onto our journey and now had to rush to make it to Spa.

"How long will it take?" I asked the attendant.

"Normally one hour. But in that," he continued, smiling and pointing his nose at the Ferrari, "maybe less".

We set off again and ensured no more deviations from the main road until we got to Spa, the voice from the sat nav greeting us as though she never went away and directing us on towards Verviers before local signage and the literature provided in the Spa-Francorchamps welcome pack guided us the rest of the way.

We arrived at exactly 5pm and were immediately ushered through the gates by a security guard. We couldn't relax yet as we had no idea where to go and where to leave the car. It appeared that there were no staff around to help us, only the constant roar of engine noise coming from the track and a large number of supercars milling around the paddock. We moved further along and discovered a group of people chatting near the back entrance to one of the pit garages. Ned pulled up behind a Swiss-registered Ferrari 430 Scuderia as I braved the rain to run over and get some directions. Frustratingly no one knew what I was talking about. There was a one-week Swiss track driving course in full flow and none of the people involved had any official affiliation with the race circuit. I ran outside again just as a black Ferrari 458 pulled up alongside a grey Aston Martin DBS, me torn between staring at the assembled exotica and pressing on with my hunt for answers. Just as I was about to start skipping over puddles and heading back over to Ned in the car one of the Swiss guys called after me.

"See that man in the orange jacket?" I nodded in response once I had spotted him. "Speak to him. He works here."

After some instructions, a bit more running around and me getting angry with a locked door, Ned and I made it upstairs and signed the relevant forms while a group of people were shown around the control room that monitors what is happening on the track. We missed that bit, not really knowing what was going on but not feeling as though we were missing out on anything of real interest. It wasn't what we had come for. Minutes later we were all ushered downstairs to another one of the pit garages. The idea was that we would each have two passenger laps in a Renaultsport Megane with one of their drivers and then have two laps behind the safety car in our own car.

Spa-Francorchamps wasn't a track that I knew much about. I had picked up from magazines that it was seen as one of the best and most interesting tracks to drive and that was enough to entice me there. The modern-day circuit, on which we were about to drive, only dates back to 1979 and is best known as the home of the Belgian Grand Prix, but the story goes back much further than that. In the early 1920s Jules de Thier and Henri Langlois Van Ophem created a circuit out of a triangle of local roads, creating a track of more than 14km in length that quickly became known for its long straights and fast corners. It would allow higher speeds than almost any other circuit. It was embraced by motorcyclists first but was soon taken up for Grand Prix racing, the first race taking place in 1925.

In time, as racing cars developed and were able to reach higher speeds, it began to be seen as unsafe, particularly as there were few run-off areas. The 1960s and 1970s saw multiple fatalities in both Formula 1 and touring car races such as the 24 Hours of Spa, and soon drivers and organisers were no longer willing to take the risks. Plans were eventually drawn up and agreed upon to redevelop the circuit, taking into account the safety concerns that had been aired and attempting to maintain the characteristics of the original circuit. The new track was around half the length at 7km and incorporated more technical corners and more run-off areas. It was opened in 1979 with Formula 1 returning four years later.

It is known today as having some of the best corners of any circuit in the world, including the legendary Eau Rouge – a descending straight that pulls to the left before climbing upwards and to the right, leading to a blind summit. To take this effectively most professional drivers will go as fast as possible, relying on the downforce created by the aerodynamics of their car to provide greater grip as they fire themselves uphill and prepare themselves for the unseen turn beyond the crest. Getting it right is crucial for a racing driver.

For me Spa-Francorchamps was about to take on some personal significance as this would be the first circuit that I had ever driven on. The experience was due to be very introductory in nature – a passenger ride followed by two laps that I presumed would be very slow – but I didn't care. I was excited, pleased that this would be my first such experience. The more serious track driving would come on another day when there would be no such speed restrictions. Hopefully it would not seem such an alien environment after this.

It wasn't raining too heavily now but it had been coming down slowly all day. I wasn't sure if that was a good or bad thing at first until it occurred to me that a wet circuit would mean less grip and potentially more fun. Stepping out onto the pitlane to watch the Renaultsport Meganes fly past with some of the other participants strapped into the passenger seat, it was clear that the drivers were very comfortable in these conditions. Every now and again you would hear the squeal of rubber on tarmac as the drivers would show off on some unseen damp corner with a bit of exuberance and a bit of oversteer. All we could see were the cars coming around the corner and then blasting along the short straight that would mark the start and finish line if this were a race. The difficulty of racing in such conditions became clear to me when I saw the amount of water spraying up from the backs of the tyres of these cars. Visibility must be almost impossible unless you are leading the pack in a competitive race in the wet.

I found myself getting a little apprehensive as the Meganes came and went from the pits every two laps, each time picking up someone else and depositing a slightly wobbly but smiling person back to their friends or family in the garage. My name was soon called out. I went and found a helmet and waited eagerly for my first passenger experience on track.

"As long as I'm not sick," I said to Ned. He simply smiled before going back to taking photographs some of the race-prepared Ferraris that were dotted around the garage, sensibly sheltering from the rain until his name was called.

I settled into the passenger seat and introduced myself to the driver. As we pulled off we started chatting. I told him about the European pilgrimage I had planned and that this was my first track experience. He was a man of few words. That was a good thing as I needed to focus on breathing properly to control my motion sickness. It's quite an affliction for a car enthusiast but thankfully it only affects me when I'm not the one driving.

He was a phenomenal driver and clearly knew the circuit and the car like the back of his hand. I had never been in a car when it has been driven so hard before and I was blown away by the levels of grip that the Renaultsport Megane delivered in these conditions, though I would imagine the car wasn't using standard road tyres. Thankfully the rain was allowing my driver to do some outrageous cornering, pointing the nose into the apex early and then powering around the corner, controlling the oversteer as the back end of the car seemed to clip the edge of the track behind us, moving in a perfect arc. The feeling of going through the Eau Rouge corner was worth the whole experience alone; the way that it dips and turns before you experience a feeling of increased mass, the compression pushing you down into your seat at the point where the road starts rising again. It felt like I was part of a strange physics experiment. I turned to the driver at one point and asked if the rain made it more fun for him. He looked back to me with a slightly demented smile and a face that said, "You've got me!" before throwing the car into another corner and riding out an immense slide, the tyres arcing across the rain-soaked asphalt again.

Afterwards I thanked him and stepped out of the car with a little wobble before finding my balance and saw Ned heading toward the second car for his two laps. As the passenger laps were almost over I was sent to collect the Ferrari to line up and get ready for the two laps we would be driving behind the safety car. We had already spoken to the woman organising us to make sure that they knew we would need to switch drivers at some point so Ned could take over and do his two laps. I was directed to pull up behind a Porsche 911 after I drove through the garage to the pit lane. I got out to set up my video camera so that I could try to capture the experience.

"You should charge people for rides in that," came a booming voice from behind me.

I turned around to see a middle-aged man with white hair who appeared to be milling around aimlessly, presumably waiting for a family member to finish their Spa experience. A bit anxious about the prospect of driving on track, I managed little more than a laugh and a smile before jumping back into the driver's seat so that I could wait for Ned in the dry. The encounter was another reminder of the broad appeal of this car, the attention it draws meaning that you never forget you are driving something special.

"I don't know how he goes so fast!" said Ned, tumbling into the car having jogged down the pit lane to join me after his passenger laps.

We waited a bit longer before the three cars in front of us pulled away, savouring the moment as we followed them out of the pit lane and onto the circuit, spray kicking up gently from the rear tyres of the Porsche in front. We were eager to see how our own skills would stack up after the master class we had witnessed during the passenger laps but as we trundled along, heading for Eau Rouge, with memories of the compressed feeling you experience going through there flat out still fresh in our minds, it became clear that we weren't going to be allowed to get any speed up. So far I had barely got into third gear. If anything I was struggling to go slowly enough to maintain any distance between us and the cars in front. I understood from the outset that it would not resemble a proper track day but we were crawling unnecessarily slowly for most of the time, barely able to get any feeling of speed or excitement.

About halfway through the second lap the Porsche in front of me seemed to slow down even more. I wasn't impressed.

"What the hell is this idiot doing now?" I said to Ned. "I'm not even allowed to overtake him."

"Maybe you can slow down even more and make some space between us and him," ventured Ned, it becoming clear at that moment that the Porsche driver had the same idea.

As we rounded the corner the Porsche launched off in front of us, the rear spoiler rising for the first time since we had been on track, indicating that he had breached 75mph. For the first time I got a chance to hear the throaty bellow from the Porsche's flat-six engine before I eased down my right foot and the sound of the F355's V8 took over, the revs rising more urgently as the road straightened. I made the most of the brief straight, snatching another gear before the next turn approached and I was forced to come off the power and brake instead.

"That guy's a genius, Ned. We should have done that from the beginning!"

It was too little too late as we caught up with the two cars in front and then rolled into the pit lane a few turns later. My frustration soon turned to jealousy when we switched seats and Ned took over. Everyone else had done their track experiences so it was just us and the safety car on the track. We pulled out of the pits for a second time and the white Renaultsport Megane seemed to accelerate with a little more intent than before, taking corners harder too. Maybe it was because there was only the Ferrari behind him now or perhaps due to the driver having a few passengers in the car to show off to. Either way, he didn't hold back in the way that he had before. With the pace turned up a notch, Ned had a chance to really enjoy Spa-Francorchamps and to get a feel for driving on track, watching the choice of racing line taken by the professional just metres in front. It was good to hear the Ferrari zing through the rev range and listen to the "click-clack" sound of the gear change even if I wasn't doing the driving. Jealousy aside, I was pleased that Ned had this experience knowing that he would be leaving for home once we reached Zurich and would miss out on the Alpine passes that myself and Spencer would be crossing.

For my part, I was no longer a track virgin and was now ready for some serious track driving. Luckily the next day would see us heading over the border to Germany and tackling the legendary Nürburgring but first we had to find our hotel for the night.

Onwards to Green Hell

Spa-Nürburg

With only a short drive between us and the town of Nürburg, we weren't in much of a rush the next morning. We headed off past the Spa-Francorchamps race circuit for the last time, the road rising around and behind it, giving us snapshots of what the track looks like in its entirety through the dense greenery that lined the road. We pressed on towards Sankt-Vith and the south-eastern corner of Belgium before crossing over the border to Germany. There we stuck to the main roads until we could break off into the countryside. Ned switched off the sat nav and picked up the directions I had downloaded back at the hotel; he was on navigation duty and I was at the wheel. It was great to get onto some proper roads after the failed attempt at a cross-country drive the previous day. The roads here wiggled their way north-east, climbing gently in altitude as we cut our way across the lush green landscape. It was still a little overcast but the rain that had followed us across Belgium seemed to have lifted now that we were in Germany and we could only hope that it would stay that way for our visit to the Nürburgring later that day.

Of all the items on my itinerary, a visit to the Nürburgring was probably the biggest rite of passage on my path to becoming a petrolhead. It was certainly high in Juergen Obermann's recommendations when I spoke to him in Monaco and it was regularly discussed by motoring journalists in the magazines I read. It wasn't just the professionals either. Car blogs and forums regularly held discussions around planned trips to the 'Ring, those that had been already often sharing photos of their visit. It has taken on legendary status over the years and now it seems that you're not serious about cars and driving if you haven't been there and experienced it for yourself. The fact that British racing driver Jackie Stewart nicknamed it the 'green hell' in the 1960s – when Formula 1 races still took place on the Nordschleife (northern loop) – gives you an idea of how serious this track is. Today it is seen to be one of the most demanding circuits in the world.

The Nordschleife dates back to 1927 and is classed as a derestricted public toll road, providing access to the public during *touristenfahrten* sessions which often take place at evenings and weekends. It is almost 13 miles long and has huge changes in altitude – the track dropping around 300 metres before you have even reached the halfway point. The length means that it is very difficult to learn all the corners, of which many are blind, and there are many accidents throughout the year from enthusiastic drivers that have over-committed on the way into a corner only to get caught out.

Today a multitude of car manufacturers test their cars at the Nürburgring to hone their dynamics for the road. Many performance-orientated vehicles use lap times as a form of benchmarking in order to make claims of superiority over their competitors. As a result, many of the so-called "spy shots" of disguised cars that appear in the motoring press are captured around the town of Nürburg.

Having ensured that we had accurate directions before leaving Spa, we were certainly better equipped to find our way to our destination than the previous day. However, it seemed as though the car was having different ideas. Since we had set off that morning the oil pressure needle had slowly moved closer to the red line, indicating that it was too high. I didn't know why. I was still learning the ins and outs of running this 15 year-old Ferrari and was quite concerned. I found myself questioning whether I had made the right choice in buying a mid-90s supercar for this epic trip. Would it actually be capable of completing the journey?

I lifted off the throttle and drove a gear higher than normal to ensure the engine was running at lower revs. I wanted to avoid putting undue pressure on the engine but it didn't make any difference to the dial reading. At the small town of Walsdorf I pulled over to take a look at the oil level but the metal cap was too hot and too tight for me to unscrew. Anxious about the possibility of damaging my car, and any potentially ruinous repair bills that might follow, I fired up my phone to search online Ferrari forums. I wanted to know if this was a common complaint and could be ignored but I found nothing to reassure me, the consensus being that high oil pressure was abnormal. That much I knew already. Unlike most cars, the F355 requires you to check oil levels when the engine is warm rather than cold but even with a t-shirt wrapped around my hand I was making no progress on the hot metal cap. We pressed on to Nürburg and hoped that everything would be alright. Besides, it didn't look like we had far to go.

I had read that the roads around Nürburg were almost as good as the track itself in places and as we got closer we were treated to long tree-lined roads with well-sighted sweeping corners that encouraged spirited driving. Soon we were following signs for the Nürburgring, leaving Ned to relax after a morning of navigating from a mobile phone. The oil pressure didn't seem to be getting any worse so I took the opportunity to make the most of the situation whenever the road opened up in front of me. Certain sections were arrow straight, dipping and gently undulating between corners. This meant that the biggest challenge was to avoid getting carried away and going too fast just in case any local police were lurking in wait of speeding Brits to pull over and fine. Soon we spotted the edges of the Nordschleife circuit and the pace dropped as the excitement began to rise. In a few hours we would be taking on the green hell ourselves.

Choosing accommodation for a night in Nürburg had been easy. The Hotel am Tiergarten was by far the best known place in town and a top recommendation in many of the guides published by motoring magazines and websites. One of the reasons for this is that the hotel is owned by the family of Sabine Schmitz, the "Queen of the Nürburgring".

Having grown up next to the Nürburgring it is perhaps no surprise that Sabine became a racing driver. She has had much success on the track, including being the first woman to win the Nürburgring 24 Hours race, and is now known for driving one of the Ring Taxis that provide high speed passenger laps around the Nordschleife. She continues to race today and has become a bit of celebrity, even appearing on the television show *Top Gear* a number of times.

The other reason for staying at Hotel am Tiergarten is that the Pistenklause restaurant is directly underneath. It is an institution in these parts, being very well known amongst the motorsport community as well as with tourists. It is the place where teams and racing drivers come to celebrate success at the 'Ring. Ned and I hadn't heard of it before we arrived but soon discovered that it is best known for its signature dish – steak served while still cooking on a hot stone.

I had intentionally devised the trip to allow us to visit the Nürburgring during one of the mid-week evening *touristenfahrten* sessions in late spring. If the track was as challenging and as popular as I had been led to believe then I would prefer my first visit to take place at as quiet a time as possible.

As Ned and I rolled into the sleepy town of Nürburg on a Tuesday lunchtime it seemed as though my planning had been spot on. There were barely any cars on the roads, few people on the streets, and only the occasional hint that we had arrived in a town that has become a second home for many petrolheads. It meant that finding the hotel was easy and we were soon turning off the main road that runs through the town, downhill towards the back of the circuit.

Thankfully we had arrived just in time to catch the end of the buffet lunch and went and sat up on the balcony to enjoy the good weather once we had loaded plates with samples from each of the heated, metal serving bowls. Due to its altitude this area has a reputation for being wet and dreary but not on this day. The weather had improved markedly as we made our way from Francorchamps, the late spring sunshine bright and warming and the sky cloudless. All this suggested that we would be enjoying the Nordscleife in the dry, which would certainly be preferable for us first-timers.

It felt almost Alpine outside and was unbelievably tranquil. The green fields that lined the edge of town were scattered with flowers and dissected by trees. An old castle sat on top of a hill surveying the town. Once we had walked up Hauptstrasse, the main road that runs through the centre of Nürburg, the motoring focus of the town became clearer. One hotel was painted up to show a scene from a race, its huge mural seeming both garish and alluring at the same time. Almost next door was BMW's M Sport test centre, a clear indicator of the role that the Nürburgring plays in the development of the company's most sporting road cars. Just up the road, near the entrance to the Grand Prix circuit, we began to spot some development cars for the first time, many painted with black and white stripes, zig-zags and swirls to create optical illusions that masked the exact shape of the new car. It was clearly a big testing day, with many soon-to-be-launched Mercedes and BMWs out in full force. A week or so later we would see photos of some of these cars on websites and in magazines. We stood for a while and watched the cars come and go, trying to work out what we were looking at.

"There goes the new BMW M5," I would say, probably a bit too excitedly, my habitual magazine reading momentarily paying off. "Look, it's the new GT version of the Audi R8 Spyder," Ned reacting to my announcement and catching a quick blurred photo as the car sped under a bridge and out of sight.

We made our way back to the hotel, the town seeming more or less deserted. We didn't quite understand everything we saw, such as a Christmas tree at the top of a long pole in May, but we walked slowly and soaked up all the details anyway. We had time to kill before picking up our rental car and heading to the 'Ring and we simply wanted to enjoy the sunshine.

It was frustrating to discover that British insurance companies have exclusions in place regarding cover on the Nürburgring but perhaps no surprise. I knew it was classed as a public toll road but it was clear that accidents happen regularly. If you crash on the circuit it is not only your car you have to worry about, you are also liable for recovery costs, damage to Armco barriers and loss of revenue if they have to close the circuit for any length of time. I can understand why British insurers don't want to open themselves up to dealing with something like that, particularly when language barriers come into play. I did find a company that would insure my car but only on a closed track event as opposed to the public sessions. It just wasn't worth the risk, especially when you consider the strain that such a circuit can put on a car, tyres and brakes in particular taking a battering. I decided to hire something fun but not too expensive or so fast that we'd end up killing ourselves, settling on a right-hand drive Renaultsport Clio from RSR, a local company that provided local tours, driver training and rental cars for the 'Ring. I had once owned a previous generation Renaultsport Clio and was well aware of how capable they are on challenging roads from my experiences driving it in Scotland. I was sure that the current model would be as capable here.

Like everything else in Nürburg, RSR seemed to be tucked away behind some trees on the edge of a field. As we approached we saw some of their engineers working on a car outside. They were focused on their work and ignored us. As there was no one else around we decided to spend some time looking around at the different cars they had to hire out to visitors like us. Inside the garage sat a Lotus Exige S painted in white and heavily branded with RSR logos. It was in these cars that you could tour around the local area. Always having wanted to drive one, I might have considered it if we had more time. This one was being worked on. The small rear cover was open, exposing the workings of this mid-engined road racer, and a piece of bodywork sat behind it on the ground. Elsewhere inside there was a track-prepared Porsche 911 GT3, something I didn't recognise that looked like a prototype racing car, and an 80s Ferrari tucked away in the back. Most of the cars were outside and here we spotted a handful of the Renaultsport Clios that RSR have available, one of which we would soon be driving.

A young couple arrived and went upstairs from the workshop so we followed them and soon found ourselves sitting on a large leather sofa listening to a fairly comprehensive briefing. It was here that we first learned of the significant changes in altitude on the Nordschleife and, as such, that our brakes would be under considerable strain during the first section of the circuit before it starts climbing again. We were given a number of other pointers. Only overtake on the left-hand side and if someone wants to overtake you, indicate and pull to the right so they know you have seen them. Do not go lower than third gear when on the circuit as lower gears are simply not needed when driving something like the Clio. If you crash, call these numbers... It went on but I didn't mind.

Both Ned and I were pleased to have a bit of expert insight before we set off. We selected appropriate sized helmets and were handed cotton balaclavas to wear underneath before setting off out into the bright sunshine again. Finally, we were handed a plastic circuit entry card that was already topped-up with the four lap allowance I had paid for alongside the car rental. This would be required at the entry barrier at the circuit.

Strapped into our silver Clio, we set off for the short drive to the entrance with Ned at the wheel. As we approached we finally saw the action we had been expecting, the car park full of all sorts of cars and a lot of people just hanging around, presumably in between laps or about to head out. It seemed busy in comparison to the empty streets around the town we had explored earlier but I knew that we had picked a good time to come, the guys at RSR confirming that it should be perfect conditions and relatively quiet. On a weekday afternoon it was only the really committed petrolheads that were there, mostly visitors from out of town and mostly men between the ages of 20 and 50.

Ned and I had decided to do one lap each and then switch, meaning that we would have a bit of a breather from the intense focus that would be required to get round the circuit safely but at a decent pace. Having paused in the car park to get a feel for the situation Ned pulled away towards the barriers, dodging incoming traffic and the many people that were chatting and checking out the more exotic cars in the car park. One of the stewards, an older man and one of the happiest-looking people that I saw during the whole trip, spotted that the car was right-hand drive and directed us to the appropriate barrier so that Ned could hold the plastic card to the reader and get going. We were initially forced to zig-zag through some cones before being deposited out on the track. I'm not sure what we were expecting but it came as a bit of a surprise to have the circuit open up in front of us for 13 miles of pure, focused driving. Ned didn't hesitate though. Foot to the floor, waiting for the beep that indicated it was time to shift up, and then working through the gears until the first corner. He focused. I focused. We didn't time it but I'm guessing it took around 10 minutes to complete that first lap before the cones funnelled us off the circuit and back out towards the barriers and the car park. The fastest hatchbacks, driven by professionals that know the circuit well, can complete a lap in a little over 8 minutes. I'd like to think we were no more than a couple of minutes off that. You'd think it would pass quite quickly and in many ways it does but it really feels like 13 miles in length and no less. You are conscious of every turn, camber change and overtake as you progress. It really is intense.

I'm not sure what Ned was thinking during that first lap but I was simultaneously doing about three things. Firstly, I was admiring Ned's driving. He might only have been 21 and new to track driving but he drove as though he had much more experience. Secondly, I was trying not to be sick, turning up the air con and pulling the balaclava down below my mouth so that I could breath in and out steadily. Not knowing what was coming meant that you could never prepare yourself for where the car was going to move next and that became quite nauseating quite quickly. Thirdly, I was trying to learn the track as we went around it and I'm sure Ned was doing the same.

They say that you can only learn the first handful of corners until you come to be more familiar with the circuit but Ned and I found ourselves picking up the key points quickly so that we were at least aware when we were approaching a particularly challenging section even if we couldn't quite remember in what way it was challenging.

Ned pulled into the car park for the changeover and I took the opportunity to take off the helmet and have a bit of a breather.

"I'm afraid that I'm not the best passenger," I said to Ned, explaining that I'm prone to car sickness at the best of times if I'm not in control.

"Well you can do all the remaining laps if you like," Ned replied, ever the gentleman. But that's not what I wanted. This was supposed to be a shared experience and a little nausea was all part of the fun I reasoned.

I found myself feeling both excited and nervous as I leant out of the window and held the plastic card up to the reader, the barrier instantly rising to let me through. I knew roughly what to expect now as I wiggled through the cones, taking a second to wipe the sweat from my palms on my trousers and then out onto the wide straight that dips downhill. What is it like to drive the Nürburgring? After years of wondering, it was time to find out for myself.

I kept to the right in case anything came up behind us, the road rising again before pulling left. I found myself instinctively lifting off the throttle as the road vanished ahead. All I knew was that there was a turn coming up and it looked as though it was going right. In the end it wasn't as bad as I had feared but I wouldn't let that lull me into thinking the next 11 or 12 miles would be predictable. Very soon we were upon a right-left-right combo, the final turn of this sequence being tighter than it looked and the large run-off area suggesting that not everyone gets it right.

Soon I found some rhythm, broken only by faster cars coming past us on the left and stealing the racing line through the corners. I began to look at the cambers of the road ahead, working the inclines to help corner faster and trying to make the most of the straights. But I didn't dare get cocky with my driving; there were too many blind crests and deceiving dips for that. Instead I kept the zingy 2 litre engine high up the rev range so that I had the power ready to pull us through and out of the corners.

I had been told that it is not unusual to see all sorts of vehicles on the circuit during *touristenfahrten*, even buses, but we had timed our visit well and it was fairly quiet. There were plenty of Porsches and BMWs speeding around the track, hustling us to the side and shortly gone from vision. There were also some Brits, one group in an old diesel Volkswagen Golf powering past and leaving a trail of smoke from the ageing car's exhaust pipes.

We weren't the slowest on the track and both Ned and I managed at least one overtake each, the limited power of the Clio and many faster cars behind us meaning we had to wait for the optimal moment on a well-sighted straight. I had a chance to do just that as the track started to drop down into a tree-lined valley before it bottomed-out. I dropped a gear, ready for the corner and the climb that followed, leading to one of the fastest sections of the circuit. After a while of flowing with this section of the road, never pushing too hard or thinking that I knew what was coming, we reached Caracciola-

Karussell – an iconic banked corner. Here the inside of the turn was lighter in colour and felt like a rougher surface than the rest of the circuit, providing the traction to power around it and slingshot out of the other side.

Throughout the circuit you can't help but notice writing on the road surface, words painted sporadically in whites, reds, greens and yellow. At first we wondered whether they were some kind of hieroglyphs, markings intended to let construction people know where repairs were required or for marshals to know where to stand during races. Then they became more frequent and suddenly we were upon sections of the circuit on which words or even sentences were painted, though we had little time to work out what it was that they said. Instead they remained fleeting statements that flew beneath our wheels as they would for the racing drivers that have more pressing things on their minds, such as the next corner. As a passenger you have more time to pick out a word, maybe the name of a car manufacturer but it was never quite clear what was all about.

In actual fact these markings are simply pieces of graffiti of different sorts. Much of it is painted around the time of the 24 hours race when people camp within the circuit, presumably jumping the barriers the night before the race to get creative with some paint. Some markings are pure vandalism and apparently so rude that they have intentionally been left out of driving-based video games by the developers. Sadly Ferrari wasn't so careful when it released a press photo of its 599-derived FXX car breaking one of the lap records, one graffiti artists' impression of male genitalia painted on the road behind the car. Some are markings and messages written by excited driving enthusiasts that want to record that they were once at the 'Ring. Other markings are messages to drivers that are taking part in races there or simply a show of support for a specific manufacturer. Some markings are promotional, including company names and website addresses. Some, sadly, are memorial in nature and are tribute messages to those that have died on the circuit. There are no official figures released but it is thought that anywhere between three and twelve people die during public sessions each year.

As we neared the end of the circuit we came to another banked corner, this one feeling bumpier, almost as though it was paved as an afterthought. We jiggled around it and then I got back on the power, around to the left, slightly uphill and through a sweeping right-hander before hitting the final straight of the Nordschleife. The road dropped gently in front of us and I knew I finally had the time and space to run through the gears, up into sixth for the first time before the cones funnelled us back out towards the car park and the choice of taking a breather or going for another lap.

We took another break and went to have a look around the other cars in the car park before heading for a quick drink. The Devil's Diner is the cafe that overlooks the car park and the entry to the circuit and it is inexplicably decorated to emulate a stereotypical American diner despite being associated with a German racing circuit. The surprise at this discovery was soon replaced by confusion when the woman at the till requested the card that we were using to get onto the circuit and which I had left in the car. I jogged back a couple of minutes later with it and she swiped it and refused to accept any money. After some back and forth and a subsequent conversation with another member of staff, Ned managed to deduce that we were entitled to two free drinks with our four lap card and we retreated back out into the warm evening sun, joining a group of people that were checking out a new McLaren MP4-12C which was obviously fresh off the production line. Sensibly, the owner didn't seem to be taking on track, merely basking in the glory of his purchase. Elsewhere a group of 20-something men were hanging out with their various sporty hatchbacks, a tall blonde girl in a short skirt seemingly holding court in the centre of the group.

Our second laps were different from the first – less tentative, more analytical and measured, and faster. We knew what to expect now and we would remind each other about particularly tough corners, otherwise remaining focused on taking the best line for each turn and extracting the best from the car. We now knew that downshifting from fourth to third gear needed a moment more than was ideal, this change always feeling notchy, so we would compensate accordingly. We also knew that the little Clio would grip hard in the corners and would give its best at the top end of the rev range. There was little other traffic, meaning that we would only rarely be bothered by a rapid Porsche driver appearing over our left shoulders, eager to pass. All this added up. We could enjoy the experience much more fully and focus on our own progress.

As with the first laps, I went second following a little breather in the car park. I pushed and pushed on each corner, trying to turn in earlier and more decisively. I was smiling underneath my helmet and balaclava whenever the tyres squealed as I pushed the limits of adhesion on some of the tighter, well-sighted turns. It became about rhythm; carrying in the right entry speed to any given corner so that I could dispatch it as effectively as possible and maintain maximum momentum for the following straight or ensure I was in the right position to take the best line through the next corner. The experience was truly exhilarating and by the time Ned and I had handed back the car to RSR and made our way back to the hotel, we knew that we would have to come back sometime soon.

We reflected on the experience over beers and food at the bustling Pistenklaus restaurant a little while later, glancing around at the other diners and the vast array of motoring memorabilia adorning the walls. To our right sat a group of Japanese guys in Mitsubishi-branded clothing but we were never quite sure whether they worked for the manufacturer or were just big fans of the marque. Elsewhere the group of young British guys that we had seen earlier sat at a long table, the pretty blonde girl still seemingly the leader of the group. There was barely any unused wall or shelf space to be seen. Instead there were hundreds of pictures, stickers, banners, bits of car bodywork, signed photographs, trophies, plaques and even brake disks creating a cacophony of motorsport imagery and a million places to rest your eyes. In between these items, the walls themselves had been signed by racing drivers and teams that had passed through over the years. This subterranean den for driving enthusiasts seemed like a fitting place to end the day and we soon retired to our rooms full, sleepy and ready for another day on the road.

Rude Awakening

Nürburg–Stuttgart–Zurich

I don't know what time it was but the noise was intense and instantly recognisable. The smooth drone would wind up, rising in both pitch and volume, holding the high point of this crescendo for a little while before dropping again. A pause. Again it would start low, building up steadily. Surely everyone was awake now.

Why the hell was there an air raid siren going off in the small German town of Nürburg in the early hours of a Wednesday morning? Had war been declared since I had left the UK and some attacking force had targeted Germany's most famous driving circuit? I hadn't looked at a newspaper so it was remotely possible. Perhaps we were near a nuclear power plant and something had gone wrong meaning that it was time to evacuate quickly before meltdown. Half awake and in mild shock my mind continued to make assumptions as to the meaning of this horrific noise. I told myself that it was ok because I could hear no one else moving in the hotel, none of the staff running around to explain to guests that it was time to escape, no movement outside even. And then it sounded as though a car was speeding off down the street. Then some running outside. This was a residential street leading to a field, surely the movement outside was not a good sign even though the siren had now stopped, a final whirring noise making it sound as though it had broken rather than been switched off. Some more cars sped past and some more running but the hotel remained silent.

And then it all became clear as another siren sounded and a larger vehicle flew past the hotel, flashing blue lights clear through the curtains. A fire engine. I had completely forgotten in my semi-conscious stupor that there was a fire station in between the hotel and RSR's car rental premises. Even so, was it necessary to wake the whole town? Surely using pagers to alert the relevant people would have been sufficient.

I met Ned for breakfast some hours later having managed to go back to sleep without further interruption, the sun already shining and promising another warm day for our drive south through Germany. I scoped out the extent of the buffet breakfast which comprised of the usual – fruit juices, some pastries, fruit, and cereals – before sitting opposite Ned a little wearily and throwing my sunglasses and room key on the table.

"How did you sleep," I asked, more out of habit than anything.

"Air raid siren?" Ned replied, as much statement as question. He was clearly as unimpressed as I was.

We discussed it briefly but had more important things to consider, such as the 200 mile journey that would take us to Zurich via Stuttgart. We were soon back on the road. Ned took the wheel for the drive out of Nürburg on what would be his last day of the trip, me having done all of the driving between Francorchamps and Nürburg the day before. He would fly back to the UK from Zurich later that evening and Spencer would fly in at roughly the same time to join me for the next stage of the journey.

I'm sure that the five minutes we let the car run out-side of the hotel in Nürburg had annoyed many of the other residents but we didn't care. You can take some liberties with a car like the F355 in a town so focused on cars and driving. The route out of Nürburg took us around the other side of the straight that marks the start and finish of the Nordschleife and we looked at it some-what longingly, both of us ready for a few more laps. I regretted for a moment building such a precise itinerary. Another day in Nürburg was very tempting but that would have to wait for another visit. For now it was a simple run towards Koblenz, before heading south on the network of motorways that would lead us to Stuttgart.

These days would always start with a relaxed cruise as the Ferrari warmed through, us not wanting to put any undue stress on the engine, especially after the con-cerns around oil pressure the prior day. Once onto the motorways we were able to make relentless progress, simply holding position in the fast lane and ploughing onwards. Every now and again we would get out of the way of one of the large German saloon cars that seemed to be designed for this type of travel but otherwise we were unchallenged. In a car like that you simply float onwards at high velocity and arrive at your destination cool and calm. Our experience was a little more intense and required a lot more focus, especially once we found our way onto the derestricted sections of the autobahn for the first time. I had imagined that these sections of road would be perfectly smooth sheets of tarmac that would encourage confidence for high speed driving. In practice it was nothing like that. The roads were similar to British motorways, being broken and rutted in parts and shaking both the stability of the car and the confidence of the driver. I wanted to go fast, really fast but I couldn't bring myself to do it. It was simply too nerve-wracking in a car that felt so responsive to changes in the surface of the road. I went up to 130mph a few times but it wasn't pleasant and I was happy to make way for more BMWs, Audis and Mercedes to pass by. Instead I settled at around 110mph feeling that this was sufficient, even though I remained a little annoyed not to have discovered the utopian high-speed road that I had imagined.

Even so, at this speed progress was swift. I smiled every time Ned or I would pilot the car into a derestricted section and the sat nav – now working as we were back on main roads – suddenly showed a blank where the speed limit would normally be. This would correspond with a round white sign with two diagonal black lines cutting across it on the side of the road, like a slightly tweaked version of the sign you might see leaving a town in the UK whose one diagonal line means you are able to go a comparatively boring 60mph or 70mph. This became a sign for us to go as fast as we were comfortable with and no faster.

I was quite excited as we came off the motorway and started seeing signs to the Porsche museum having become increasingly keen on the company's cars as I had grown older. As a youngster I would look at the Porsche 911 and find it ugly. I just couldn't understand how it could be deemed aesthetically pleasing but, of course, tastes change. Now I love 911s. I love the way that they seem to have maintained their design heritage more than any other car on the road. You could sit a 1970s 911 next to the newest one to roll out of the factory and you would recognise that the DNA is the same. I also love the fact that Porsche continues to produce real drivers' cars, focusing on the interaction between man and machine. Of course that level of interaction may have diminished over the years as technology has moved on, but the dynamics of sporting Porsches still regularly set the benchmark for other manufacturers.

I drove a Porsche Boxster S for around a year while living and working in Aberdeen and I loved it. It was the 987 version, the second generation car which Porsche apparently put significant time and money into after the success of the 986 version which was, reportedly, rushed through to production on a shoestring budget. The 987 was well-made, had a boot in the front and the back so surprisingly convenient, looked good (with the roof down at least), and was fun to drive. I even found my local dealership to provide excellent customer service. All these things left me knowing that I would one day own another Porsche. In the meantime I would take the opportunity of driving through Germany to visit the home of this motoring icon in the Zuffenhausen area of Stuttgart. Despite efforts to organise a factory tour Ned and I would have to make do with the museum, all tours having been booked up already and the visitor relations people not willing to make any allowances.

As we got closer to the museum it became increasingly clear whose territory we were in. The signposts repeatedly indicated Porsche's domination of Zuffenhausen as we made our way towards Porscheplatz – the aptly named site of the museum. Before spotting the museum we saw a large, wide grey building emblazoned with the Porsche logo, it only becoming clear as we moved closer that this was the company's flagship dealership, the windows at the bottom of the building showing lines of the latest cars in every possible colour. And then we locked eyes on the museum itself, looming like an alien monolith, all angles, mirrors and spaces. It was genuinely impressive. Ned and I did a circuit of the roundabout and caught glimpses of the bright red Ferrari in the reflective, angled surfaces of the building. It appeared lopsided from some angles and once we came to know the interior layout it seemed like a cross between Dr Who's tardis and an Escher drawing – the lines that the eye sees not quite reconciling with the physics of the reality. I loved it. I think it makes sense that a company like Porsche – whose work is as design-based as it is mechanical – would create something so modern and challenging. It was actually designed by Delugan Meissl Associated Architects of Vienna and completed in 2008. According to the firm, "The Porsche Museum was conceived as a dynamically formed organism, inviting new ideas on the use of gravity and space to establish a new basis in the foundations of architecture". Driving around the museum that description seemed remarkably accurate.

I should probably say at this point that we felt like complete imposters driving into the Porsche heartland in a very conspicuous Italian supercar. It felt a bit naughty, but in a good way. Of course there is always someone that likes to make an even bigger statement and I couldn't help but laugh as we made our way to the underground car park that lay beneath the museum and spotted an Aston Martin Rapide parked audaciously on the pavement directly in front of the museum, no other cars anywhere near it.

Inside the museum the modern, futuristic feel continued. Everything was white, clean and well ordered. Next to the smaller of the two cafés was a glass partition which allowed visitors to look through to the Museum Workshop where Porsche Classic mechanics worked on cars of all vintages. The inevitable Porsche gift shop was nearby, visitors being offered everything from t-shirts to books to model cars. But it was the large escalator and staircase that really caught the eye. There was something strangely enticing about the way it rose up towards the hidden exhibition space above, never giving any hint as to what might be up there. As you might expect the floors above were filled with every Porsche car imaginable, from the oldest to the newest and from the rarest to the most common. There was plenty of information about the cars so we could get a good feel for their relevance to the company and their reason for being. It was particularly interesting to see some of the concept cars that were later tweaked for mainstream release and there were plenty of motorsport examples too.

There were some clever technological touches as well. I approached one such feature with trepidation, it looking like a teleportation device from *Star Trek*. Circular pads sat on the floor beneath white ceiling-mounted cylindrical fittings, names and dates of Porsche vehicles scrolling in red text inside the black interior. As I stepped on the pad engine noise erupted from above, the text rotating above my head telling me which model I was listening to. Stepping off and on again meant I had the pleasure of hearing a different car. There was also a great graphic on the wall that showed the outlines of all generations of the 911, a light highlighting one after the other to show the evolution of the shape and size of the car. There was even a cross section of a car that looked like it had been cut perfectly by lasers, a segment placed in a glass tank like a technology-orientated Damian Hirst exhibit. You could see everything, from the thickness of the seat padding to the wires that would normally be hidden under the dashboard.

After a late lunch in the café I stood outside looking up at my distorted reflection in the mirrored surface way above my head while Ned took some photos of the building. I couldn't help but feel that Porsche had got this museum just right. Maybe it had something to do with us visiting midweek and out of holiday season but I liked it not being too busy. It meant we had time to explore the space and the many cars on our own terms. The food was good, the staff were polite and it was amazingly easy to find. Above all it gave great insight into the broad and diverse heritage of Porsche, a company best known for the enduring appeal of one model: the 911.

The drive from Stuttgart to Zurich was never going to be an interesting one, being predominantly made up of autobahn, though cutting through endless greenery and under blue skies it certainly could have been worse. We had a chance to progress at high speed once again but it felt like a necessary part of the trip as opposed to anything more exciting. Aside from the convenience of the airport for both Ned and Spencer, I had chosen to stop in Zurich because we would wake with the Alps only a stone's throw away and Spencer and I would be on some good driving roads in no time.

I hadn't really considered that we'd be heading briefly out of the European Union but I was reminded quite suddenly when the speed limit-free autobahn drew to a close with a roundabout that pointed right towards Switzerland or left towards more Germany. Almost immediately afterwards were the checkpoints and we quickly rummaged for our passports so as to hand them over to an official that looked less than impressed at a UK registered Ferrari entering his country. I can only guess that was why he decided to pull us to the side and went off with our passports for a while, returning with a slightly disappointed look on his face. Presumably he had discovered we were not wanted by the authorities for any arrestable crime.

We pressed onwards into an increasingly industrial landscape and were soon trapped in a rush hour traffic jam on the outskirts of Zurich.

Heading for the hills

Zurich–Flüela Pass–Brescia

"Isn't Robert Wagner the name of an actor?" Spencer whispered to me over the noise of a coach-load of chatting India tourists.

We were checking in to the Renaissance Hotel in Zurich and, sure enough, that was the name of the guy behind the desk processing our details. I knew Robert Wagner to be a bit of a Hollywood legend but I thought I would keep it simple and choose the example best known to my generation.

"Yes," me also whispering. "He was in Austin Powers."

The guy behind the desk looked up. We obviously hadn't been quiet enough. "Yes, it's me! I'm Number Two!" he exclaimed, referring to the role Wagner plays in Mike Myers' spoof spy movie and undoing any preconceptions that the Swiss don't have a sense of humour.

Ned and I had taken the tram to the airport a bit earlier that evening, meeting Spencer and then having a quick farewell beer before parting ways. I was really pleased that Ned had done the first section of the journey with me. He was an excellent companion, a competent driver, and it gave me an opportunity to build a relationship with a cousin that I really hadn't known that well beforehand. I think that the experience made quite an impact on him as well. A few days later I received a message saying that he had now found himself looking at Renaultsport Clios for sale and upcoming track days near his home. The addiction had set in. Ned might have blamed me but I blamed the Nürburgring.

I had been at a bit of a loss when it came to booking a hotel in Zurich and settled on the Renaissance due to its proximity to the airport and underground parking provision. I had toyed with the idea of choosing somewhere that would allow us to explore the city that evening but I knew that a good night's sleep would be the main priority even if I hadn't realised that would be partly as a result of the Nürburg air raid siren. Frustratingly, as we checked-in it became clear that there was only one room booked for the two of us. I couldn't remember if this was something that I had arranged intentionally to keep the costs down in the first place, Zurich being far and away the most expensive of our overnight stops. Robert Wagner offered to find us another room but I declined, something that turned out to be an awful idea some hours later when Spencer began to snore. I'm surprised that none of his girlfriends have tried to assassinate him before now as it was pretty much unbearable. There was no rhythm, no consistency, just random bursts of noise. I very nearly went to reception to ask for another room in the early hours of the morning but decided this might be a waste of money even if I might be grumpy the next day. That would be Spencer's punishment.

Snoring aside, I was pleased that Spencer had managed to join me on my motoring pilgrimage. As a person he is considerate, generous and has a wicked sense of humour which meant that our trips away were generally filled with laughter. I was sure this journey would be no different.

Perhaps more importantly for a trip like this one, from the first time I met Spencer it was obvious that he loved cars, particularly Ferraris. I knew that the experiences we would share together in Switzerland, Italy and France would mean as much to him as they would to me.

I had been looking forward to Spa-Francorchamps and was very excited about the Nürburgring but this was what I had really been waiting for. I had built a number of Europe's most highly rated driving roads into the itinerary and it began with the departure from Zurich and the roads that would lead us directly to the Alps and beyond.

Spencer took the wheel to start with. He had driven my car back in the UK and was eager to reacquaint himself before we hit the good roads. It suited me perfectly and allowed me to relax for a little while after a second disturbed night's sleep. Once we had made it through the morning rush hour and out of the city the vista began to open up around us. Huge lakes lined the road for mile after mile, their light blue sheen mirroring the colour of the sky above. Once again the sun was shining brightly, warming the cabin of the Ferrari and elevating our spirits even further.

The sat nav would cover the Alpine roads and so I could really just enjoy the scenery as we proceeded swiftly down the motorway and towards the mountains that were looming ever larger through the windscreen in front of us. The buildings and signs of commerce became more sporadic, replaced by quaint farms and tree-covered hills. Every now and again a sign of local industry would remind us of our proximity to Zurich but would disappear again just as quickly. Ever bluer lakes glinted at us as we passed, the deep colours hinting at their depth and their glacial origins. There was little traffic but as we got closer to the mountains a brand new Ferrari 458 pulled up behind us – the first Italian car I had seen since Spa-Francorchamps in Belgium. Soon we had lost it as the driver turned off at a junction, leaving us to continue on through ever more impressive and imposing valleys, climbing in altitude the whole time. We turned off the main road shortly after Bad Ragaz. A little further and we spotted a red train trundling along beside the road, hinting at our approach to the skiing resorts of Klosters and Davos.

At Davos we turned off for the start of the Flüela Pass, a road rated as one of Europe's best for driving enjoyment. At first it climbed gently, the long corners sweeping us further into the mountains, a few cars and eager motorcyclists soaking up the views and providing us with time to do the same. Before long, patches of snow began appearing on the roadside around us and the air became thinner and cooler, the car reacting by losing a bit of power and feeling slightly sluggish but the engine sounding as furious as ever whenever pushed; a stark contrast to the sense of peace and emptiness around us. Sections of wider road with good visibility emerged every now and then, providing sought after opportunities to pass the traffic that had been holding us up and allowing us to begin to find some rhythm with the road. With it we twisted, turned and climbed, blasting forwards into the snowy landscape with Spencer still at the controls and relishing the opportunity to work through the gears almost constantly as to maintain the desired momentum.

We decided to pull over in a lay-by that sat on a small plateau, taking a few minutes to enjoy the combination of cool, clean air and warm, unfiltered sunshine. Photos were taken and positions were swapped as the engine popped and ticked as it cooled, the noise puncturing the silence. Now it was my turn.

We started climbing steeply, snow now forming small banks on the side of the road in some places. The landscape settled into a combination of white and brown, the grass not yet having had a chance to reclaim its vitality after a long hard winter. Passing slower traffic was a challenge as more and more blind corners featured. The key was to be patient and a straight would soon appear or a considerate driver would recognise my intentions and pull into a lay-by. Then I had the chance to flow with the road once more and to understand why it is so highly rated.

There was every type of corner imaginable here – some well-sighted, some blind and some with sheer drops on one side. There were uphill and downhill sections. There were fast sections and slower, more challenging sections. And there were sections that seemed to link all of the above together in quick succession. The road surface remained relatively consistent and was surprisingly good considering the extreme weather that impacts this area across the changing seasons. The scenery was stunning throughout. The Ferrari seemed perfectly at home here. Its ability to execute sharp direction changes, its strong brakes and effortless acceleration were ideal for such varied roads, while its tidy proportions meant that I didn't find myself breathing in every time that a car came the other way.

Soon we found ourselves descending, the road twisting and turning tightly and the drops on the other side of the metal barriers looking more precipitous than ever. Water from melted snow would occasionally snake across the road but didn't seem to affect grip. Then overall speed fell and the brakes began to play an increasingly important role, the mass of the car greater with gravity against us. Even so, the diversity of the road continued as we pressed on to Zemez and beyond, and there were still plenty of occasions to exploit the addictive pace of the F355.

Trees and small cliffs now lined the road once again as we found ourselves in a valley, snow no longer a presence, the threat of ice replaced with rocks lying on the road. I was soon forced to pull over having gone over the top of one of these, a sickening bang filtering through the cabin as it struck the underside of the car despite not looking big enough to have caused any problems. I leapt out of the driver's seat and searched for signs of damage but couldn't see anything, the aerodynamic undertray that is fitted to the F355 presumably bearing the brunt of the impact.

Spencer took over again as we headed into the Swiss National Park, the road dropping steadily down the side of a tree-lined mountain, a river visible somewhere below as we rounded hairpins where ongoing roadworks had reduced the surface to rubble. It felt as though we were gradually rejoining civilisation but sections of road remained challenging and the brakes were now fading from sustained use. It was as we approached the Pass dal Fuorn – another great mountain pass just south-west of Flüela – that the brakes locked-up during a long left-hander giving us a split second of panic before normal service was resumed and Spencer powered onwards around the corner. It was clearly time for a break; both us and the car needed it. Thankfully the restaurant on the top of the pass served excellent schnitzel and strong coffee and we would soon be ready for the blast to the Italian border and then on to the legendary Stelvio Pass.

We were both still buzzing from the previous hour or so of hard driving. It was exactly this feeling that I had been searching for, the experience that I craved and had dreamt about as I sat at my desk in a dreary office in Aberdeen.

Why did I crave these kinds of experiences? I didn't really know then and I'm not sure I know now. It must be the combination of excitement and anxiety that comes with driving a car at speed, and the fact that a great driver's car comes to feel like an extension of your body in the way that it reacts to the movement of your arms and legs. There is a strange, intrinsic relationship between man and machine that directly reflects the characteristics of the car and the skill of the driver. The right combination can be exhilarating. The only thing that I know for sure is that blasting along an Alpine pass in an Italian supercar was everything I had hoped for. I wasn't disappointed with the experience so far and I knew that Spencer was enjoying it as much as me. It was hard to believe that there was so much more to come as we pressed on in accordance with my master plan. Our descent into larger, greener valleys continued beyond Fuorn and before we knew it we were being waved nonchalantly across the Italian border, the official here clearly far less concerned about a Ferrari entering his realm than his Swiss counterpart. But then again a Ferrari is royalty in Italy, its home land, something that I would come to learn again and again over the coming days. Roadside workers would urge us on so that they could hear the throaty rasp as we passed by. Traffic would evacuate the fast lane of the motorway so that we could maintain speed unimpeded. On one occasion the local police stopped the traffic so that we could do a three-point turn in the middle of a city street. But all that was still to come...

For a short while we drove through the small villages and towns that punctuated the fields, the lush green of the grass seemingly facing an onslaught from white and yellow flowers, all of them being drenched by the numerous sprinkler systems that seemed to erupt continuously. Stone spires rose from churches, sometimes close by or sometimes the only sign of a community that was visible off towards the horizon, each of the towns seemingly ex-pressing its individuality through differing spire design. It was one of the most tranquil sections of the entire journey. It almost seemed appropriate, the calm before the storm that would be the Stelvio Pass – one of the highest passes in the Alps at 2,757 metres, with 48 hairpin turns that zig-zag down the hillside like a piece of unfurled grey ribbon. Various television programmes and magazines had la-belled it a must do experience for petrolheads even though it is seen as more of a spectacle than a true drivers' road by many people. I wasn't convinced that it would be that fun to drive, particularly when compared with some of the other roads we would be experiencing in the course of this adventure, but there was no doubt that we'd give it a go and tick it off the list. No doubt, that is, until we saw the sign saying that the road was closed.

The road had started to climb quickly again after the small town of Prato alla Stelvio. We had turned right at the crossroads, signposts leading us onwards and up-wards again. It was then that we spotted the sign but I carried on regardless. Surely it couldn't be true. Shortly afterwards we passed by a strange garden in which mys-terious totems and sculptures stood as though part of a personal exhibition, all apparently made from wood and animal skeletons. A tall, colourfully-painted totem pole stood next to a tree on which a vast amount of bones seemed to be suspended. We could only assume that the bones were from animals, even if the place looked like something out of a horror movie.

The road continued to thin as it carried us through small villages that seemed more or less deserted, large hotels standing in lonely isolation next to the snow-capped mountains, presumably waiting for the summer season to arrive and mountain bikers and hill walkers to bring life back to the area. We wanted to press on in the hope that the sign telling us that the Stelvio Pass was closed was wrong. Perhaps someone had forgotten to up-date it. I couldn't believe it; didn't *want* to believe it. After all, the Flüela Pass had been open and that was 2,383 metres high. Could those 374 metres really make such a difference to the road in the middle of May?

We came to another town, bigger but similarly de-serted. This was Trafoi. We would cross the Stelvio Pass from here, make our way to Bormio on the other side, and then we would wiggle southwards towards Brescia from there, our stop for the night. That was the plan anyway but as we were winding up the hill on the other side of Trafoi we spotted a second sign stating that the road was closed. Again I pressed on in disbelief, though this time only for another 20 metres before Spencer talked some sense into me and we went in search of someone to speak to. Deciding against trying one of the deserted hotels we made our way to the Natura Trafoi visitor centre where a little girl was playing outside, one of only two people we had seen in the town. Spencer jumped out and went inside, beckoning me in a minute or two later. It turned out that the Stelvio Pass would be shut for around ten more days whilst they waited for the ice to melt. It was mid-May and the great weather I had experienced since leaving Belgium meant that I had assumed snow would be an issue on this journey, even on higher ground.

A friendly young woman talked us through our options on a map of the local area as her other child, a young boy, ran around behind her. The route that she suggested meant going back to Prato alla Stelvio and then back into Switzerland, retracing our footsteps until we could head south to St Moritz and on to the Italian border, before finally rejoining our route to Brescia at Edolo. We were really frustrated. We had come to this remote part of northern Italy just to drive one of the world's most famous roads and were essentially being turned away, my itinerary no longer looking so well thought out. Back in the car we looked at our own map.

"Mate, there is no way I'm going back into Switzerland," I said to Spencer. "How about this route?" I pointed to an alternative that would take us east to Bolzano, south towards Verona and then west to Brescia. It was clearly a big detour but shouldn't add too much time.

"Fine. Let's get on the motorway and we can make up some ground there," Spencer replied. "A bit of high speed cruising can be fun as well."

I couldn't help but smile at his positive spin on the

situation though I actually felt really guilty. I had let us both down through poor planning. I shouldn't have assumed that the road would be open. In retrospect, we were probably lucky that the Flüela Pass had been.

We set off again, stopping by the scary bone sculptures to take a photo or two. The artist ran out to claim some money from us for photographing his work and invited us in to his garden to have a look around. In there we could take as many photos as we liked, he assured us. I would have considered the invitation as I was intrigued. Spencer wasn't keen on taking the risk on the off-chance that he was a serial killer and wanted some new bones for his sculptures. He politely declined on both our behalves. I passed him a few coins for the photos we had taken and then sped off before we got embroiled in a longer discussion.

We soon found ourselves back in rolling agricultural land and feeling a bit calmer once again. The weather remained good, the sun shining in a clear sky. Strange castles and turreted structures passed by our windows as we made for the motorway. Here it was just a matter of patience once again as we attempted to maintain a high but sensible speed, other motorists making way as soon as they recognised the prancing horse of the Ferrari logo in their rear-view mirror. But ours wasn't the only Ferrari on the road. Spencer, the eagle-eyed Ferrari enthusiast, spotted an F40 up ahead and what looked like a Porsche 964 Turbo right behind it.

"Al! Look, an F40!" I did as I was told and looked up from the map and saw the two cars. They appeared to be taking the same exit as us.

"Can you catch up with it?" I asked. Spencer was already on the case, me trying to keep one eye on the road signs to ensure we actually were still going the right direction and the other eye on the progress.

The Ferrari F40 is an automotive legend, a car launched in 1987 to correspond with the company's 40th anniversary. It was also the last car that Enzo Ferrari would himself sign-off. The twin-turbocharged V8 engine is capable of propelling the F40 to 202mph. It was designed as a road-going racer and its design, both inside and out, reflects that. Although planned as a very limited edition model, eventually 1,315 cars were produced – still not enough to diminish its rarity, residual values and allure to motoring enthusiasts around the world. Even today, many motoring journalists and collectors rate it as one of their favourite cars. By all accounts, it really gets under your skin with its no nonsense approach and road-racer aura, even if there are more technologically-advanced cars out there today.

Soon we were part of this convoy of supercars and I could only hope that it looked as cool to nearby car enthusiasts as it felt to us – the gleaming red Ferrari F40 leading a black Porsche and red F355. The two cars in front weren't holding back. We watched as other motorists instinctively evacuated the fast lane and the leading Ferrari approached a tunnel, our windows already down so that we could appreciate the noise. I had never seen an F40 on the road before and I was genuinely shocked by the noise it made as it charged through that tunnel. It wasn't dissimilar to that of the F355 in some respects but it was somehow more feral, less restrained and very race car like. It filled the tunnel with sound, to us an exquisite sound that had us laughing in appreciation, a vocal applause. There was no way of hearing the Porsche over the two Italian V8s but it certainly looked the part, its body-work wide and taut over the back wheels, its huge spoiler jutting out at the rear. It was undoubtedly capable of a few fireworks of its own but the F40 ahead stole the show, its shape akin to something a young boy might come up with if you asked him to draw a fast car and its colour drawing attention away from the monotony of regular commuter traffic. It had also managed to draw our attention away from the route we should have been taking and now we were heading the wrong way. We had to peel off the main road, turn around and find the correct route to Brescia and a well-earned beer. I couldn't help but hope the two drivers would talk about us later.

"Did you see that F355 behind us earlier?" They might say. "That was pretty cool when we were all blasting through the tunnel together."

I had never spent any time in Italy before and had been looking forward to it. My mother had been urging me to visit for some time, having fallen in love with Tuscany herself. Rita's Italian ancestry and love of art meant that she was also a keen and regular visitor to Italy. For my part, I had only spent a couple of hours in Rome one hot summer's day between international flights and a few hours in Venice before a boat trip along the Dalmatian coast, arriving in St Mark's Square at midnight when everything seemed to be closing. These visits didn't count as far as I was concerned and I was hoping the next few days would give me a feel for Italy even if I knew I would only be scratching the surface of this diverse country.

I had decided to arrange a night in Brescia based upon its role as the start and finish point for the Mille

Miglia – a thousand mile tribute race open to those cars and models that took part in the original races between 1927 and 1957. I had originally hoped to be there for the start of this race but there was no way it was going to fit into the itinerary when my co-drivers had such tight time constraints. Still, the town sounded pleasant enough and Spencer and I were ready to relax after a long day behind the wheel and after the disappointment of missing out on experiencing the Stelvio Pass.

I had booked us into a centrally-located hotel with secure parking and we also had separate rooms this time which was a relief. Wanting to enjoy the warm evening sun we set off for the old town almost immediately, past a kitchen showroom and a couple of nondescript shops before entering a tunnel that appeared never-ending and eerily devoid of people or traffic. Walking out the other end reminded me of the movie *Who Framed Roger Rabbit?*, in which the tunnel acts as a sort of portal between the grimy real world and clean, colourful Toontown. In our case it was a matter of a shift from a pleasant but unremarkable part of the city to a place that reflected my preconceptions of what Italy *should* look like. Here the streets were smaller and young couples wandered around slowly, hand-in-hand. The buildings looked to be built at different times using different materials but all had character and oozed history. Some had old and exposed brickwork and some were painted in faded terracotta or burnt orange, their shutters contrasting with a grey-blue colour that matched the evening sky.

We turned off into a piazza where a large building sat imposingly, dominatingly. Its columns, domes and sheer size marked it out as something of significance, though we didn't know what. We took one of the small side streets and soon found ourselves in a peaceful yet thriving network of restaurants, bars and cafés. The Locanda dei Guasconi sat on one such street, Via Cesare Beccaria, and looked ideal. We were given a seat on the terrace, under the awning where we proceeded to enjoy some excellent Italian cuisine and wine, watching people pass by and reflecting on the day's adventure. We would never have guessed from the generic seating that lined the road but the interior of this restaurant was fabulously mediaeval in design. The low ceilings, wooden features and exposed brickwork were given context by the pieces of armour and paintings of noblemen from days gone by. You could imagine spending a long and boozy night in here with friends in the winter months but on such a pleasant warm night it was empty, everyone pressed towards the street instead.

We explored the area a little more after a superb dinner in an effort to walk off some of the local food and wine before bed. Despite being midweek there was a real buzz in the air. One tiny street was packed with people from both ends, everyone crowding around a small bar which sat in the middle and enjoying a lively local band. The tune was vaguely familiar but I couldn't tell you what it was. Those lucky enough to have a table were swaying with the music and sipping slowly on their drinks, others would sing along with the chorus. It was a wonderful feeling of community.

I walked away looking around at the diverse and beautiful buildings that make up this part of Brescia with the sound of late night revellers behind me and with some understanding of the passion my mother and Rita had expressed for this country.

Homecoming

Brescia-Maranello-Castelfranco
Emilia-Modena

I might have been visiting Italy for the first time but this was a return home for my Ferrari, it having rolled out of the factory in Maranello some 15 years previously before being shipped to the UK. The romantic in me had been really looking forward to driving it back through its home town even if I had failed to organise a factory tour, despite exploring numerous avenues when planning the trip. I had even discovered that members of the Ferrari Owners' Club UK, which I had joined almost immediately after buying my car, would be visiting the factory that very same day but there was no room for Spencer and myself at such short notice. I had received some friendly advice from the Ferrari North Europe Press Office but it didn't help. We would have to make do with a visit to the museum and lunch at Il Cavallino instead.

Thankfully I had managed to arrange a tour of the nearby Pagani factory later the same day and there was a slim chance of meeting Horacio Pagani, the man that turned the supercar world order on its head when he launched the Zonda in 1999. But first there was the matter of getting to Maranello and the two hours we had allocated for the journey was looking increasingly ambitious as we became held up in traffic jams on the approach from Brescia. To complicate things further the sat nav decided that we were now far enough away from Europe's main roads and the Alps that we would have to fend for ourselves, the road map pulled out from behind the seat once again.

Despite running late there was no way that we would be driving into Maranello in a dirty Ferrari and so I convinced Spencer to help me wash the car. The journey so far had taken its toll and, if nothing else, the wheels needed the brake dust cleaning off and a kamikaze bird needed to be removed from the air vent on the bonnet. We found an old service station with a basic jet wash system and a dirty bucket, setting to work using the cleaning products that I had brought along for just such an occasion. With the car now gleaming we were soon driving into Maranello, the home of one of the world's most iconic car manufacturers.

I'm not too sure what I expected to see on arrival but I had assumed that it would be obvious where we needed to go, particularly after the many road signs that had helped Ned and I find the Porsche museum in Stuttgart. We followed the traffic initially and knew that we were on the right track once we spotted what appeared to be the back of the Ferrari factory, a huge yellow sign hovering over an industrial-looking complex and a vast car park. Spencer had been to Maranello once before but this didn't look at all familiar to him and there was no sign of anything that looked visitor-orientated. We passed a number of Ferrari 458s, presumably out with potential customers or on factory test drives but it was clear that we needed to be somewhere else. There was nothing for it but to keep our faith and follow the signs that would theoretically lead us to the Museo Ferrari and from there to see the hallowed factory gates. A few turns later we found ourselves on a street where every other shop seemed to be utilising the name of Ferrari. Here people were walking around excitedly and more and more Ferraris flowed past us on the road. We had arrived in the home of Ferrari and were in the perfect car for the visit, a stark contrast to the feeling of being an imposter in Porsche territory when Ned and I had arrived in Stuttgart. We were running very late now as a result of the traffic jams and would not have long before needing to leave for Castelfranco Emilia and the Pagani factory. Thankfully the museum was easy to find now that we were in the right place and we decided to have a quick look before having lunch.

Walking in, I found it a bit underwhelming in comparison with Porsche's excellent museum, both architecturally and with regard to the exhibition itself. There were some wonderful road cars and plenty of examples from Ferrari's decades of motorsport success but there was plenty missing as well. If you come here hoping to see a comprehensive collection of Ferraris from past to present then you will be disappointed. However, if you've never really looked closely at an Enzo or F40 before, or if you're a big fan of motorsport, then it is certainly worth a visit. For me, the Formula 1 room was the highlight with its display of recent race cars and a vast trophy collection. The video that is played on a loop in the background was also a very good feature; the music, cheers, engine noise and commentary telling you a little about the passion and pride associated with past glories.

We jumped back in the car and drove around a little more to try to find the factory gates, initially taking a wrong turn and ending up at the back of Pista Fiorano,

Ferrari's test track. Back the other way we passed by a number of Ferrari Californias that were providing tourist test drive experiences but soon we were parked up outside Il Cavallino, opposite the gates to the Ferrari factory, the place where Enzo Ferrari is known to have often taken his lunch. It was all a bit rushed from here. We ate a quick bowl of pasta, smiling as the waiting staff moved around unfazed and ever professional despite a power cut that lasted the duration of our meal, and then had a peek in the Ferrari merchandise shop over the road to buy gifts for girlfriends but we left empty handed. We took a few photos of my car in front of the factory gates and then set off to find our way to Castelfranco Emilia, struggling as usual without the sat nav and a road map that didn't go into enough detail. I apologised to Spencer for us having to rush as I hadn't realised that Maranello would be somewhere we could happily spend half a day pottering around, soaking up the atmosphere and simply watching all the Ferraris roll by. We had hoped to get to Sant'Agata to visit the Lamborghini museum as well but that was simply struck off the itinerary. After all, Pagani was the one manufacturer that had agreed to give us a tour of their facilities and we were both excited about seeing the new Huayra in the metal and the possibility of meeting Horacio.

This was supposed to be quite a relaxing day after the serious driving across the Alps and through northern Italy the previous day but we were soon lost again, meandering along rural Modenese roads, past fields and small cottages, in and out of towns. We tried to navigate with the road map and the road signs that decorated every junction but we were literally going around in circles. We eventually found our way there having stopped to ask three sets of people the way, pulling up outside Pagani's modest premises in an industrial estate on the edge of town. You would have no way of knowing, standing here on the side of the road and looking through the gates, that some of the world's most exclusive, high performance cars were created here. Get a little closer and the cars parked in front of the entrance hint at something different – a Maserati GranTurismo, a Pagani Zonda, and a Pagani Huayra that would turn out to be Horacio Pagani's daily driver; one of the perks of creating a car that was only just beginning to be featured by the world's motoring press. Stepping inside we were greeted by the sight of two Pagani Zonda Rs – track-orientated versions of the company's last road car, looking menacing in carbon fibre finish with huge rear wings, roof scoops and gold alloy wheels. Having introduced ourselves to Caterina, the receptionist, we were formally greeted by Luca Venturi, one of the press team. We were frustrated to discover that we were not going to be able to speak with Horacio after all. He had apparently just returned from a business trip to China – presumably a key market – and was now catching up on some work. We were still welcome to tour the premises though, first taking a proper look around the showroom-like foyer.

There was a small plaque on one wall highlighting the many awards that various editions of the Zonda have won over the past 11 years, starting with *evo* magazine's Car of the Year award in 2000 for the Zonda C12 S. More recently, record lap times for the Zonda F on the Nürburgring Nordscleife are listed, the quickest being 7:22:44 in August 2008. By the window sat a high-end home stereo system inspired by the Zonda but looking more like a gleaming chrome robot than a music machine, and next to the stereo were abstract paintings that fused images of wheels, brake pads and other design cues from the Zonda. Finally, by the door to the workshop sat a single-seater racing car.

"This was the first car that Horacio built," Caterina explained to us, shifting expertly from the role of welcoming receptionist to tour guide.

Having been told to put our cameras away, Spencer and I followed Caterina into the workshop. She seemed to know a great deal about the various processes taking place despite being very modest when we told her so. A few cars were up on ramps being worked on, the atmosphere relaxed yet professional. We were shown the V12 engines that are used in both the Zonda and Huayra and are supplied by Mercedes' AMG outfit, bespoke items that provide these cars with their immense power and resulting pace. Other components are drawn from suppliers elsewhere, both locally and globally. In many respects you expect that from a small company like this, the relevant expertise being outsourced to ensure that every model Pagani produces is world class. But it was in this workshop that much of the carbon fibre bodywork was constructed, the material giving the car its structural rigidity yet remaining comparatively lightweight. A small room was set off from the main workshop, a few people inside manipulating and shaping the material which only gains its rigidity once heated, something that is also done on site. We peeked through the window for a second before taking a closer look at the semi-complete cars up on the ramps, picking out details that we would never have known existed even if one of us owned one of these fabulous machines. It was certainly interesting to see how a successful manufacturer of high-end performance cars creates its products, even if their small workshop meant that the tour was a short one.

Caterina led us outside to have a closer look at Horacio's Huayra, presumably one of the few in the world at that point in time. Its gullwing-style doors were already open and we were offered the opportunity to sit inside and take some photos. Assuming that it might be my one and only chance to sit in a Huayra, I didn't hesitate.

The finish of the car was simply exquisite, all leather, chrome and carbon fibre. Numerous switches looked as though they were taken from a plane, something which made sense when we learnt that the exterior design was inspired by the moment that a plane takes-off. I loved the way that the bodywork seemed to taper rearwards from the roof, culminating at the four exhaust pipes that sit two-by-two above the number plate. Caterina explained that the wing mirrors, which protrude from the flanks of the car on carbon fibre stalks, are based on the shape of an eye. At the front and rear of the car are active panels that shift continuously as you drive to ensure optimal aerodynamics, particularly at high speed. It was very exciting to be able to sit in a car that very few other people had even seen outside of magazines, knowing that it would soon make it to the top of many people's dream garage lists.

Having been uninspired by the options on offer at the Ferrari shop in Maranello I thought I would buy a little gift for Rita from here. The only thing that I could afford was a t-shirt and so I chose to go for the design that Caterina had been expertly modelling all afternoon. After expressing our thanks and saying goodbye, Spencer and I took one last lustful look at the Huayra and set off for Modena and our hotel for the night.

The half hour drive was no problem this time though my navigation skills soon came under strain as we found ourselves doing circuits of the old town, avoiding one way streets and learning to ignore any recommendations given by the sat nav which was pointing us the wrong way. There must have been a local military passing out ceremony going on somewhere as we spotted quite a few uniformed young men walking around, with what we could only assume were proud parents. I phoned the hotel but the advice didn't help much and so we were forced to stop on the side of the road so that I could leap out and ask a group of policemen if they knew the hotel. One of them seemed genuinely pleased to show off to his colleagues that, yes, he could speak English. Not only did he give us the directions we required but he stopped all oncoming cars so that we could do a three-point turn in the middle of the road and head back the other direction. One of the perks of driving a Ferrari in Italy I guess.

The Hotel Real Fini on via Emilia had been recommended in a number of guides I had read both in print and online, it apparently being one of the places that Ferrari uses to put up visiting journalists. It had a feel of fading grandeur. The design and the furniture were a little tired but the staff were excellent and the coffee some of the best I've had anywhere, more than punchy enough to keep me going until dinner.

I didn't know much about Modena aside from its proximity to some of the world's most revered supercar makers and the fact that Ferrari used its name for the successor to my F355 Berlinetta – the Ferrari 360 Modena. It soon became clear that it was a university town, the University of Modena in fact being one of the oldest in the world having been founded in 1175. Lots of young people were walking around, groups of friends chatting animatedly and couples meandering hand-in-hand. Everyone was enjoying the warm evening, many presumably off to make the most of the many bars and restaurants on offer. It turned out that Modena was also the home of the Italian Military Academy which explained why we had seen the newly appointed officers strutting proudly in their uniforms.

As with Brescia we hit a very obvious transition point at which the cheap-looking shops and busy roads were replaced by old stone buildings and cobbled streets. There was something pleasant and cosseting about the way that these ancient buildings – with their columns, ornate decorations and shuttered windows – suddenly closed in around us, funnelling Spencer and I towards large piazzas and ornate churches.

After an underwhelming meal in a very pleasant setting, we made our way back to the hotel for a nightcap in the deserted bar and then to bed some much needed rest amongst the imposing dark wood furniture that decorated the rooms.

Beyond expectations

Modena–Lake Como–Turin

I wasn't in a great mood the next morning as we cruised up the motorway out of Modena and north-west towards Parma, Piacenza and Milan. The prospect of driving to Lake Como to see some cars at the Concorso d'Eleganza and then pressing on to Turin for the night seemed boring after all the wonderful driving of the past few days. I was probably just tired from the repeated adrenalin hits and subsequent comedowns but it was the first time in the course of the trip that I really couldn't be bothered and the first time that the thought of driving the F355, even on dull roads like these, wasn't enough to perk me up.

Spencer took the wheel first and ensured that we made swift progress. Driving on the motorways in Italy was always a fairly pleasant experience. Lorries appeared to stay on the outside lane, not overtaking each other and causing hold-ups to car drivers as they often do in the UK. Cars would only use the inside lane for overtaking as opposed to sitting there and slowing down faster traffic. There was always a feeling that being in a Ferrari somehow earned us some kudos on Italian motorways and we were able to proceed at a high speed without hold up, other motorists more than happy to get out of the way. This view was something I had been made aware of in a number of motoring magazines back home, instances when even the police would urge supercar drivers to show what their cars were capable of. This love of cars seems to flow through the veins of the Italian people, born out of a long history of producing some of the world's most desirable vehicles and a strong relationship with motorsport.

Of course there are always some idiots on the roads, no matter where in the world you are. Spencer and I watched with a combination of shock and amusement as a cigarette-smoking Mercedes driver pulled right up behind us in the fast lane of the motorway at what could be described as 'a reasonable speed', before proceeding to undertake us and then scything through the traffic ahead, to-ing and fro-ing across the lanes as far as the eye could see.

For us these sections of the journey were a matter of efficiency rather than idiocy; a means to get us between places of interest and to the real drivers' roads I had built into the itinerary. The plan today was to stick to the main roads and go for lunch by Lake Como before looking at the auction cars at Villa Erba. Later that night they would go under the hammer as part of the Villa d'Este Concorso d'Eleganza. We had left it too late to get passes for the actual concours event at Villa d'Este and this meant missing out on seeing some of the world's most exclusive cars, such as the Aston Martin V12 Zagato which would later come to grab all the headlines.

Peeling off the main roads and approaching Lake Como for the first time quickly dispelled any doubts I may have had about our plans for the day. I was at the wheel now and went through tunnel after tunnel before Spencer drew my attention to the lake on my right. I caught glimpses of the deep, inky blue that sat at the bottom of the surrounding hills, snapshots between trees and through the fences and houses that lined the road. The traffic began to slow and the view opened up, vivid green trees crawling up the hillside to our left and the immense size of the lake now becoming clear, it meandering like a large, still river as we progressed onwards along its westerly edge. It was immediately clear why this is seen as such a desirable place to visit and why many of the more discerning movie stars choose to have homes here.

Spencer had been given the recommendation to check out Locanda dell'Isola Comacina, a restaurant on an island on Lake Como at which they have been serving the same set menu since the 1940s. With a parking space found at Sala Comacina, after a bit of trial and error, we worked our way down to the shore and took a small boat over to the island which sat in the middle of the lake and appeared to contain nothing but an outcrop of trees. I couldn't help but feel relaxed in this setting. Looking at the shifting colours of the calm waters around us and the pinks, yellows and terracottas of the buildings lining the shore, I was pleased that this excursion had made it onto the itinerary. For a while my car was still visible. Once again it seemed like the perfect vehicle for this trip and once again the decision to embark on this journey somehow seemed justified.

A few minutes later and we were on the island. We paused for a moment to watch trout swimming in the shallows before climbing the steps up to the restaurant which is nestled amongst rocks and lush greenery. Sat amongst couples out for a romantic Saturday lunch - and subject to a few questioning glances as to our own relationship - we were soon tucking into fresh local food and enjoying a glass of wine, me feeling pretty good about life after my grumpy start to the day. The five course meal was excellent, the food simple but fresh and tasty. We were both excited to see some fresh fish on the menu having not seen any listed in the restaurants we visited in Modena or Brescia. Here, on the lake, there is an abundance of trout which would be grilled and served to us after the first course – an antipasto of bread, fresh vegetables, prosciutto ham, and half a tomato served with a very thin slice of lemon and virgin olive oil on top. The meal was a leisurely affair, the bottle of local wine that came as part of the fixed price meal doing a good job of washing down the food as we sat and gazed over the lake, kept cool from the hot afternoon sun by the trees overhead. We enjoyed the chicken course, nibbled on huge lumps of parmesan that had been spooned out of a huge section of the cheese by our waiter and devoured the sweet fruit and ice cream.

The meal traditionally ends with a ceremony during which the owner of the restaurant burns brandy in a pot, tells the story of the island and then adds coffee and sugar before serving to the diners and ringing a bell. I had missed the explanation of this process at the beginning of the meal having gone straight to the bathroom when Spencer was being seated. It sounded a bit excessive, particularly as there was driving to be done, so we simply made do with a normal coffee, paid the bill and left.

What I hadn't realised was that this was actually a special ritual to attempt to undo a curse put on the island by Vidulfo, a 12th century Bishop of Como. There are different readings of the bishop's curse but the sentiment is clear: "The bells will not ring again. No stone shall be put on stone. No one shall ever be host, under pain of unnatural death." The island was subsequently abandoned, no innkeeper or restaurateur willing to take the risk of hosting guests, at least until the middle of the 20th century when Lino Nessi was contacted by Carlo Sacchi and Sandro De Col with the proposal of opening a restaurant. De Col, a racer of speedboats, soon died in a speedboat accident and Sacchi was killed by his lover, Countess Pia Bellentani, at a gala at nearby Villa d'Este in 1948. Nessi gave up on the idea of opening a restaurant until writer Frances Dale suggested an exorcism of fire, a ritual that he could perform at the end of each meal ("il rito del fuoco" in Italian). That is what we had seemingly missed out on by requesting a standard coffee and I must confess that I had a moment of panic when I learned this until I came to understand that the curse is put on the host rather than the guest. At least I hoped that is what it meant.

Arriving at Villa Erba, some 15 minutes further down the lake in the town of Cernobbio, we managed to park in an area reserved for supercars and classics, located only a stone's throw from the entrance. We knew we only had an hour before the event closed and before the organisers made their final preparations for the auction that evening but that would be more than enough to get a feel for things.

Villa Erba itself is a grand 19th century building that sits imposingly at the water's edge, its design apparently inspired by Renaissance Mannerist architecture. Today it is an events venue and a sort of overspill location for Villa d'Este during the concours event. From the front it looked ordered and symmetrical, a central staircase running down towards the lake, fan-like in the way its width expanded. At the side a portico and turreted tower rose from the light grey and beige-coloured stone, large sections covered in deep green ivy that had been expertly trimmed around the large rectangular windows and their ornate stonework detailing.

Before we reached the gardens we found ourselves in a large exhibition space which was being utilised for a BMW retrospective, the company being one of the main sponsors of the event. It turned out that this was the Congress Centre that has been purpose-built for such events. It was very modern in design and its ability to accommodate large capacity groups meant that it dwarfed the nearby villa. In this air conditioned, glass-domed building the focus was on BMW road cars from the 1960s, although some older and younger models were present. There were also Rolls Royces and Minis, the latter eye-catchingly decorated in designs by Paul Smith, Kate Moss and Calvin Klein. I enjoyed seeing some of BMW's older cars for the first time but Spencer and I were both more interested in seeing the RM Auctions collection and made our way out to the impeccably well-kept grounds, past some more BMWs and a collection of motorbikes that were competing as part of the Motorcycle Concours event. The auction cars were displayed in what felt to be a greenhouse, a glass roofed, open-sided building that sat next to the villa itself. It was absurdly warm in there. Even with the breeze coming off the nearby lake we were both sweating within minutes.

My passion for cars is predominantly orientated around the experience of driving but I do enjoy looking at rare and interesting cars from time to time, even when they are stationary. The collection of cars for sale here was quite extraordinary, the most memorable cars being a number of weird and wonderful Bertone concept cars, such as the 1977 Lancia Stratos HF Zero which looked as though it had been designed for a science fiction movie. Despite being one of the most revered design houses in the automotive world – having created the Lamborghini Countach and Miura, the latter often rated as one of the world's most beautiful cars of all time by other designers – Bertone had become insolvent and was forced to sell off a number of prototypes from its heritage collection in order to raise funds. But it wasn't just Bertone designs that were drawing attention from the crowds and, in due course, the buyers at the auction. The gorgeous Talbot-Lago Teardrop is a work of art and an icon of car design and the Ferrari 375 MM Berlinetta rare and beautiful. Even so, it might come as some surprise that these cars sold for €3,136,000 and €3,360,000 respectively. That is big money for a car no matter how wealthy you are. It is an indicator of the kind of people that attend these events and the serious collectability of the most special cars on the planet.

This wasn't the first time that I had found myself looking around auction cars in the course of the year. Before I had gone out to Monaco, bought the Ferrari or even considered this petrolhead's pilgrimage around Europe, I discovered that there was an auction taking place locally to me and decided to take a look.

I had never visited the Royal Horticultural Halls before but I immediately saw that it was an ideal venue for a classic car auction. Its high vaulted ceilings, multiple windows and bright lighting were perfect for showing off highly polished cars. I thumbed through the brochure as I passed the deserted turnstiles and made my way toward the cars; it informed me that I was about to see "an important collection of fine historic automobiles", though "rare collector film posters" were also going to be auctioned later that afternoon.

It was quite a sight, this hugely diverse collection of cars. The oldest dated back to 1913 and the newest to 2002 but most seemed to come from the 60s, 70s and 80s. I looked around at the small number of people that had bothered to come to the preview. Being some four hours before the actual auction was due to start it was perhaps unsurprising that the auction staff outnumbered the catalogue-clutching visitors. There were some middle-aged couples milling around, perhaps looking for something in particular. There were a few small groups of men chatting in one section of the hall who I presumed to be traders of some sort. Some cars were being closely inspected, people with heads wedged under bonnets or down on one knee peeking underneath to check for rust. And then there was me.

There was nothing else to do but follow the lead of the others and go to look at the cars that interested me, cross-referencing each time with the brief history and guide price from the brochure. This was a technique that I would later employ at Villa Erba.

I was impressed at the number of British cars on display – old Bentleys, MGBs, Aston Martins and Jaguars. They seemed to make up a significant proportion of the collection and it was hard not to think about who owned them and why they were selling them. I paused by an eye-catching Cornish Gold-coloured Aston Martin V8 from 1974 and read the details as I moved around the car. "Estimate £18,000 - £22,000", the brochure informed me.

Wait a moment! Theoretically I could afford this. It would be stupid and irresponsible but having sold my flat in Scotland to move to London it was possible.

Suddenly the auction took on a new dimension for me. I worked my way around the hall looking only at those cars under £20,000 and tried to fool myself into thinking that I might come back at 7.00pm and bid for one of them. There was a nice looking TVR Tuscan S, a couple of Jags, a Lotus Elan but I had arrived with no intention of buying anything and I was adamant it would remain that way. I did come back but strictly to witness some of the auction, which turned out to be much more popular than one might have guessed earlier in the day.

There were clearly some veterans there now, young and old. There were families, couples, friends, individuals and probably some business partners too. Many were seated in front of the stage following progress intently, waiting for the car they wanted to come up or, if that time had come, raising their hands sporadically to indicate a bid. Other groups were still having a good look around the cars or lurking on the fringes of the seating area, signalling discreetly when they wanted to bid, maybe a nod, maybe a slight raise of the brochure. Progress was steady but not in line with the stereotypical rapidity that I associated with auctions from films and television shows.

Many cars did not sell, the reserve having not been met due to lack of demand. Others seemed to do quite well. The atmosphere was actually quite pleasant. There was a buzz of the sort that you might expect at the races or a casino – anywhere people are gambling to some degree with their money.

I didn't hang around for too long, pausing on the way out to buy a movie poster of Brigitte Bardot that I thought Rita might like and then heading home. I had seen what I wanted and had begun to understand the draw of classic car auctions, particularly if you are actually there to buy something.

Back in Italy it was soon time for Spencer and myself to leave beautiful Como behind and make our way to Turin. That was to be our base for the night and our starting point for the drive over the border to France and across the Col de la Bonette the next morning. My only impression of the city had come from watching *The Italian Job* in my youth. For some reason I imagined it as a dull, industrial place and had added it to the itinerary purely for geographic convenience rather than any longing to visit.

Leaving Erba, we strode past the parked supercars that surrounded my Ferrari and made our way back towards the motorway, south towards Milan and then westwards towards Turin, or Torino as it is known locally. We passed by a few memorable cars on the way but it was, once again, a section of journey that simply had to be done and so we set about covering the ground as quickly and safely as possible.

As we approached Turin we found ourselves keeping an eye on the fuel gauge as we would soon need to stop for petrol. The problem was that none of the motorway service stations in the area had 99 octane unleaded petrol, something we had discovered on arriving in Italy and immediately realised that it suited the car better than any lesser quality fuel. In fact, the 99 octane petrol seemed not only to give the car some extra punch but also ensured that the oil pressure – which I had been so concerned about in Belgium and northern Germany – remained stable, even at altitude. It was one of the many intricacies of my car that I had the chance to learn about during this epic trip. I later mentioned this to a friend that was training to be a pilot. He explained that it made sense as it would, theoretically, put less strain on the engine by burning more efficiently. Whether that is true or not, I don't know. As we would be tackling one of Europe's highest roads the next day I thought we should persevere until we found some of the good stuff but it simply wasn't to be and we were forced to go for standard unleaded on the outskirts of town rather than risk running out of fuel altogether.

The Parco Hotel Sassi was probably the strangest of all the places I stayed at during this trip. I had chosen it on the basis of favourable reviews found on the internet and due to the provision of off-road parking, but it wasn't quite what I was expecting. It was certainly positioned in a peaceful spot but it was further away from the city centre than I had appreciated. Inside it appeared as if one member of staff was running the place all on his own. There was no bar and no restaurant. If you wanted a beer then the guy that was manning the front desk would bring it to you. Spencer had a chat with him while I caught up on some emails, discovering that we needed to take a taxi into town and that we might struggle to find anywhere to eat because Saturday nights were busy. A little pestering and a dinner reservation was made by the pessimistic, all-in-one hotel man and a taxi booked to get us there in time for a few drinks.

Turin is a much more attractive city than I had ever imagined, the old centre far removed from my assumption that it would be a cold, ugly, industrial place. The buildings were as grand and as quintessentially Italian as I had seen anywhere else on my travels yet here it was all on a larger scale. We were dropped off in a large rectangular piazza, a wide cobbled street flanked by pedestrian areas. Covered walkways lined the piazza, hiding shops and restaurants that were visible behind each of the arches that looped down towards the river ahead. It was the Piazza Vittorio Veneto. At one end the magnificent domed church, Chiesa della Gran Madre di Dio, sat dominatingly on the other side of the water. It is so clearly visible at the end of the street you would be forgiven for not realising there was a river in between.

The atmosphere was lively but relaxed. Many of the cafes and restaurants that lined the piazza were filled with people enjoying the warm evening and talking animatedly over drinks and food. Spencer and I found a nice place about halfway down one side of the piazza, enticed by the sound of good music being pumped out of the open-fronted building and reaching out to the customers sat at tables spreading out towards the road. It was an interesting place. Cocktails were being made to order and served in plastic cups by stylish young staff. A second room had tables laid out with food, a sort of buffet that was obviously appealing to many of the students that were around. Sitting with cocktail in hand and watching people pass by it became clear that Turin was a very diverse place. Groups of young Goths, meandering couples, giggling trios of girls, gay guys in tight jeans, this area had it all.

Dinner was on the other side of the square, the restaurant holding a more mature crowd that seemed as happy as we were to be bordering the action and soaking up the atmosphere over dinner. The food itself was pleasant but far from memorable. Even so, I returned to the hotel thinking that Turin is a place I would like to return to one day.

Scaling New Heights

Turin–Col de la Bonette–Vence

A fter a few good days in Italy it was time to head over the border to France. We had planned to meet some friends at a small town half an hour inland from Nice for a late lunch and so it was necessary to make a prompt start. Thankfully the Sunday morning roads in Turin were quiet and we were soon heading out of the city and off towards the hills. The quickest route meant heading south then east, before following the coastal road westwards through Imperia, San Remo and Ventimiglia and then hitting the French border. The more interesting route meant turning inland towards Cuneo and then south at Jausiers over the Col de la Bonette – Europe's highest through road. Naturally that is what I wanted to do. I had finally downloaded some appropriate maps for the sat nav system which meant we shouldn't have a problem with getting lost and could simply enjoy the journey and the views without scrabbling at the not-quite-detailed-enough map.

I had high hopes for the Col de la Bonette having heard it to be one of Europe's best driving roads. After the disappointment of the Stelvio Pass being closed I had made sure to check numerous websites to confirm that it was open. Thankfully it was. Better still, the sun was shining as we set off and once again I started the day with a real appetite for being on the road after my low moment the previous morning. If yesterday had taught me anything, a day on the road with a good friend and a Ferrari is never a bad day.

The first section of the journey was unremarkable but things improved almost instantly once we had passed Cuneo. Although I hadn't known this at the time, we had stumbled across the Colle della Maddalena, a road which would lead us through small villages and past green fields and ever more jagged hills. The hills were green to start with, covered in trees where we were but increasingly rocky off into the distance until the largest and furthest away were tinged with white. We found ourselves caught behind weekend traffic, forced to follow patiently on meandering roads, overtaking when we could. Each town or village we passed seemed to suck up some of the traffic and poured us out onto ever tighter but quieter roads.

The snow-capped mountains were soon rising up around us, cliff edges creeping closer to the roadside. The villages too became smaller, the roads that cut past the buildings barely big enough for two cars. Banners and flags seemed popular here. Every village we passed had bunting crossing the small streets, Italian flags asserting their identity so close to the border with France. We were seeing more cyclists and motorcyclists now as well, they as keen to enjoy a good road as we were.

As the road began to climb the surface became more changeable but the opportunity to have fun increased significantly. This was a great road; as good a road as I had experienced in the course of the trip and a bit of a surprise as we thought it was just a means of getting to the Col de la Bonette. There were straights and long sweeping corners. There were well-sighted hairpins and long tunnels that seemed to carry you into the rock face, each time giving us an excuse to drop a gear and run through the rev range, savouring the engine noise as it ricocheted off the walls. Sometimes one side of the tunnel would open up, light pouring in between the pillars, giving the impression of passing a huge filmstrip as we powered towards the mountains that lay ahead. Yellow and black poles lined the road up here, snow markers hinting at the weather that locals have to endure during the winter months and the reason for the broken tarmac.

We had gradually climbed up into the mountains by the time we crossed over into France, the lush greenery now replaced with more muted colours, rocky outcrops, snow patches and small dark lakes. The popularity of this area among bikers became clear just before the border, groups of motorbikes and their owners huddled together in a restaurant car park, presumably readying themselves for the drive to France or back from where they had come. We found ourselves following them from time to time on the road that dropped down towards Jausiers, back into the trees and through more small towns. They were fast on the straights but slower on the corners, causing frustration for short periods of time until they let us pass. Finally we turned off towards the Col de la Bonette, the road to ourselves for the first time that day. The road began to climb, zig-zagging at first as we made our way up the first hill. The mountains loomed in the distance and the weather was looking far from welcoming there. The tarmac was smooth up here, as though the road had been recently resurfaced. Frustratingly, visibility wasn't good. There were too many blind corners to really get any speed up on this unfamiliar road.

It opened up again for a while as the road stopped climbing and sidled along a valley. That meant we could start getting into more of a rhythm, making the most of the excellent throttle response, steering and brakes of the F355.

After a short while the road started rising again steadily and continuously. There were points during which we were faced with hairpin after hairpin, with butterfly-inducing drops to the side. It became clear very quickly that although it was a great road to drive it was no drivers' road. It did not compare to the enjoyment of the previous couple of hours from an out-and-out driving perspective but once we made our peace with that it was easy to settle back, take it easy and enjoy the spectacular scenery.

As we climbed, the trees thinned again and the once distant snow began to appear in patches on the side of the road. We weren't alone up there either. Aside from the occasional car, cyclist or biker, Spencer and I had noticed large rodent-like creatures running across the road or away from the roadside as we sped by. I genuinely had no idea what they were but Spencer felt that they might be marmots and he was right. There were a huge amount of them about, just scampering around on the snow and rocks that lined the side of the road, looking for food and amusing me in the process.

The landscape became more and more barren until it was just rocks and snow and soon felt like a place divorced from the France we felt we knew. In fact, it could have been anywhere in the world from Asia or Russia to South America; anywhere with mountains. The roads had obviously been recently ploughed and this created huge

glacial-looking banks on the side of the road. We proceeded, climbing and climbing, onwards and upwards,
wondering if it was ever going to come to a summit. Of
course it does eventually. Once we had passed some brave
cyclists and the obligatory motorbike parade we reached
the top, the road peaking at an altitude of 2,715 metres
and the views spectacular even with the slightly threat-
ening clouds that lay over the mountains casting everything in a sinister grey light. There was another small
road that went up around the peak and a little higher
still to 2,802m but it was still snow-covered at the time, a
group of motorcyclists hanging out and chatting by its
edge. It turned out that this small, scenic tarmac loop is
what endows this road with the label of Europe's highest
through road.

Photos taken and driver switch-over completed, we
were soon heading down the other side towards the Cote
D'Azur, this time Spencer at the wheel. This section of
the road seemed to have been more affected by rocks and
gravel than the north side, it having either fallen off the
mountain or been carried by melting snow. It meant
stopping more than once to move rocks out of the road
just so that we could continue downwards to the greenery
below.

As much as I trust Spencer behind the wheel I was a
bit nervous as we descended the tight, twisting roads.
There was less snow on the side of the pass but the sheer
drops and scattering of small stones on the surface made
me a little fearful, my issues of wanting to be in control
kicking-in as they had at the Nürburgring. There was
nothing to worry about though and soon the road improved, snaking down the mountainside and providing

opportunities for more spirited driving due to long, well-sighted sections. There were some more hairpins and sections of broken tarmac to contend with but we were soon in another valley, flying past waterfalls and forests until we hit the small town of St Etienne de Tinee and stopped for a bit of refreshment before setting off for the final push towards Vence.

We found that the roads leading away from the Col de la Bonette on the south side were better for driving enjoyment than the Col itself. In fact, these roads were as good as those experienced earlier on the Colle della Maddelena. The roads that ran past the ski town of Isola and on, down valleys that followed bright blue rivers to the sea were spectacular. They were beautiful, well-surfaced, varied and almost deserted. The fact that this route was scattered with tunnels gave us plenty of chance to really enjoy the wailing sound of the F355 as we pushed through each of the gears to 8,250rpm where the car's peak power of 380bhp is delivered.

Before we knew it, we were back amongst the Sunday traffic and seeing signs for places we recognised, the sat nav now redundant. We got caught behind a tourist bus on the winding roads that follow the hills of the Cote d'Azur towards Vence, slowing the final miles of the journey. We rolled up the driveway of the villa where we would be staying for the night and switched off the engine, listening to the ticking sounds as it cooled in the shade of the trees.

We had time for a beer and a swim before our friends were due to arrive for what turned into a very boozy evening. It was great to unwind but I was already feeling a little flat after the adrenaline-fuelled adventure. My

European trip was going to be paused for a little while and leaving for London by plane the next morning just didn't appeal. I felt as though I could carry on driving around Europe endlessly and as the sun set I couldn't quite understand why it had taken me until now to get out there and embrace my passion for cars and driving. I was thoroughly enjoying every mile.

An Old Friend

Driving the Aston Martin DB7 Vantage

I'm not normally one for attending events organised by my old schools or universities. For some reason I've never been tempted, normally preferring to wait for someone to get married to provide an opportunity to temporarily renew lapsed friendships. As my younger brother attended the same school as I did, I have also been back many times so there hasn't really been the novelty factor for me that I imagine others have. That said, I have my weaknesses and the discovery that the school was organising its first classic car rally and concours event was something that piqued my interest. I knew immediately that I wanted to take part, particularly as it was taking place shortly after my return from France.

The event sounded fun rather than being a serious challenge, and the focus was squarely on raising money for charity as opposed to out-and-out competition. That suited me perfectly having never taken part in a car rally before but eager to find out how they work. It was also not going to be particularly time consuming, with a black tie dinner planned for the Friday night at a Highland castle, and then half a day's driving followed by the concours event on the Saturday, all designed to fit in with the junior school's annual Highland Games. With my car still in France, my step-father, Alasdair, offered his Aston Martin so that I could take part, though he himself didn't fancy the role of co-driver. My good friend Ross was less hesitant, feeling this would be the perfect way to visit the school again for the first time since leaving in 1999. Some forms filled in, deposits sent, jacket sizes and car description given over and we were quickly signed-up and left wondering who else might be there and what they would be driving.

I arrived back in London from France only a day or two before my birthday and Rita had kindly arranged a surprise party for me. After the excitement of seeing Rita and catching up with all my friends had passed, I found myself feeling pretty down. I just wasn't prepared for how low I might be feeling after ten days driving across Europe. It had been all I could focus on for weeks beforehand and was also draining during the trip itself, both physically and emotionally. The adrenalin had now gone and there was no Italian V8 engine keeping me buzzing. Thankfully I didn't have long to mope around feeling sorry for myself as Rita and I were due to fly to Scotland to spend some time with my family before the rally. I wasn't convinced that peace and quiet was the answer but it proved to be perfect for getting over the road trip come-down.

We arrived just in time to enjoy a rare occurrence – a period during which the weather is better in the northeast of Scotland than it is in London. Britain is a stunningly beautiful place when the sun shines and Morayshire is no exception. At the beginning of June everything is a lush green, with daisies and buttercups glazing the fields white and yellow, and the hills and distant snow-capped mountains of the Cairngorms giving an Alpine feel. Like the Alps, the air is clean, the skies clear and the peace and quiet a dominant feature, particularly if you step outside at night. I knew all these things already but it had been almost six months since I had been in Scotland and nearer nine months since I had been home to visit my parents. I immediately understood why my friends from London had been so insistent to arrange visits to my family home during the years I had lived in Aberdeen – the contrast from London is huge, something I had never really appreciated on brief visits to the south and back again. The space and peace is almost overwhelming, particularly if you normally begin your day travelling on the London Underground.

The other thing that caught me off guard was how friendly everyone is. I had always felt like a bit of an outsider in Scotland, particularly having maintained a very English accent despite spending more than half my life there. Returning from the hustle and bustle of London I soon realised how polite and interested everyone is. Maybe it's something that happens in all smaller communities where the pace of life is slower but it is certainly no less refreshing for that.

It seemed fitting that I had come back to Scotland to take part in a classic motoring event. My passion for cars and driving owed a lot to my fifteen years living in the north-east of Scotland and it felt good to be back in the guise of a car enthusiast. Lifelong interests can often start with your family and Alasdair can certainly shoulder some of the blame for setting me on the path I was on now. It wasn't long after moving to Scotland that Alasdair bought an Aston Martin DB7 in British Racing Green, perhaps the ultimate British sports car of the time. As teenage boys my friends and I all knew that an Aston Martin was a James Bond car, even if Bond seemed to be inexplicably driving BMWs under Pierce Brosnan's stewardship. That kind of simple association stood for a lot at that age. Maybe it still does. It was certainly the first truly exotic and special car I had ever been in. It might not have had the drama of some of its Italian contemporaries but it still had me under its spell from the first moment that I saw it. Simple things like getting dropped off at school became an event in an Aston Martin and I subconsciously learnt that a feeling of occasion is a desirable attribute in a sports car, no matter what brand it might be or how expensive it is to buy.

Mum's pride and joy was a bright red Saab 900i convertible. It looked like a proper Saab, built before they put on weight and began looking ungainly. It was the car that I initially learned to drive in and a huge contrast to the slow and clunky diesel Renault Clio I had to contend with during my paid-for driving lessons. I always looked forward to going out for a drive with Mum even if she was a fairly edgy passenger. We had the benefit of the quiet, winding, undulating roads of the Scottish Highlands on our doorstep. On roads like these you quickly learn that the quickest way to get from one place to another is to flow almost meditatively with the road, in the summer at least. The winter months provide different challenges in that part of the world, snow and ice a common occurrence and four-wheel drive vehicles often a necessity. Familiarity with driving in such conditions was a useful lesson in itself.

By the time I left sixth form Alasdair had upgraded to a silver DB7 Vantage. It was even more eye-catching and more muscular than the standard version and able to emit a spectacular sound due to its 6 litre V12 engine and sports exhaust. That car still turns heads today. Even those who are not interested in cars seem to recognise that it is a truly handsome piece of design, while those in the know will nod approvingly or even start conversations about the car at petrol pumps.

It wasn't just the cars that inspired me. Learning to drive in Morayshire is a necessity if you want to have any kind of freedom. My friends were scattered all over the place and public transport was rarely a feasible option; the train lines missed out large areas and bus travel took far too long and required numerous changes. As a result the car quickly became a symbol of liberation for my friends and me. I grew to love the feeling of setting off on a journey, any journey that would simply allow me to drive, uninterrupted. Thankfully, living in Scotland meant that I could quickly be on a great driving road, somewhere off in the countryside, across the hills and through the valleys that make up much of the country north of Edinburgh and Glasgow. I would regularly go for drives simply for the pleasure of it and with no destination in mind. My choice of car evolved, becoming more performance-centric and with a focus on best enjoying these challenging roads. But you could never quite guess when you would have a truly memorable drive. Driving over the hills between Forres and Dufftown in a VW Golf 1.6 SE, following the contours of the Pentland Hills outside of Edinburgh in an Audi TT, and charging up towards the Lecht ski centre in a Porsche Boxster S; these were all outstanding drives. Borrowing the Aston Martin to drive around the Highlands and the west coast of Scotland with Spencer for three days was a particular high point, an experience which went some way to emulating the road trips I had read about in my favourite magazines over the years and left me eager for more driving-focused road trips of the kind I had just returned from.

It was certainly relaxing being back home – walks with the dogs, fishing on the Spey, good food and even better wine – but I wanted to get back on the road. Thankfully arriving in Scotland early gave me a chance to plan a trip to Edinburgh with Rita, providing a welcome opportunity to reacquaint myself with the Aston Martin DB7 Vantage ahead of the classic car rally. Better yet, I had heard that a garden party was taking place near Aberdeen which included an exhibition of a very special private car collection in aid of Save the Children.

I didn't really need any excuse to take out the Aston. It's a car that you take every opportunity to enjoy; the svelte shape, the knowledge that it has a 12-cylinder engine underneath the bonnet and the fact it is an Aston Martin allure enough to get most drivers and car enthusiasts a little hot under the collar.

Having not read the motoring press much during my high school years, I never really knew how the DB7 was received when it was launched, although I was aware that it is recognised as having 'saved' Aston Martin through sales success, in turn developing a new level of consumer desire for the brand. Looking back now and re-reading some of the articles and road tests from the 90s, you quickly notice how much of a big deal this new car was at the time.

The standard DB7, with its supercharged V8 engine, arrived to a mixture of fanfare and criticism. It was the first car in over 20 years to be named with the DB prefix – a nod to Sir David Brown who ran the company from 1947 until 1972. Ian Callum's design seemed to offer a modern interpretation of the earlier DB cars, once again looking smooth and curvey and a significant departure from the blunt muscle car looks of the recent V8 Astons. The design quickly became recognised as a classic and stood in subtle contrast to some of the DB7s brasher peers of the time.

Critics weren't so sure about what was underneath though. At the time Aston Martin and Jaguar were owned by Ford and there was a feeling that the DB7 would be no more than a Ford/Jaguar parts bin special. The fact that the chassis was derived from the unrealised Jaguar F-type concept didn't help this perception, itself a development of the dated XJS platform. The Jaguar XK8 that did go into production also had a chassis derived from the XJS, marking the DB7 out as nothing more than a sexed-up and overpriced Jaguar in many peoples' eyes. In fact, steering aside, it was seen to drive well enough, particularly in terms of how it soaked up bumps and road imperfections more capably than some of its competitors. However, it just wasn't special enough to stand as the company's flagship product and left some people a bit cold.

The introduction of the V12-engined DB7 Vantage in 1999 changed things significantly. Delivering 420bhp, 0-60mph in 5.0 seconds and a claimed top speed of 180mph, Aston Martin delivered a car with supercar credentials and a slightly more muscular version of the celebrated design of its V8-engined sibling. The engine is actually engineered from two Ford V6s of the sort used in the top of the range Mondeo of the time. This work was under-taken by engineering company Cosworth, whose mo-torsport success and special edition road cars during the 80s and 90s endowed the firm with a lot of respect both within the industry and amongst consumers. Other areas of the car were reworked and improved as well but it will always be recognised for its engine. At the time, motoring journalist Andrew Frankel suggested that:

"...two Ford V6 engines make a more charismatic V12 than any made by Ferrari today. It's not quite so smooth as that fitted to a 550 Maranello but if it's that multi-layered V12 symphony you're after, that which Ferrari used to make its own, you'll now find it under the bonnet of an Aston Martin. This is one of the world's great powerplants, flexible, urbane and unobtrusive when needed, sharp edged and snarling when wanted."

After a couple of days of quiet country living, Rita and I prepared to head off to Edinburgh. There are two ways to get to Edinburgh from the area of Scotland that skirts the Morayshire and Aberdeenshire border – to Aberdeen and along the main roads that run south through Dundee, or across to Aviemore and then down the A9 towards Perth. With the sun shining and no time constraints the scenic route beckoned. Luggage, CDs and girlfriend all loaded into the car and we were ready to go. The idea of a decent drive for the first time since reaching the south of France in the Ferrari was really appealing and the combination of car, place and weather all felt spot-on.

The DB7 Vantage still looks great. The aggressive front end provides strong road presence and purpose but it remains graceful and understated, particularly in the slightly conservative metallic grey of this car. I've always been a fan of the ten-spoke design of the alloy wheels. Their slightly spiky front edge seems to hint at the sporting intent of what is essentially a grand-tourer rather than pure sports car, though at 18 inches they are smaller than some of today's hot hatches let alone cars of this pedigree.

Press the key icon on the plastic fob, open the solid-feeling door, and you are greeted with a cocoon of contrasting grey and cream leather, wood panelling and a simple black steering wheel. I personally find the lacquered wood to look a bit dated, something not helped by the basic-looking switchgear. Step over the sill – with its "DB7 Vantage" plaque – and drop down into the seats and things improve. The seats are nicely sculpted and well-bolstered and give the feel of having been designed for long journeys. There are rear seats but these are best saved for emergencies, jackets and only very small children. Overall it is a pleasant place to be and does a good job of insulating you from the outside world, if that's what you want. I would recommend keeping the window or door open, at least until after you have started the engine.

Turn the DB7-logoed key and you are met with an airplane-like "bong, bong, bong" sound for a few seconds and then left with a dull background buzz that indicates the car is primed, ready for you to start it up. No matter how many times you have done it before, reaching for the bright red, unlabelled starter button is a moment to be savoured and anticipation allowed to build that bit higher. Depress the button and, for a second and no more, it sounds like a Transformer clearing its throat before the roar of the engine erupts into life with a deep growl, then settling into a steady, reserved idle. Stick your head out-side and you can detect a sonorous burble that hints at what is under the bonnet, then blip the throttle and you'll be under no doubt that there's a 6-litre V12 in front of you.

The seating position is good and it doesn't take long to get comfortable, and visibility is good all around. De-spite being a V12 Aston Martin and inherently feeling 'a little special', it really feels like a car designed to be used every day. A majority of these cars were sold with the Touchtronic gearbox which acts as a five-speed automatic with both a normal mode and a higher-revving, more re-sponsive sport mode. Pull the gearstick back to drive, lift your foot off the brake and it rolls off positively before you apply a bit of throttle. That's when things get interesting, particularly as far as the sound is concerned and particu-larly with this car's optional sports exhaust. Like many high performance cars the DB7 Vantage seems to have a variety of 'voices' as you take it through the rev range. It starts low, like the sound of a squad of six-foot tall bees with an attitude problem, and it keeps escalating in pitch in a linear fashion. It never screams like a Ferrari V8 or an F1 car. Instead there is a rounded, bassy sound all the way through the rev range but it is also laced with a whine that makes it sound like a jet engine. It is intoxi-cating and makes you want to rev through the gears as much as possible. Luckily the Touchtronic system also allows the driver to change gear by tilting the gearstick forwards or backwards, or by using the '+' and '-' buttons on the steering wheel. In many respects it is a dated sys-tem and I would prefer a manual. That said, it is in keep-ing with the nature of the car and allows you to drive the car much more actively, with downshifts slowing engine speed as you brake into corners – something that modern dual clutch systems seem to avoid with their engineered throttle blips.

Heading from Speyside towards Aviemore provides an opportunity to experience some really good driving roads. We sped past numerous distilleries, through lush green glens and onwards towards the snow-capped mountains of the Cairngorms. There were moments when the vista seemed to suddenly open out around us; an elevated plain scattered with streams, sheep and the occasional building, all helping to demonstrate the sheer scale of the landscape. I couldn't help but think how bleak it must be to live up there in the depths of winter but that wasn't a concern for Rita and I. The sun was shining brightly and the sense of space and the vibrancy of the greens against the blue of the sky made it seem as though we had stumbled into a Visit Scotland advert.

The roads blended decent straights with plenty of third and fourth gear bends, providing a perfect recipe for some fast but relaxed driving. Once we got going I was quickly reminded that this car treads a fine line between soaking up the imperfections of the road and providing some feedback as to what is going on beneath the wheels. The steering feels a little vague, which doesn't help, and taking corners at any kind of speed becomes about believing in the grip the tyres are able to generate rather than there being any seat-of-the-pants indication as to where the limits lie. If you get in to the DB7 Vantage and try to drive it like a Lotus Elise, you'll be disappointed. Instead, approach it more along the lines of a Bentley and you'll be impressed. In essence, it is more about finding a rhythm than beating the road into submission; more about carrying good average speed than it is about accelerating hard, braking hard and trying to throw the car round the corners with complete abandon. Drive it steadily and you'll find it is capable of crushing any distance with minimum drama and dispatching any slower traffic with disdain, the only problem being speed limits.

Eventually the pace slowed and the traffic increased, then the road closed in and the scenery was replaced with dull, generic modern housing. This shift marked our approach to Aviemore, a place that acts as a hub for Scotland's outdoor activities. In the winter it is essentially a skiing town and apparently has been since the 1960s. In the summer it attracts those interested in walking, mountain biking, climbing and doing water sports in the nearby mountains and lochs. Its position between Perth and Inverness, both by road and rail, means it is an obvious point of access for those wanting to visit the Highlands and has allowed it to continue building itself as a centre for outdoor types. Truth be told, it is not a pretty place. It feels very 'fit for purpose', providing enough outdoor clothing shops, restaurants and bars to satisfy visitors and the local community and nothing more. Driving through, it often feels like a quiet outpost town but I am told it's lively and good fun during the ski season. We rolled through slowly, looking around to see what was going on before turning out onto the A9 and heading south towards Perth.

The A9 is a frustrating road. It is long, straight and well-sighted but it seems to be an area that the authorities are eager to protect from the dangers of speeding cars. This means that there are a handful of fixed speed cameras and a number of mobile units lurking on any given day. It is also beautiful, particularly in the transition from the mountains down into the lush green countryside of Perthshire. The DB7 Vantage was the perfect car for the journey. It was sedate and refined for the slower sections when we were simply cruising and enjoying the views, yet it was always ready to react with a surge of power if I spotted an overtaking opportunity or reached one of the rare sections of dual carriageway that would allow us to pass the inevitable lorries and caravans. Road signs warned of the dual carriageways some two miles in advance and then again shortly beforehand, providing me with plenty of time to push the gearstick over to Sport mode and to warn Rita about the impending fireworks. The piling on of speed that followed never lost its appeal.

After about half an hour of skirting the Cairngorms, before Pitlochry and seemingly in the middle of nowhere, is a restaurant and retail outlet complex called House of Bruar. It was here that Rita and I stopped to stretch our legs. We enjoyed a hearty lunch in the courtyard before getting back on the road, just managing to avoid the lure of sweets and ice cream in the food hall. A bit further on along the winding A9 we peeled off onto the M90, joining the traffic that had come down the east coast from Aberdeen and Dundee. From there it was a straightforward run towards the Firth of Forth, over the bridge and beyond, to Edinburgh.

I always enjoy visiting Edinburgh, particularly in the summer when it is abuzz with numerous festivals and the many international visitors that they draw. We were too early in the year for the festivities but with the summer holidays looming it seemed as though the city's students were winding down already and making the most of the good weather. In the parks, plumes of smoke rose from the many disposable barbeques that were placed at the centre of small tribes of students, all engaged in animated conversations and sipping on beers or plastic cups filled with wine. Others were darting around chasing balls or leaping to catch Frisbees. There would be some good parties going on in Edinburgh later that night but it looked like Rita and I would be missing out.

Almost as soon as we had arrived at our base for the night, I managed to hit my head on the mantelpiece. Gone were any plans of taking Rita for dinner down at the waterfront in Leith or showing her my favourite cocktail bars. Instead she would be accompanying me to the local hospital and then joining me on the sofa for a takeaway and some TV. It transpired that I had given myself a mild concussion and a night on the town was not a good idea. On the upside, at least I wouldn't have a hangover for the drive home the next day.

The road back north via Dundee is pleasant enough and you can make brisk progress once you've battled with the weekend traffic, poorly surfaced roads, and numerous road works before saying goodbye to Edinburgh and crossing the bridge. Just after Stonehaven we took the opportunity of avoiding Aberdeen itself, instead turning off the dual carriageway near Cammachmore and taking the country lanes towards the River Dee. We had just enough time for a quick stop at the Lairhillock Inn for some lunch in the conservatory before throwing ourselves into an Aberdeenshire garden party already in full swing.

Truth be told, we were running pretty late following the hour-long hold-up getting out of Edinburgh and even

181

the Aston couldn't make amends without me driving at silly, license-losing speeds. On small country lanes the car does a good job of damping the road imperfections caused by numerous hard winters, the steering wheel-mounted buttons again delivering a welcome level of control and interaction after two hours of high speed motorway cruising.

It is a great car to attend any kind of event in, always receiving admiring glances from people of all ages. However, it was very quickly overshadowed by the excellent car collection lined up inside the gardens, a stunning array of motorsport examples and some very special road cars. The first thing we saw having sneaked away from the charity auction to the quiet section of garden where the cars were arranged was Alain Prost's 1991 Ferrari 643 Formula 1 car. It stood side-by-side with Rubens Barrichello's Ferrari F2003-GA car from 2003. Beyond that a number of Ferrari-based GT series race cars were grouped together in full racing livery, with two road-going Ferrari 550 Barchettas lurking behind them. You rarely see one of these topless derivatives of Maranello's V12-engined grand-tourer, let alone two in one place. I was amused to discover that the left-hand drive example was destined for the owner's California house and the right-hand drive version would be staying at the UK home. Amongst the other cars in this impressive collection sat something that I had never seen in the flesh before – a Ferrari FXX.

Based on the Enzo supercar, the FXX was launched in 2005 with 29 cars built for some of Ferrari's most dedicated customers and one for a certain Mr. Schumacher. The idea was for the owners to act as 'Client Test Drivers' alongside Ferrari's technical team and professional test drivers, all as part of an ongoing research and development programme. The findings would then be fed into the development of future extreme road cars. The FXX is a track-only car that draws heavily on Ferrari's Formula 1 technology. It has a 6.3 litre V12 engine that puts out 800bhp, a gearbox that can shift in 80ms, and bespoke Bridgestone tyres and Brembo brakes. Each driver would be given a driving suit, helmet, gloves and boots, receive an introduction session at the Fiorano test track in Maranello, and have a tailored set up for seat and pedals. The package, which cost €1.5 million plus taxes, included six non-competitive track events in three continents over the course of two years, as well as events at the Ferrari World Finals in 2006 and 2007, all with full support from a team of engineers and technicians. The programme was seen as a success and in 2007 Ferrari launched an Evoluzione package that included upgrades based upon the data collected, including a power rise to 860bhp, quicker gearshift times and more options for the traction control settings.

I tried to catch our host and the owner of these wonderful cars to find out more about his experiences with the FXX but he was circulating furiously around his guests, seemingly fuelled by an afternoon of champagne consumption. We managed some pleasantries before his attention was drawn elsewhere leaving Rita and I to say goodbye to some acquaintances from my Aberdeen days before going home. I feared that the DB7 Vantage might feel very ordinary after time spent gawping at the FXX. All I had to do was thumb that red starter button once more and I was immediately reminded that there is nothing ordinary about a V12 Aston Martin.

Whisky, Castles and Cars

An introduction to classic car rallying

I knew that it was non-competitive and would only include half a day's worth of actual driving but I still found myself getting increasingly excited by the prospect of the classic car rally. A lot of that excitement was undoubtedly related to the fact that this would be my first social event as a car enthusiast and I was looking forward to spending some time with like-minded people.

Rita had left and Ross had arrived the night before the rally. We had spent a little time going over the itinerary, catching up and sipping on a beer or two. We were due to arrive at Drummuir Castle sometime before the 6pm briefing on the Friday evening. The castle was owned by a local family but was being run by Diageo for corporate hospitality purposes. We assumed that this meant dinner would be a boozy affair, teeing the participants up for an after dinner speech by guest John Brigden. Among his many interests and experiences, including a stint as councillor for Sevenoaks District Council, we had been informed that John owned and ran Worldwide Classic Car Rallies and had toured much of Asia and Central America in classic cars. The following morning would see timed departures starting at 8.30am, giving us a chance for a bite to eat and a chance to attach our rally plate to the front of the car before setting off. The route – which had apparently been chosen to show off the best bits of Morayshire – would be revealed in due course in the form of tulip diagrams, distances and supporting maps. We would finish at the school and would then parade to the playing field, through the junior Highland Games, to be judged as part of the concours event.

I wanted Ross to do the short drive to Drummuir Castle as it would be his first time behind the wheel of the Aston and it made sense for him to acclimatise a little before things really kicked-off the following morning. It may have only been a ten minute journey but it is quite a revealing road, combining a little bit of everything and, I felt, probably indicative of the roads we would experience the next day. The DB7 Vantage is in no way a difficult car to drive but it is no less exciting for that. Judging by the smile on Ross's face when we stopped it was clear that he would enjoy this experience as much as I would.

Ross is a true gentleman and the most stylishly dressed of all my friends. With his Scottish roots and sophisticated taste, I knew that a night at a Highland castle and a classic motoring event in an Aston Martin would appeal to him. It was also important to me that he was involved in at least one element of my journey and it wasn't just because he had endured many hours listening to Spencer and myself talking about cars. Ross and I had shared adventures in Europe, Africa and Australasia over the years, during which we had been arrested, conquered mountains and got into all sorts of mischief. Ross had even spent a week sitting with me as I recovered from a horrible skiing accident in the Alps. After all that it seemed fitting that he play a role on my journey into the world of car enthusiasm.

Pulling off the road which led us from Dufftown to Keith, trundling down a leafy lane, over an old railway line and onto the driveway, Drummuir Castle was revealed, nestled within well kempt grounds and looking stereotypically Scottish. We were clearly one of the last cars to arrive, with six or seven already lined up in a row facing the castle and a few owners fiddling with the attachments for the rally plates which would need to be mounted before we left. A young man – who turned out to be a current sixth-former and the mastermind behind the rally – directed us to wait behind a car which was tucked under a *porte-cochère* at the front of the building. Soon the space was cleared for us and we rolled forward, attempted to squeeze out of the car without catching the doors on any of the stonework, and greeted a couple of teachers that we recognised from our school days. Our former economics teacher was there in the guise of Events Coordinator for the former pupils' association. He greeted us warmly before inviting us inside and steering us into the combined library and snooker room which sat just off a magnificent hallway, its central lantern tower rising three or four stories high. Either side of a large window at the back of the room were fitted shelves stacked with bottles, primarily of single malt whisky. Looking more closely it became clear that Diageo's entire catalogue of brands was represented, everything from unheard of foreign beers to mint-flavoured Baileys. My eyes must have widened considerably when it was explained that we could help ourselves to as much as we liked during our stay, though we should attempt to be sober the following morning. Our host made to offer us a cup of coffee each, pausing as though he had processed the implications of what he had just told us before gesturing to the whisky.

"Why don't you start with one of these?" he asked.

Moments later we were back outside admiring the other cars and sipping on a very generous measure of Mortlach 32 year-old single malt; a pleasant but ominous start to the evening.

Disappointingly, it turned out that there would only be ten cars taking part in the rally, a little less than I was anticipating. Already outside were a number of MGs, a Jaguar XJS, an Alfa Romeo Spider, an old Mercedes SL 'Pagoda', a Morgan, and a bright orange Caterham R300 which would probably be the most fun on these roads if it stayed dry. The drivers and co-drivers of the cars were a similarly eclectic bunch. Many were local but some were returning to the area for the first time since leaving the school over 40 years ago. Ross and I weren't quite the youngest as we had predicted, though we were somewhat below the average age.

It was great to see the Aston getting so much positive attention. As one of the newer cars there I feared it would have been looked upon with contempt, as not being a true classic, but people seemed to be interested in it, some even photographing themselves next to it.

Over a pre-briefing whisky, Ross and I got an opportunity to meet the other participants properly, discovering everyone to be extremely friendly and very passionate about their cars. Most were old boys attending with their wives, who would act as navigators, rather than friends sharing the driving and navigating as Ross and I were. There was certainly a lot of specialised knowledge and experience in the group which was soon completed by the arrival of the final participant, John Grant. John not only ran the Glenfarclas distillery but was also the proud owner of a gorgeous 1934 Bentley Van den Plas Open Tourer. Once we had peeked out the window to have a look we were convinced it would take the honours at the concours event the next day even if it wouldn't be the fastest car in the group.

In many ways that ten minute spell before the briefing set the tone for the night ahead – good conversation and plentiful drinks. The revelry continued through the black tie dinner and on into the early hours of the morning, despite the 10.30pm 'close' indicated on the agenda.

Inevitably there would be an 'I should have known better' moment the next day. It happened an hour or so after the timed departures from Drummuir as we hurtled to Ballindalloch Castle from Tomintoul. I was sat in the passenger seat, nose pointed to the window for fresh air, desperately trying to get past my significant nausea and thumping headache. Ross, by contrast, was revelling in the great driving roads, the car lunging ahead every now and again as he spotted a straight or an overtaking opportunity, the car automatically dropping a gear or two to facilitate the surge of power required.

The day had actually started very well and, thankfully, would improve along with my hangover after the Ballindalloch stop. My alarm had failed to go off and I had awoken, completely by chance, just in time for breakfast. I subsequently woke up Ross twice and convinced one of the school pupils that were helping run the event to attach our rally plate to the front grill of the Aston while I looked on bleary-eyed, coffee in hand. I would be taking the wheel for the first section and Ross would be in charge of navigating using the tulip diagrams and routes we had been given the night before. First he was attempting to alleviate my concerns as to whether he knew what he was doing or not, a fear prompted by him having been asleep fifteen minutes before we were due to leave. Though neither of us had used them before, Ross was adamant that he was comfortable with the tulip diagrams and insisted I relax.

We were placed somewhere near the back of the pack despite, or because of, having one of the fastest cars there and watched as each of the others threaded through the *porte-cochère* at the front of the castle, ready to be flagged off at two minute intervals. We would be following the vintage Bentley. A support car had set off a little earlier than the rest of the group. It was a Marlin kit car built and driven by one of the teachers with the young mastermind Will as his passenger, presumably in case anyone got lost *en route*.

When our turn came I immediately pushed the gear lever over to the left and into sports mode, trundled along the gravel and past the group of school pupils that were lining the driveway taking photos. Once we hit the tarmac I flexed my right ankle and ripped off towards the gate in the hope that everyone behind us was enjoying the sound of the engine as much as we were.

The first sector ran towards Dufftown before turning off up to Cabrach, a road that I last drove in my old Porsche Boxster S on a crisp spring day some 14 months previously. The weather on the day of our rally wasn't looking so good and the predicted rain certainly wouldn't be pleasant for our open-topped colleagues. We were cosy in the Aston Martin and ready to make our mark, overtaking the Bentley just after one of the turnings before getting caught behind an Audi A3 that had infiltrated our convoy. Despite the road being barely wide enough for two cars our frustration didn't last too long as the Audi pulled aside to let us past. Hazard lights on to say thank you, I accelerated hard to the next corner only to find the Jaguar XJS cruising along at a leisurely pace ahead. Before we even got particularly close the Jaguar pulled over to let us past and only then did I realise that I still had the hazards on, the driver thinking we were demanding for him to get out of the way. I tried explaining later but I'm not sure he believed me, particularly as we were quickly building a reputation for overtaking whenever we could. We couldn't help but feel a bit competitive and enjoyed each overtaking manoeuvre as though we were really being timed, our more mature colleagues putting it down to the impatience of youth.

The section of road from Rhynie to Glenkindie and the first checkpoint was indicative of what we would enjoy for the rest of the morning – quiet, fast-flowing, relatively well-surfaced roads that cut and circled around the countryside. Settling into a steady rhythm was essential for brisk progress. There was no point in barrelling into corners too fast on roads like these, the Aston always leaving you guessing where the limits of grip lay. Although our average speed must have been one of the highest in the group it was great to see the Caterham teach us a lesson in cornering at one point. It is clearly a devastatingly effective tool on the right road and watching it carve through the tight turns left me itching to drive one.

With our route card signed and Ross installed at the wheel we took the high road to Tomintoul which climbs steeply after Cockbridge, dragging you out of the murky greenery and up to the Lecht ski centre. It's a fabulous section of road that unfurls in front of you, climbing upwards towards the horizon, then slithering back downhill just as suddenly as it rose. We paused at Tomintoul shortly afterwards so that I could jump out and get our route card signed once more, before pressing on for the short run to Ballindalloch Castle and our late morning coffee break.

On arrival to Ballindalloch we were warmly welcomed by Claire Macpherson-Grant Russell, Lord Lieutenant of Banffshire, and her husband Oliver Russell before being shown upstairs and taking the opportunity to compare notes with the other teams. Sadly we didn't get an opportunity to see much of the castle, known as the 'Pearl of the North', but we were impressed with what we saw. It is clearly very well looked after. I had never before seen such clinical grass verges as those lining the lawn in front of the castle.

Various photos taken and we were off again. I was relieved to be back at the wheel in my self-inflicted fragile state and I was actually feeling a lot better by this point thanks to coffee and shortbread. We were both happy to be on the move again, even if it was only a few miles to the next checkpoint at Glenfarclas Distillery where we happily accepted a small gift box containing some miniature whisky bottles.

It was raining quite heavily as we made our way to Dallas, a rural village that is about as far removed from the US oil capital in terms of glamour and weather as it's possible to get. The Morgan pulled over in front of us to raise its hood, husband and wife team declining our offer of assistance and leaving us to continue to the next check point. In our case it was simply a matter of lights, wipers and demister on. We might have been feeling a little smug about having a roof but this section of road demands commitment in the dry and respect in the wet, whatever you're driving. We pressed on steadily, soon passing the open-topped Marlin on the side of the road, driver and passenger cowering under an umbrella waiting for the worst to pass. A little further along and one of the MGs pulled over to let us past, our reputation firmly established at this point.

The next and final checkpoint was at Pluscarden Abbey. It is a magnificent building. Parts of it date back to the 13th century and it is actually still inhabited by Benedictine monks. We were in full flow now and preferred to press on rather than take a look around. Judging by the procession of cars behind us now, our fellow participants shared that view.

Ross took the wheel for this final section of the rally, it seeming appropriate that he return to school for the first time in 12 years driving an Aston Martin. As we made our way towards the finish line we missed a turning for the first time all day but we were on the road to Elgin by this point and in territory that I knew well. From here I could navigate without tulip diagrams and would hopefully get us there without losing too much ground to those travelling cross country. I feared that the Saturday lunchtime traffic might hold us up as we skirted through the edge of town but as we rolled down the school driveway, attempting to avoid school pupils and brutal speed bumps, it became clear that we were the first to arrive. The other cars started trickling in behind us almost immediately and there was now some time to catch-up with each other and to have a little walk around the place where we had spent five years of our youth before parading the cars up to the playing field, past the attractions and fire service display, where the Highland Games were in full flow.

The concours event was a foregone conclusion and, as we had predicted the previous evening, John Grant's Bentley took first prize, us taking a respectable sixth place. Despite not being the judges' favourite there was a lot of interest in the Aston from pupils and their parents alike, so we popped open the bonnet to expose the engine and left the doors unlocked so that people could sit inside if they wanted; something that quite a few people took advantage of as we sneaked off to the burger stall.

Motoring had remained a relatively solitary pursuit for me before taking part in this event. I knew that I enjoyed driving good cars on good roads but I had no idea that the social side of driving could be so fun, so rewarding. Ross and I hadn't been in the most dynamically-accomplished car by today's standards, neither had we been driving excessively fast, but we had discovered that there was great satisfaction to be had in being part of something bigger. It was all about the camaraderie, the shared experiences and a shared passion for cars. If a 24 hour event like this could be so enjoyable, it was no wonder that longer rallies and international tours had become so popular.

Every Dog Has Its Day

Foolish purchases and borrowed cars

I t would be all too easy to pretend that my experiences were all well-planned and strategically thought out but the truth is far from that. There were some things that were out of my hands, some meetings that never came to fruition and some requests that were denied. There were also one or two clear mistakes on my part. One such mistake was not checking whether the Stelvio Pass was open on the day that Spencer and I planned to drive it. Buying an early 90s Porsche without really thinking it through and then struggling for months to sell it was another, much larger mistake.

Almost as soon as I had returned home from the classic car rally I had a sudden panic, a feeling that I needed to get out there and experience more from behind the wheel before the year had passed me by. I was feeling hugely inspired by my recent adventures in both the Ferrari and the Aston Martin and I didn't like the feeling that all the excitement for the year had passed already. I needed something else to look forward to and so I started looking at options to entertain me until it was time to pick up my Ferrari from France, itself partly dependent upon me finding a garage space to rent in London.

Without a car to hand there wasn't a huge amount that I could do. Even a dull drive around the block wasn't

possible. It occurred to me that I could buy a little run-
around and maybe do some trackdays, or rent a car and
do a UK-based road trip to Scotland or the Isle of Man.
But these things didn't really excite me. I had also been
reading more and more about budget, or "banger", rallies
in the motoring press and took a snap decision to sign up
for one, thinking it to be a good experience for a budding
car enthusiast like me. I would be driving from the UK to
Prague over the course of ten days, following a given
route and taking part in various challenges along the
way. I would finally have the chance to drive the Stelvio
Pass and I would also get to experience more of the camaraderie and competition that I had enjoyed during the
classic car rally. The fact that photos from previous years
showed a propensity for participants to dress in ridicu-
lous outfits didn't put me off. Neither did my not having a
co-driver or a car that fit the criteria of being either under £250 in value or over 20 years old.

First of all I roped in my friend Tom Jelley. I knew
he might be up for doing something random and adventurous. There was no pressure on him as I had offered to
sort everything out, including our car, so all he had to do
was turn up. For my part, finding the right car wasn't
quite as easy as I thought it would be. I went back to my
habit of spending hours scanning through the classifieds
online, first at cars that were cheap enough to be eligible
and then at cars old enough to be eligible but not overly
expensive. There appeared to be very little that met the
criteria in and around London and I had no intention of
travelling around the country to find a car that I didn't
really care about. All I wanted was something that would
be fun and reliable for a jaunt around Europe. I knew

what some of the roads would be like after my adventures with Ned and Spencer and I was adamant that we would be travelling in something that would make the good driving roads enjoyable. Having considered the cheaper and, in retrospect, much more sensible Mazda MX-5, I somehow settled on a 1990 Porsche 944 S2 cabriolet.

Porsche made the 944 from 1982 to 1991, producing around 150,000 cars across the range available. Today its design and residual prices reflect its 80s heritage, with lack of exclusivity meaning that it has come to be seen as a good entry point to Porsche ownership. At various points in its production cycle it was available in coupe and cabriolet forms, and with either a turbocharged or normally aspirated engine.

I have a bit of a soft spot for Porsches and increasingly lusted after various incarnations of the iconic 911 but I had never considered buying a 944 until this point. I had always thought it an ugly car, far too 80s in style for my liking, but it seemed that other owners loved theirs and they were clearly a bit of a bargain. It would mean paying slightly more than I had originally intended for a car that would potentially be abused during the course of the planned rally, though I presumed I would be able to make much of the value back when I came to sell it. Hopefully I could manage to convince a Czech car dealer that he needed a right-hand drive early 90s Porsche on his forecourt when the time came, even if my initial enquiries had proved fruitless. It was either sell it there or drive it all the way back.

Being a Porsche it should be reliable if it had been looked after and therefore wouldn't test Jelley and my non-existent car maintenance skills. This would be important if we were to avoid getting stranded on the scenic route across western Europe. It had a 3 litre engine that should be punchy enough, even if it had lost some of its original 211bhp over the years. It even had near 50:50 weight distribution so would be perfectly balanced for enjoying the mountain roads and the Stelvio Pass. The more I thought about it, the more I came to like its looks as well, coming to see it as 'retro' rather than 'ugly'.

I would like to be able to tell you that laziness never came into the equation but I can't. I was far too heavily influenced by the fact that there was a car for sale down the road from my flat which appeared to meet my requirements. I went to look at the car and thought it to be quite handsome in maroon paint, with its long regal bonnet and wide stance. There was a bit of rust, which didn't surprise me too much at 20 years old, and the interior had been reupholstered in dubious taste and to a standard poor enough for the original tartan material to still be visible beneath. The owner took me around the block and it ran well. There were also plenty of receipts showing all the money that had been spent on it and I think I was more or less sold on the idea at that point. Even so, I found the nearest independent Porsche specialist and had them carry out an inspection. It was at this point that things started to go wrong.

The inspection report was delivered to me over the phone and it turned out there were a good few things that needed doing but apparently the car was in reasonable order overall. I used the work required as a foundation on which to haggle the price down slightly. Then I took the plunge, withdrawing the required money from my account and heading back to south London, praying that I wouldn't get mugged on the way. We did the exchange and I drove away, trying to get a feel for the car, working around the limits on its visibility in city driving. It felt as though its best days were far behind it but everything seemed to work, one or two switches aside. Once home I contacted the specialist again and asked about booking it in to get the work done but the owner of the garage had now lost the inspection report and couldn't remember what had been required.

"It's probably on my desk somewhere. Maybe under some other paperwork," he told me. "I don't suppose you remember what needed doing?" I didn't.

I should have found another specialist at this point but I didn't have a chance. The very next day it turned out the roof or door frames had leaked under heavy rain, the driver's seat was wet and water was dripping down the inside of the windows. It was now clear why the previous owner had kept it under a car cover. I was furious, both with myself for buying a car that leaked and at the previous owner for selling it to me in this condition. I even called up the local Trading Standards Service but there was nothing that I could do in the situation. If I could have given the car back to the guy I had bought it off at that moment I would have done so but I was stuck with it now. I had to attend to the leaking fairly urgently so I took it back to the specialist who had first inspected it and told them to sort it out before the interior sustained any permanent damage from the rain, also listing a couple of things I did know needed attention. I walked away to the tube station hoping that I wouldn't come to regret my focus on convenience, either in terms of the specialist or the car itself. As long as it would get me to Prague, then I could sell it.

I think I first came across the word 'dog' as a description for a car on an internet forum. The implication was that everyone bought a dog at some point or another. I inherently knew what the phrase meant even though it was quite hard to pin down. It wouldn't be sufficient to say that a dog, in car terms, is simply a crap car because you can have what might be perceived as a crap car that runs perfectly, is reliable, and doesn't cost a fortune to maintain. A dog is the polar opposite. It might once have been a good car, something quite desirable. However, now it could be unreliable and unsafe; it might cost a small fortune to keep on the road; it might be the kind of car that keeps revealing new faults that you weren't aware of when you bought it. In short, a dog is the kind of car that you would never have bought if you'd done your homework.

If buying a dog was something that most car enthusiasts do at some point, it was the one experience that I would happily have done without. It certainly didn't help that I had chosen the most incompetent Porsche specialists in the country. Within a week of the leaking roof incident (which they didn't actually ever attend to), the 944 had to go back in to have some more work done. This time the engine was not running properly and the steering wheel was vibrating violently at motorway speeds. I was sinking more and more money into a car that I didn't care about only to drive it across Europe and sell it and I was kicking myself for having rushed into such a poor purchase.

Significant maintenance issues aside, having the car sitting around in central London never really gave me the chance to enjoy it and see whether it was the perfectly balanced sports car that fellow owners seemed to think it was. In fact I found myself struggling to bond with it in a way that I never had with any other car. That was predominantly a result of the shock and disappointment of having to spend so much money on it just to ensure it was safe for the road, though the driving position never seemed quite right for me either. Perhaps it was designed around the long-legged, short-armed people that must have inhabited Stuttgart in the 80s and 90s as opposed to me, a short-legged, long-armed creature more suited to Italian cars. The engine seemed ok though. It needed a lot of revs to get moving but the controls were fairly well-weighted, even if the steering felt a little heavy in traffic. That feeling was partly exacerbated by having to guide the long bonnet around potholes and cyclists.

On the occasions I did get the car out of the city I was able to catch a glimpse of the 944's true character and there were a couple of drives during which the car suddenly made sense to me. Out on a winding country road in Berkshire, roof down, I worked my way up and down the beautifully smooth gearbox and enjoyed the ample torque from the ageing 3 litre engine. Throwing it into corners revealed its neutral balance and decent grip, the suspension not as stiff as today's sports cars and so soaking up road imperfections without removing all feedback. It seemed smooth and effortless and I remember thinking that it would be great for driving across continents and blasting down long open roads and across epic landscapes. These moments of enjoyment were fleeting but made me realise that I would probably have kept the car and gradually restored it if I had lived somewhere with a big enough garage to keep it in and had the money to afford a second potentially expensive car. An imperfect car can clearly get under your skin, as many owners of classic cars and restorative projects would attest to. I never reached that stage with this Porsche but I liked its road presence and had grown to respect the charm of its late 80s/early 90s brashness.

It wasn't enough though, and the perfectionist in me could never make my peace with a car that was far from perfect. The whole ownership experience had really frustrated me already. No one likes to feel as though they have been stupid enough to be cheated and the decision to buy the car hung over me as an unnecessary and expensive mistake in a year that was already spiralling out of control. I had become a slave to my two cars. I seemed to be orientating all my activities around getting the best of out these dubious investments in the hope of a few moments of exhilaration and adventure out on the open road. It occurred to me on more than one occasion to cancel the lease on my flat, flog the Porsche and run away somewhere peaceful where I could offer communication strategy support to local businesses. In practice there was no way I was going anywhere without Rita. In this case the only thing that I could do was to admit my mistakes, sell the car and withdraw from the banger rally. The 944 would never have the chance to show me how capable a cross-country companion it might have been but I didn't care anymore.

It felt in keeping with my general mood regarding the 944 that no one else seemed to want it. I attempted to sell it to Porsche specialists, through online classified adverts and even on eBay. I spent a bit more money on it to ensure it was as desirable as possible but I was having no luck. The car was in much better condition than when I bought it but it looked unlikely that I would be able to make back what I originally paid for it. The only other option was to try and trade it in for something else of a similar value, ideally something more modern, something safer and more practical that I could let Rita use for her daily commute. Many traders were reluctant, simply not knowing the market for modern classics such as the 944 and therefore not willing to take a chance on it. After lots of unsuccessful phone calls and unanswered emails I found a dealer willing to offer part-exchange for a Renaultsport Clio 182, almost identical to a car that I had owned and loved in the past. I know I should have tried to find something with a nice economical diesel engine, as opposed to the buzzy and thirsty 2 litre petrol engine in the Clio, but the emerging petrolhead in me managed to put fun at the top of the agenda even in this undesirable situation. Besides, I knew Rita would love driving something a little punchier, particularly as my enthusiasm for cars seemed to be rubbing off on her.

Driving away from the dealership in the Clio was a genuine relief for me as an end to one of the real low-points of my journey to becoming a petrolhead. It was good to have the whole episode closed, particularly as I have a bad habit for getting wound-up about things until there has been some kind of resolution. The rally would certainly have been good fun but the momentary decision to sign up had led me to throw away a significant amount of money and waste precious time. I felt no regrets about pulling out of it. It was time to move on.

Over the weeks that followed the 944 saga I took every opportunity to get behind the wheel, no matter what the car might be and where I might borrow it from. I wasn't fussy about brand, power or design and I didn't care if it was a big off-roader, a hatchback or a supercar. I simply enjoyed the experience of driving different cars, as I always had. The critic in me valued the opportunity of being able to better contrast and compare cars against each other. The petrolhead in me just wanted to drive.

I had a very brief encounter with Rita's mum's Citroen C1 in Berkshire and found it to be a good, honest little car and perfectly suitable for zipping around town. I drove an ageing Saab 93 convertible in the south of France and found it to handle like a boat, its shortcomings alleviated somewhat by its ability to expose passengers to the sunshine. I drove a Porsche Panamera S and a diesel Cayenne around central London and was very surprised to find that I thought the Cayenne a better and more responsive car, though I imagine the Panamera might have come into its own on a more spirited drive out of town. I drove a Bentley Arnage and discovered it to be one of the thirstiest cars I had ever driven as well as having huge road presence and luxuriously thick floor mats. I did a little off-roading in a Land Rover Defender during a fishing trip in Scotland and also began to understand the appeal of the Range Rover for the first time as I drove between Inverness and Aberdeen in miserable conditions feeling unstoppable.

Despite these experiences, I found myself increasingly looking forward to heading back to France so that I could be reunited with the Ferrari and begin the drive back, though that was as much through a yearning for some adventure as it was to do with missing the car. In the meantime, I hadn't given up on pursuing a couple of leads in the UK and was delighted when a long discussed visit to the Morgan factory was finally added to my diary. As well as a tour of the factory, Charles Morgan had kindly agreed to spend some time chatting with me about the company, its heritage and its future direction. As the company had just re-launched its iconic 3 Wheeler it would undoubtedly be a fascinating time to visit. With my car still in France and the train journey from London looking horribly complicated Spencer came to the rescue, offering me the use of his recently-purchased Ferrari 575M for the day.

Ever since we had returned from France, Spencer had found himself tormented by the idea of Ferrari ownership. He was a Ferrari fan long before me but, it seemed, he had managed to talk himself out of the idea of owning one until he experienced roads like the Flüela Pass at the wheel of my F355. After much deliberation as to which model to go for – he had originally fancied the four-seat 456 – and whether or not he could really talk himself into it, Spencer travelled down to the West Country to buy one.

It wasn't all plain sailing. Within the first week he sent me a photo of his new car being loaded onto the back of a truck. I had experienced a couple of teething problems of my own and it just goes to show that these cars really do need to be driven regularly to keep everything running sweetly. Thankfully it wasn't long before he was calling me up and raving about it. The speed was phenomenal, he said. The F1 paddle-shift gear change was a bit clunky and dated but the sports exhaust that the previous owner had fitted meant that it sounded incredible. I was looking forward to experiencing these things for myself even if I was a bit apprehensive about driving someone else's new Ferrari through London.

Ferraris might hold certain connotations these days and, it is true, their iconic status has meant that the brand attracts posers as well as enthusiasts. Ventures like the Ferrari World theme park in Dubai don't help the view that the company is happy to dumb down or sell out in the pursuit of profits. But it is a business after all and these developments are built on success and a simple truth: Ferrari has been making some of the world's best performing, best handling and most desirable sports cars for decades. It's a company that strives to be the best, whether in Formula 1 or on the road, and they work hard to make amends if they don't get it right first time. And so it was with the 575M, the successor to the 550 Maranello, a car which is rated as one of the ultimate GT cars of modern times.

Like its predecessor, the 575M is a front-engined, two-seater, rear-wheel drive car powered by a V12 engine, in this case 5.75 litres in size. It has 508bhp and is capable of hitting 60mph in a little over four seconds before going on to a top speed of around 200mph. These are big numbers but ideal for a car that is designed to catapult you across continents in style and comfort. The criticism levelled at the car was not to do with its straight-line performance but its handling. Critics found it too soft, not taut enough to really enjoy driving more challenging roads. In short, it wasn't the car that it should have been.

Ferrari's response was to release the Fiorano handling pack - named after the test circuit in Maranello - which included lower and stiffer springs and revised programming for the dampers and steering. By all accounts it transformed the car into a much more precise and sharper-handling machine. Spencer was well aware of this when he began looking for a car, ensuring that the one he chose had this desirable option fitted.

It was an overcast Tuesday morning as I approached Spencer's car for the first time, parked on a quiet residential street not far from my London flat and ready for a drive to the Malvern Hills. I personally think it is a very handsome car, its svelte shape somehow made more menacing by the long bonnet, the integrated air scoop hinting at the huge engine beneath and its appetite for cool air. The gleaming Argento Nurburgring paintwork is such a light colour of silver that it appears almost white from some angles and does a good job of showing you a distorted reflection of the car's surroundings when clean. Inside it feels very high-end and well made, with black leather everywhere and sculpted, intricately-stitched Daytona-style seats. As you settle you realise that not only is it comfortable but visibility is good, giving you a good idea of where that long bonnet stops. From what Spencer had told me, his car wasn't as bad for grazing its nose as the F355 so there would be less breath-holding moments over speed bumps.

Many 575Ms were specified with Ferrari's F1 paddle-shift gearbox which is seen to make it a more liveable car, though being a slightly dated single-clutch system means it feels a bit clunky today, even compared to a modern VW Golf with its dual-clutch system. I like it though. It feels in keeping with the drama of the car and undoubtedly makes urban progress that bit easier, particularly when you are getting to grips with the dimensions of the car for the first time. It is a remarkably easy car to drive and is much more calming and cosseting during city driving than the F355. It is also more subtle due to its colour. That said, the sports exhaust system adds a serious dollop of aural drama. It still has the smooth, hearty purring sound of the standard car but is overlaid with a sharper, gruffer edge. Any blip of revs causes a bark that would scare off the hound of the Baskervilles and upshifts are almost amusing for the loud "pop" that accompanies each one, making it sound more like a race car than a road car. I was fearful of causing heart attacks amongst elderly passers-by as I made my way through commuter traffic and out towards the motorway for my journey west, unsure if I would have traded the relative subtlety of this car in standard form for that snarling exhaust note. I probably would. There's something slightly addictive about a raw exhaust note when coupled with huge power, even if it's best experienced when unleashed from the limitations of the city.

That power really makes itself known on the motorway. I had never before driven a car that builds speed so easily and relentlessly. It is the kind of car that would boss the autobahn but on UK roads it has you at license-losing speeds before you even have a chance to glance at the speedometer. It's one of those cars that makes you feel a bit naughty; you constantly find yourself slowing right down and pulling the left-hand paddle that sits behind the steering wheel so that you can drop a couple of gears, before planting your foot just to feel the surge of acceleration once more. Frustratingly, my route didn't take in any country roads so I was unable to learn about the 575M's dynamics when you're pushing on and able to string a few corners together.

"It's a bit of a handful," Spencer explained when we discussed it later. "I almost lost it down a country lane when the tail snapped out without warning. It's not nearly as progressive or communicative as the F355 and, of course, it weighs much more."

I wasn't too disappointed about not having a chance to push the car harder. I was driving a V12-engined Ferrari to visit the Morgan factory and these were the kind of days that I dreamed of as I sat in Aberdeen writing communications policies.

Generation Game

Three-wheeled fun with Charles Morgan

I f you spotted UK rapper Dizzee Rascal grinning whilst pootling along in a Morgan 3 Wheeler at the 2011 Goodwood Festival of Speed and chatting with company owner Charles Morgan, you would be forgiven for assuming that the company was desperate for publicity, just another manufacturer trying to utilise popular culture to reach a new audience. In fact, the excitement that surrounded the 3 Wheeler had started long before Goodwood and would continue long after, with or without the approval of Mr Rascal. The plan was to build between 200 and 250 of the Morgan 3 Wheelers per year but over 500 eager customers had already placed deposits by the time of my visit. That was a good couple of months before production would even begin.

On arrival I was ushered into a large reception room with various pictures, cars and a looped film introducing visitors to the marque. To my surprise it was Charles Morgan himself who came to greet me and walked me around to the building in which his office was located. He began by showing me a presentation and then we talked for a while over sandwiches and coffee about the Morgan Motor Company and his enthusiasm for cars and driving. The tour would come later.

Charles Morgan obviously loves his job. It's an impression that begins from the moment that he strode confidently into the visitor centre to shake my hand and continued throughout the three hours he took out of his day to talk to me. You can quickly understand why the cars produced at Morgan's Malvern factory continue to exude a timeless British style under Charles' guidance. He has an aura of confidence that is reflected in the cars his company makes. He is well spoken, well dressed and very much the English gentleman. He smiles a lot and laughs a lot. You would imagine him to be good fun at a dinner party and it is no surprise to hear that he has regularly attended the annual dinner of the Japanese Morgan owners' club in the past, promoting the extended family ethos that runs through the company.

Of course there is no reason why he shouldn't be enjoying himself. He is doing the job that he was quite literally born to do, following in the footsteps of his ancestors and guiding the company his grandfather started over one hundred years ago through one of the most successful periods in its long history. One factor of this success is that Morgan has remained a family company. It is something that extends way beyond the company's ownership to include the workforce, owners and fans of the marque. There is a camaraderie, Charles feels, that connects owners of Morgan cars as well as those simply passionate about them. It is something which every Morgan employee you meet seems very proud of.

International sales have played a big part in Morgan's continuing success; the draw of the styling, excellent build quality and the performance that a Morgan car offers not uniquely recognised by UK customers. In fact Charles is very clear that many international customers – whether they are from France or China – would only consider buying a sports car of the kind Morgan produces from a British company. These customers believe that "made in Britain" is something that indicates quality. "Not enough is made of this," Charles tells me.

I suggested to Charles that his company seems to tread a fine line between the influence of the past and the possibilities and legislative requirements of the future, perhaps more so than any other manufacturer. After all, you only have to look at the design of a car like the Morgan 4/4 to know that it is influenced by the past. His response was simple: "Nothing from the past is inherently valuable but you can be inspired by it."

Customers clearly agree, the 4/4 being an evolution of the company's first four-wheeled car launched 70 years ago and demand still strong today. "A lot of people would like something old but they want something that works," Charles asserts.

Charles and his team seem to have got the balance between supply and demand just right. They have never flooded the market in an effort to clock up ever higher sales figures in the way other manufacturers have and this means that their cars hold their value remarkably well. The lightweight design and efficient engines go a step further to mark Morgans out as the thinking man's sports car.

Underneath the classic looks of the cars that roll out of the Malvern factory today, this ethos of lightweight performance is clear, something that comes from many years of motorsport involvement and something that most other manufacturers are only just catching up with today in an effort to comply with emissions requirements or in the constant hunt for higher speeds. Charles shows me a piece of metal from a Gulf Stream jet plane and explains that Morgan was the first car company to utilise superformed aluminium in the construction of its cars, adopting the technology in 1996 at a time when it was more commonly used on planes. It was this kind of innovation that would eventually allow Morgan cars to stand shoulder-to-shoulder with the established supercar elite and this would be proved on track.

Charles himself had a passion for racing from an early age. During his time as a news cameraman for ITN he would use his time off to get back on the race track, even winning the Production Sports Car Championship in 1978 and 1979, in a Morgan of course. When he eventually returned to the family business he set about making Morgans more competitive once again in the face of the domination of Porsche, Ferrari and Audi. The Aero 8 was produced as a more modern successor to the Plus Eight but it failed to win its class at Le Mans on two occasions, although Charles proudly tells me that a team from the Malvern workshop did manage to win a prize for being the best pit crew. Eventually they got it right though.

In 2009, the company's centenary year, the more hardcore Aero Supersports won the opening race of the FIA GT3 European Championship at Silverstone, beating all its obvious rivals in the process. "It showed that the technology we adopted in order to achieve this was probably as good as it gets," Charles said of the win.

Today Morgan is one of the last of the British-owned and British-run car manufacturers. It remains quintessentially British in terms of its style and its commitment to quality and innovation. The brand is respected across the globe and that will surely continue as long as the cars are produced to feel different, bespoke and individual, while managing to immerse owners in the joy of driving. Bigger companies have failed at that task.

What next then? Well, it's fair to assume that Xan Morgan, Charles' son, will one day take over management of the company but that's not on the cards for the foreseeable future. Instead Morgan needs to keep innovating, moving with the times and attracting new customers. "Morgan is interested in the future," Charles explains. "We're much more adventurous than most car manufacturers because we can afford to be."

One part of the strategy is to develop an electric-powered concept based on the Aero as well as a brand new model, the Eva GT – a lightweight, four seat coupe due for launch in 2013. The other part, of course, is the latest 3 Wheeler. It is what Charles refers to as a "motor tricycle". It is powered by a 2 litre V-twin engine of the kind usually found in a motorbike and its light weight (only 500kg), means that it is capable of 0-60mph in only 4.5 seconds. Charles suggests that it's "a typically Morgan approach to keeping the performance but in a much more efficient, economical way."

As for Charles, he went on to tell me that he is as passionate as ever about cars and about the company he shares his name with. He doesn't race anymore, despite still holding an international racing license, partly because he finds the latest cars too physically demanding to drive, but he does still love driving on road and track. Luckily for him the winding roads of the Malvern Hills are on his doorstep and he has access to the perfect cars to enjoy them in.

Walking around the various buildings and warehouses that make up the factory complex nestled under the Malvern Hills, I was struck by how calm it all feels, somehow relaxed yet undoubtedly productive at the same time. I was a little surprised to learn that as many as 20,000 people visit the factory each year, some of them there to decide upon the exact specifications of their own car or to watch it being built – one of the perks of buying from a welcoming low-volume manufacturer. Charles smiles as he tells me that some Japanese owners take away samples of sawdust from the workshop as souvenirs, a vial of "Morgan dust" to display in their homes.

Once Charles has caught up on a couple of work-related activities and left me to wander around the factory taking photos, he suggests that we go for a spin in one of the 3 Wheelers. Naturally I jump at the opportunity and we're soon buzzing up towards the hills, the clouds overhead looking ominous. At the top of the hill Charles pulls over and asks whether I'd like to have a go, my day seemingly getting better and better.

It is not just long-time Morgan fans and existing owners that are excited at the prospect of this new vehicle and that's partly because the 3 Wheeler is undeniably cool – especially with the Second World War bomber-style decals on the side. It will appeal to anyone with an urge to experience a pure, unfiltered driving experience at a time when many manufacturers seem to be separating the driver from the action with more and more technology. There is no way of standing next to one without desperately wanting to drive it. Even clothing label Superdry has got in on the action, designing a limited edition model that will be sold with an equally limited edition "classically styled" leather jacket.

The very process of clambering into the 3 Wheeler is an experience of its own. You step over the doorless sill and use the roll bar to lean on as you slide your body down into the seat. It's cosy in there, particularly if you have a passenger with you, but that's something you come to appreciate once you get moving. The dark green car with black leather that I'm driving is as discreet as they come. Many customers will want to take advantage of the graphics options that are available, such as the RAF-inspired livery.

To start the car you turn the key and then lift a small safety catch – inspired by a Eurofighter's bomb release Charles tells me – to expose the starter button which wakes the car up with a blast of noise. It quickly settles into an unsteady idle. The footwell is tight but the controls familiar. The five-speed gearbox is the same one as you'd find in a Mazda MX-5 and has a very positive, slick movement from the off.

Pull away and you'll find that the 3 Wheeler behaves like any other car, the difference being that there is a blaring engine hanging out in front of you delivering the sort of soundtrack you would expect to hear at a meeting of Hell's Angels. The clutch and throttle peddles are easily modulated meaning that you can move off without looking like a learner. You peer over a tiny wind-deflecting screen and can watch the two thin front wheels reacting to the movement of the Momo steering wheel. Goggles or some fairly sturdy glasses are a must, particularly when you get some speed going.

It's certainly quick. A claimed 0-60mph time of 4.5 seconds is impressive but it's the exposure to the environment around you that really adds to the sensation of speed. You quickly become aware of the purity of the driving experience. There is honesty to the controls, everything seeming unfiltered. You really notice this with the unassisted brakes which mean there's a need for thinking ahead and getting your foot down much sooner than you would at first think necessary. Once you know this, it's very easy to drive.

Heading along the Malvern Hills that overlook the Morgan factory I soon found myself in a rhythm, working up and down the gears and pushing ever harder in the corners to explore the limits of grip. The visibility means that you can pick your line through corners with great accuracy. It's the kind of car that you would enjoy driving over and over again as you learn the intricacies of its handling. You can feel what's going on beneath you and although you'll know about it if you go over a pothole, the ride is not excessively hard.

If you're the shy and retiring type then this is not the car for you. As we descended the hill, back down towards the factory, it became clear just how much attention the 3 Wheeler gets. I don't think that's a bad thing and I'm guessing the team that developed the car don't either. It's a very desirable machine and one which has the ability to appeal well beyond Morgan's traditional client base. I would love to drive one around central London on a Saturday afternoon and see how people react. I think they would love it. There really are few cars that can touch it for the fun and drama it delivers and if I had the money and some garage space it would be top of my wish list.

I walked back to the car park through the Morgan museum, taking a moment to inspect the original 3-Wheeler. Its gleaming maroon paint and gold trim were the only real hint that it might be from another era, so close is the design to the new model. It is a testament to Charles Morgan's passion for cars and driving that he has chosen to re-launch such a pure driving machine when most performance cars are getting bigger and heavier. He is a true petrolhead and that bodes well for fans of the marque.

Outside, in the car park, the silver Ferrari 575M looked conspicuously modern and stylised compared with the cars I had spent the afternoon looking at. As much as I loved the 3-Wheeler, this was the perfect proposition for the monotonous motorway journey back to London. I couldn't help but smile as the car barked into life once more and I pulled away, a huge "pop" from the sports exhaust announcing my departure as I shifted up from first to second and made my way out of Malvern.

Everyone is a Car Enthusiast

Collectors and tweeps

When I met up with Spencer to return his car after the Morgan visit he had a suggestion for me, something he had apparently forgotten to mention when he handed over the keys to the Ferrari the previous evening. He had spent a weekend in Paris with his girlfriend and had been hugely impressed by an exhibition of Ralph Lauren's cars. He urged me to check it out before it came to a close a few weeks later. Having not been to Paris since I was five-years old it seemed the perfect excuse for a romantic weekend away with Rita during which we could enjoy some good food and take a look at some classic cars. As Spencer even had a suggestion for a boutique hotel he had spotted near Musée d'Orsay everything was booked up by the time I went to bed that night.

As an art historian with a good understanding of architecture, Rita turned out to be an impressive tour guide. We had arrived early on the Saturday morning and once we had checked in to the hotel she took me on a walking tour all over the city, pointing out all the sites and referring to a book when necessary to give me the relevant history. It was August and that meant that there were probably more tourists in Paris than Parisians, seemingly unbalancing the city. It felt as though there was a distinct split between the busy hotspots that formed around the cultural landmarks and the deserted back streets that had been abandoned by the residents for the peak holiday period. The quiet streets were always a welcome sight, providing brief moments of respite from the heat and the crowds as we pressed on to the next point of interest, or *crêperie* if I was peckish. There was nowhere to hide as we approached the Eiffel Tower though, opportunistic vendors swarming *en masse*, pitching to passers-by in an effort to sell cheap-looking souvenirs. Between the huge metal legs of the tower were vast queues of people waiting for tickets to allow them onto the huge structure standing over us. We walked straight past, Rita leading me on to another part of the city rather than joining the queue. Instead I booked us a table at the Jules Verne restaurant for lunch the following day on the advice of Rita's friend. The restaurant's location on the second floor of the Eiffel Tower would mean that we would have the benefit of jumping the queues and get to enjoy the panoramic views from the comfort of our table.

I hadn't appreciated that Ralph Lauren was such a keen collector of cars before Spencer had mentioned the exhibition but I was left in no doubt as soon as Les Arts Decoratif opened its doors on the Sunday morning. The exhibition began with one of the world's most highly regarded and beautiful classic cars - the 1938 Bugatti 57 S(C) Atlantique. It sat near the entrance, separated from all the other cars as if to highlight its importance. We took our time studying the lines, Rita's artistic eye meaning she was as keen to assess the details as I was.

As we wandered around we learned that Ralph had built a significant collection of cars over the years, dating from the 1920s to the present day. This exhibition brought together 17 so-called "masterpieces" from his collection. All of the cars present had a notable influence on the automotive world through their aesthetics and their performance and I was pleased to read that Ralph is genuinely passionate about his cars. He loves the way that they drive, feel, sound, and even smell. Of course he is a designer and the way that a car looks is something that he could never ignore but when you begin to understand the types of cars that he owns you realise that he is more than a collector - he is an enthusiast. The cars that were representing his collection are each highly regarded, many of them being significant racing cars or road-orientated derivatives of racing cars.

From the Bugatti we climbed a small staircase to view the rest of the collection and emerged at the top to see all but five of the remaining cars visible in front of us. These were the racing cars, beginning with the 1929 Bentley "Blower" and ending with the gorgeous 1964 Ferrari 250 LM. In a side room, the four grand touring cars were sat on slowly turning plinths, including the iconic 1955 Mercedes-Benz 300SL "Gullwing" (or "Papillon" as the French call it). Finally, in another side room sat the 1996 McLaren F1 LM, the only modern supercar to have been included in this exhibition and a true icon.

A nice touch were the other side rooms, two of which cycled through the noises made by each of the cars – from start-up, on the move inside the cabin, drive-bys, and finally stopping – alongside images of the respective cars which were projected onto the back wall. The other room featured old film footage of the various cars, including racing footage and even early launch event footage where available.

Having read some of the interview with Ralph Lauren from the book that accompanies the exhibition, I was interested to learn that his first car was a Morgan. He apparently had to sell it so that he could afford to get an apartment with his wife and bought another one once he could afford to do so. His first Morgan had helped him to gain a reputation as "the tie salesman in the Morgan", a small thing but important in helping to build his reputation as a purveyor of stylish clothing in those early days.

My passion for cars has always stemmed from my passion for driving – the way that a car feels and sounds on the road. I love the sense of freedom you can get on the right road in the right car and I think that such experiences have affected my perceptions as to how attractive a car might be, my views on design, engineering and value being intrinsically linked to my desire to drive a given car. This has changed a bit over the years as I have learnt about the significance of many cars - in terms of influence, rarity or racing success - something that has encouraged me to start looking at cars based on their aesthetics as automotive objects and with regard to their historical significance. Owning a Ferrari for the first time had made me more interested in those cars that went before it and I loved spotting a design cue that had been carried through over the decades. Now, for the first time, I was going out of my way to check out private collections. After all, many serious collectors are some of the greatest enthusiasts you could ever hope to meet, often having a deep understanding of what makes their cars special.

The Monaco Top Cars collection I had stumbled across a little earlier in the year was a completely different experience to other private collections I had seen. If the Ralph Lauren exhibition had been widely marketed and commented upon in the motoring press, then HSH Prince Rainier III's collection was relatively unknown. I found it by complete chance. It was hidden away next to the Fontvielle shopping centre like some long-forgotten secret and it appeared that I had the place to myself aside from one middle-aged couple. Though described as a "private collection of antique cars" it is a bit more diverse than that, the most recent car dating back only a few years.

You walk in to be confronted by the striking image of a Mercedes SLR McLaren Stirling Moss edition, its impossibly long silver body gleaming under the lighting above. It has a top speed of 217mph delivered by its supercharged V8 engine, though its lack of windscreen means you would want to consider wearing a helmet if you were attempting that. As the name implies, the car was inspired by Sir Stirling Moss's victories in both Formula 1 and the Mille Miglia in Mercedes-Benz cars. In particular it pays homage to the 300 SLR in which Moss achieved a record breaking win in the 1955 Mille Miglia, during which he recorded an incredible average speed of 97.9mph over the course of the 1,000 mile race on public roads between Brescia and Rome. It is one of 75 cars produced and something that you would be lucky to see on the road. Thankfully here, with a backdrop of vintage cars, you have an opportunity to admire the details that help this car stand out as one of the most eye-catching of recent years.

Once you've had your fill of the SLR there are still plenty more cars to see. The vintage cars section makes up a large part of the collection and seemingly includes everything this side of a horse-drawn carriage but it was the more modern metal that interested me. You move from the Venturi Fetish to a Lotus Seven and then on to a wonderful selection of Ferraris and Lamborghinis. Opposite, rally-spec Lancias and Renaults in full racing livery sit next to the wonderful diesel-powered Audi R10 TDI that won its class at Le Mans in 2006. It is a wonderfully diverse collection and well worth the entry price.

Privileged collectors aside, I knew from the outset that I wasn't alone in my interest in cars. The world is full of car enthusiasts and there are many different types out there, all helping to create subcultures around specific motoring interests. You only have to walk into your local newsagent to get a feel for the breadth and diversity of car culture today. Do so and you will see magazines dedicated to buying and selling cars, those for fans of specific marques and others focused on classic cars. There are magazines about high performance cars, some about modifying and tuning cars, as well as more general publications that seem to cover all bases. If moving images are more your thing, the chances are that you can watch a rerun of Top Gear at most times of the day should you so desire. It's astonishing to think that this programme reportedly has a global audience of 350 million people, even if it is looked at with derision by some petrolheads for being nothing more than a generic entertainment product.

Over the decades, the car as an object, as the ultimate lifestyle accessory, has become woven into the very fabric of society. As Wolfgang Sach wrote in the early 90s, "The automobile is much more than a mere means of transportation; rather, it is wholly imbued with feelings and desires that raise it to the level of cultural symbol". When you start looking you can quickly see how pervasive car enthusiasm is in our culture. Each of these different interpretations of motoring subcultures, delivered through various media, is built around the actual habits and existing interests of enthusiasts. The people that engage with this content are the same people that visit the Morgan or Ferrari factories, the same people that build kit cars or spend their weekends driving on track. They are the same people that join owners' clubs, attend motorsport events or fit custom suspension set ups to their cars. They are also the people, like me, that will be drawn in and inspired to one day do many of these things even if some are not quite there yet.

As with almost all areas of modern life, the internet has taken all this to another level. Blogs, forums, YouTube and Twitter; these are some of the tools that allow car enthusiasts to better engage with each other and to share their views, opinions, photos and videos. The great thing is that it is all happening in real time and it becomes quite addictive once you engage with these communities. I found Twitter particularly gripping. I would read with interest as people shared pictures of the cars that they were driving, links to articles they had written, or brief thoughts on an event they had attended. Sometimes I would see long back-and-forth discussions taking place between journalists whose words I was used to seeing in print. On occasion the same people would simply hint at what car they would be driving and reviewing that week so that their followers could guess. Other people would openly plan to meet up at the next big track event or discuss used car propositions from adverts found online. Following petrolheads on Twitter means that you are also quickly exposed to a variety of digital magazines, websites and blogs, many of which are created by amateurs as opposed to professional journalists and might otherwise remain hidden from view. There is some exceptional content out there but you won't find it in your local newsagents.

Like any community, online or offline, you have to be proactive to get anything out of it. I had been blogging about my experiences in Europe and since my return I had been using Twitter to share my stories and pictures with an ever-developing network of petrolheads. It wasn't long after I had started to engage with some of these unknown car enthusiasts that I found myself on my way to my first Autotweetup at a cocktail bar in London's Covent Garden. I had been to a couple of tweet-ups in Scotland before, both organised by my friend Mark, who is someone I like to think of as a digital guru of sorts. These were more general social and networking events organised on Twitter, often between people who had never met before but were part of an invisible network or interest group. I had found them to be interesting, both personally and in my role as a communications strategist. I had also met some great people and the idea of such an event for motoring enthusiasts and professionals seemed ideal to me. I missed the first event, the poor weather and promise of bad traffic putting me off the drive out to Kent but there would be no such excuses for the second event.

I had no idea what to expect and so it came as a bit of a relief to get there in good time and have a chance to chat with organiser Tim Hutton. As editor of motoring website *Racing and Waiting* and a keen user of social media, Tim was indicative of the type of people I would meet that night. We stood up on the small mezzanine level that sat at the back of the Dirty Martini bar, a couple of his colleagues setting up computers and projectors so that we could all see who was tweeting about the event in real time. He told me that he had taken the initiative of bringing together disparate Twitter users that have a shared love of cars and motoring and that the crowd would be made up of journalists, bloggers and PR professionals. We were all deemed to be influencers of some sort.

After I had accepted a voucher for a free cocktail and a slip of paper providing me with the wi-fi code so that I could tweet during the event, I started striking up conversations with anyone that I could find. I can be a little reserved in these scenarios but I needn't have worried. Almost everyone I met was in a similar boat in that many of us followed each other on Twitter but we had never met face-to-face. I met a girl that managed the PR for a tyre manufacturer, a couple of young guys that were trying to break into journalism through blogging, as well as people that were already writing professionally for various motoring websites. There were people from trade bodies and others that offered consultancy services to those needing guidance on buying and looking after supercars. They were all petrolheads of one sort or another and they had all chosen slightly different ways to bring their love of cars into their working lives, some presumably making sacrifices to do so.

It was quite inspiring to hear about some of their experiences and I was flattered that people seemed genuinely interested in my adventures. When you've got a few stories to tell and a Ferrari in your garage it certainly makes conversation a little easier with people who have long embraced their own passion for motoring. Six months earlier and I would have felt completely out of my depth. Now I was in my element.

High Rolling in Northamptonshire

The British Grand Prix and

Silverstone Experience

Over the course of the year I received a lot of emails, text messages and phone calls from friends and family members wanting to tell me about motoring articles they had read or reminding me that *Top Gear* was on television. I also found that people I knew were suddenly interested in my thoughts on certain cars. Had I driven the Porsche Cayman? How did I rate the latest BMW 3 series? It was quite flattering really, being seen as an expert of sorts. I also received some generous invitations to events. Some I wasn't able to attend but Spencer's offer of joining him at the British Grand Prix at Silverstone was too good to pass up. Northamptonshire might not have the glamour of Monaco but Spencer had secured Paddock Club tickets through a charity auction and that meant we would be watching the race in comfort and luxury. The truth was that I would have gone along no matter where we would be seated as it was high time I attended a motorsport event on British soil. I did look at some other motorsport events earlier in the year but I never managed to get myself organised in time, the more hands-on experiences taking priority.

Like most of the race circuits the UK today, Silverstone is built on the site of a Second World War airfield. It was first leased by the Royal Automobile Club in 1948 for racing purposes and has seen more than six decades of top level racing since. The lease was taken over by the British Racing Drivers' Club in 1951 and it was at this point that the circuit started being tweaked to make it more suitable and safer for high speed racing, something that would continue as cars got faster over the years. It was in the 1960s that Silverstone really came of age for Formula 1 fans. It was the decade that saw the circuit hosting racing legends such as Graham Hill, Jim Clark, Jack Brabham and Jackie Stewart. Since then the circuit has seen a lot of drama, a lot of development to the track and facilities, and some superb racing. Turbocharged cars have come and gone, drivers have crashed and rivalries have been fought out. Though there have been periods during which the British Grand Prix was hosted elsewhere, it is Silverstone that has become synonymous with Formula 1 in Britain.

Spencer and I had decided to get the train to Milton Keynes and had arranged a taxi to pick us up and take us to the circuit, rightly assuming that the champagne would be flowing and driving back wouldn't be an option. The closest the driver claimed he could get us to the circuit meant a 30 minute walk across camp sites and hotel grounds, despite us having the appropriate paperwork and badges to get us much nearer our stand. I hadn't quite expected there to be so many people camping but it seemed like a very popular option, it obviously being one way to miss the worst of the traffic. I thought about what it might be like in the evenings as we traipsed quickly through, past tents and parked cars. Maybe they have boozy parties and barbeques that help create a mini festival or Le Mans-style atmosphere. Already the support for McLaren was appearing dominant over the likes of

Ferrari and Red Bull, with many people wearing branded polo shirts and hats, presumably excited at the prospect of supporting two British drivers on home turf.

We passed through as quickly as possible, not really knowing how much further we had to walk. Hitting the edge of the circuit we were very grateful that a young, friendly minibus driver we had flagged down was happy to help us. It meant going a different route from the one he had planned but none of the other staff we encountered knew the site well enough to direct us. Our driver informed us that this is because security staff are hired in for the weekend and aren't briefed properly. It was a pretty poor first impression and a far cry from the well-trained staff at other sporting events around the UK, such as Wimbledon or at Premier League football matches.

We trundled around the hugely impressive complex with our driver, only pausing to let a couple of other passengers out. The Porsche Experience Centre is clearly visible on the way in and you can watch people pilot 911s through water jets and around a dedicated circuit as they attempt to develop their handling skills and learn the limits of these rear-engined cars in a safe environment.

The race circuit itself seems to provide spectators with numerous vantage points. There are some long, well-sighted sections that allow you to watch the cars flying along straights and plenty of turns that give you a chance to hear the drivers dropping down through the gears before powering through the corners. As we arrived it was the Porsche Supercup cars that were in full flow and the speeds these modified road cars carry through corners was truly astounding, as was the sound which was clearly audible even from within the minibus.

Once through the turnstiles, hefty yellow tickets draped around our necks and earplugs ready to be inserted, we made our way along the walkway which hovers above the pit lane. This was obviously the centre point for hospitality and we found ourselves peering into the Red Bull suite, the Pirelli suite, and then Virgin, Ferrari and McLaren's as we pressed on to the Paddock Club at the end. This turned out to be the largest of all the hospitality suites. I couldn't help but wonder what it would be like to be a guest of one of the participating F1 teams. Presumably there would be a good party if one of their drivers won the race.

We were seated up on the mezzanine level and were soon sitting down with a glass of champagne, enjoying the cool air conditioning after the rush through the camping ground. We had plenty of time to get a feel for our surroundings before the race was due to start and I was pleased to see the various buffet areas offering different cuisine, everything from dim sum to cheese and desserts. In fact the hospitality in the Paddock Club was some of the best I have experienced anywhere, the staff excellent, and high quality food and drinks available all day. The windows and large balcony of the building overlooked the starting grid and the pit lane, while the grass bank and dedicated grandstand overlooked the exit from the pit lane and the first two corners. The numerous TV screens in the Paddock Club ensured that we would know what was going on with the race standings, giving context to what we would see when the cars blasted past us.

Before the race we also had an opportunity to walk around the pit lane and peek into the garages of the different teams. We didn't really get to see anything in great detail as it was only sponsors and their guests that were allowed behind the barriers and it was generally very busy around them. Even so, it was a new experience for me and certainly still interesting to have a bit of a look behind the scenes. If you made the effort to head up towards the less successful teams then there were better opportunities to peek inside the garages. Most people were focusing their attention on Ferrari, McLaren and Red Bull. We were ushered out just before the drivers came down and soon found ourselves back at the window in the Paddock Club watching the beginning of the race.

The race itself was enjoyable to watch and I felt a bit more in the loop than I had at Monaco as a result of all the TVs and different vantage points. It gave us a chance to enjoy being close to the action and to follow the 'story' of the race as it unfolded. In Monaco there were moments at which the race felt like an inconvenient break amongst the hardcore socialising, whereas at Silverstone the racing took centre stage.

There are always at least one or two dramas or points of contention in a race, no matter how boring or predictable people like to say modern racing can be. On this occasion, we were standing overlooking the exit of the pit lane – which emerged beneath a grass bank in between the Paddock Club and the grandstand – as Jenson Button was forced to stop because one of his new wheels hadn't been screwed on properly, our fellow spectators pushing up to the fence to take photos of the incident. Back inside we found ourselves watching the battle between Massa and Hamilton unfold as they came onto the final straight, us switching back and forth between the big screen and the view out of the window to try to get the best view of what was happening, falling into conversation with a very lively motorsport fan from the next table after this battle had concluded. As we sat down it suddenly became apparent that BBC Sport was about to film the follow-up discussion to their Formula 1 programme from the sofa right next to our table. This meant that we had a front row seat to hear Eddie Jordan, David Coulthard, Murray Walker, Damon Hill and Christian Horner discuss and analyse the race, all of them Formula 1 legends of one sort or another.

It was an unexpected end to a great day out but it was the cars that made the biggest impression on me. Whatever it is that is happening on the track, it's always a pleasure to witness F1 cars screaming around a race circuit. You simply can't appreciate how absurdly fast and loud they are by watching them on television. I think anyone that has a passing interest in cars must go to at least one Formula 1 race to experience this circus of speed and sound. For us, it was back to reality all too soon and we once again crossed the campsite and found our way back to the waiting taxi and then a crowded train to central London. The train gave me a chance to consider the other motorsport I events that I would have liked to attend, of which there were many. World Rally Championship, British Touring Car Championship, Mille Miglia, Le Mans... Each would presumably have its own unique atmosphere and its own group of committed petrolhead fans. I hoped to find out for myself sooner rather than later.

It wasn't long until I returned to Silverstone again, though this time I could drive right in to the car park myself rather than having to walk for half an hour through a field. I had been desperately looking for something interesting to get my father for his birthday and had settled on buying him a Nissan GT-R driving experience knowing that he has a long-held love of Japanese performance cars. In fact, he had often said that a GT-R would be his next car and this would give him an opportunity to discover how good they really are.

I was never quite sure where my interest in cars had come from. There was no specific moment in my memory, no day in my childhood when I first saw a Lamborghini and fell in love with cars or met a racing driver and began following motorsport. However, I'm fairly sure that my father is to blame in the first instance.

One of my earliest memories is nothing more than an image in my mind, like a photo etched into my memory. It was a rare occasion, at the age of two or three, when I was awake at the time Dad came home from work. I stood at the open front door with Mum and watched as this svelte, exotic-looking machine purred along the driveway towards us, cutting through the cold night. The pop-up headlights looked like blinking eyes as he flashed them at us. It was an early 80s Mazda RX7 in a frog green colour. I remember very little about it today but I do remember hating it. I couldn't see over the dashboard and always felt nauseous after going out in it. Dad used to reverse out of the driveway and then fire it along the windy roads that cut up the countryside around our house. It felt like being on a roller-coaster whilst blindfolded and I would always ask that we go out in Mum's Volvo instead.

Even when he had a company car, Dad would choose discerningly. He seemed to know much more about cars than I appreciated at the time. I never saw car magazines around and it was pre-internet so he obviously kept his ear close to the ground when it came to knowing what car to buy. I soon found myself accepting that a car needn't look sporty to be something a little special, something that would reward the passionate driver and maybe embarrass more flashy vehicles.

As far as I was concerned Dad's car choices were always cool or interesting in their way, certainly as I approached my teenage years. There was the Nissan 300ZX with the removable roof panels and twin-turbo engine that whisked us across France one holiday while my sister baked in the tiny rear seats, and the Lexus-badged Toyota Aristo import that claimed much higher performance figures than the UK equivalent due to its turbocharged engine and four-wheel steering. There are also some great photos of him from the 70s posing next to his Panther Lima, much as there are photos of me leaning on my old Porsche Boxster at around the same age as he must have been.

If Dad's interest in cars had kick-started my own, it seemed appropriate that I buy him a motoring gift for his birthday. I had enjoyed my track experience at Spa-Francorchamps and the GT-R experience at Silverstone looked far more comprehensive by comparison. I knew he would love driving on track for the first time but we were both a bit underwhelmed as we walked into the busy visitor centre, the price of the experience I had bought leading me to expect something a bit smarter, a bit more corporate perhaps. I had decided against the more expensive Porsche Experience Centre which was located on the other side of the circuit and hoped that I would not regret my decision. Dad went to sign-in, leaving me to mill around checking emails on my phone before we sat down for a coffee and waited for the relevant announcement. Groups of children were playing on a simulator while the adults sat waiting to be called for their safety briefings but the amount of people there was actually very deceptive. Many were simply accompanying those that would be taking part. Those that were going to be driving had signed-up for a variety of different experiences and it turned out that Dad was one of only three in the GT-R group. He kindly offered to pay for me to join in as well but I declined. The truth was that I would have loved to join in but my principles got in the way. This was his present and it wouldn't have felt right having him pay for me to take part in return.

The programme started with some acclimatisation in the Nissan 370Z, an evolution of the 300ZX that Dad had owned many years earlier and a much tamer car than the GT-R in which to learn the circuit. With 326bhp and a 0-60mph time of less than 5 seconds, the 370Z is not slow but it apparently felt like that on the near-deserted circuit. I had gone up to the roof of the building that we had been taken to, nestled within the circuit and offering great views of the passing cars. Each driver would have four laps in the 370Z with an instructor and I was able to watch as Dad built up speed, the instructor no doubt pushing him on and telling him to brake later and harder. When he got out he told me that is exactly what happened. Now he was ready for the GT-R.

Styled with an identical white and red paint scheme, and covered with the same Nissan and Playstation decals as the 370Z, the GT-R still managed to look like a much more serious proposition. With nearly 500bhp, a 0-60mph time of around 3.5 seconds, four-wheel drive and lots of electronic gadgetry this is a car with the performance to embarrass many of the world's so-called supercars. Dad loved it. It's exactly the type of car he has been interested in for as long as I've known him.

I ran back up to the roof as soon as Dad had put his helmet back on and settled into the driver's seat. From here I could watch and listen as he pulled onto the track for five flying laps, during which it was clear he was pushing more each lap, going faster and faster and braking harder and harder. He got out with a big smile on his face, simply astounded at the pace of the car and its ability to brake so hard from high speeds. He was going to get an even better feel for that a moment later as he was immediately ushered into the passenger seat of another GT-R to experience what the car was capable of in the hands of a professional. I knew roughly what he could expect from this after my own experiences around Spa-Francorchamps and we compared notes afterwards as we headed home.

The problem with these kinds of experiences is that you tend to come away with a greater appetite for things rather than walking away satisfied and able to move on. In my case it was a desire to do some more track driving and in Dad's case to buy a Nissan GT-R. Dad didn't have any immediate plans to get the Nissan but I would find myself driving on track sooner than I anticipated.

A Worthy Competitor

A date at the Lotus Academy

I have never really been particularly interested in competitions. It might be because the only thing that I ever won was a VHS of a song from the Teenage Mutant Ninja Turtles movie (or it might have been from the sequel). But the opportunity to win a Lotus Evora S for a year was too tempting to ignore and so I found myself entering the Lotus Diaries competition that was being run in collaboration with *evo* magazine. Having filled in some details about my credentials and subsequently been accepted to enter the competition, I had a chance to take a brief test drive in the car. The idea was to take some photos and video and to write a 200 word review which would be judged later. I had planned to put together a comprehensive video review but the Lotus salesman wasn't willing to spend his working day entertaining my directorial ambitions when I wasn't likely to be buying the car. That meant that I could simply enjoy the experience and get a feel for the car.

When Lotus put out the Evora it won many plaudits and was immediately hailed as one of the world's best handling cars. But critics always felt that it could handle more power. Lotus responded by adding a supercharger to the 3.5 litre V6 engine, giving us the 345bhp Evora S.

It will always be a matter of taste but I think that the Evora S is a good looking car. It helps that you don't see many of them on the road, making sure it is still something 'interesting' or 'unusual'. Of course it does look like a grown up Lotus Elise in many ways but that is no bad thing. However, the interior doesn't quite feel special enough for a car in this segment. It is certainly a pleasant and comfortable place to be but you might expect more flair considering the price and the competition.

The Evora S is a much purer sports car than the Porsches that critics often compare them to, even if Lotus has done a good job of making the car perfectly liveable and capable of being taken on longer trips, to mainland Europe for example. It certainly feels every bit the inertia-free sports car when you put your foot down, catapulting you towards the horizon with disdain. It's a very quick car, capable of dispatching a sub-5 seconds 0-60mph time, and it feels torquey right through the rev range. All the controls are slick and everything feels well made, though I can understand why some journalists criticised the gearshift. It is not good enough for a car of this pedigree and certainly not as good as the manual gearboxes that Porsche produces. It is far too notchy.

The ride is superb, as one would expect from a Lotus. The car seems to communicate exactly what's going on beneath you without letting road imperfections crash into the cabin or jar you offline in the way that many cars do on British roads. This means that you can make the most of the sharp and precise steering, cutting the desired driving line through any given corner.

It is quite calm and not too noisy in the cabin, though frustratingly it means that you can only really hear the supercharger whine from the engine as opposed to the exhaust but this might be a blessing for longer motorway journeys. The sports seats are certainly comfortable and feel as though they would be as good for long journeys as well as track work. You would certainly want to take this car on track to test its performance properly and to find its limits. It's a car that urges you to press harder whenever the road opens up in front of you.

I enjoyed driving it and would have happily carried on for hours as I learned its intricacies and pushed it harder, particularly in the corners. As a vehicle to enjoy British A and B roads, one that's capable of jaunts to the south of France or the Nürburgring, there can't be many better sports cars out there, particularly if you want something a bit individual.

I submitted my review of the car – holding back on a couple of concerns as to whether the Evora S might be overpriced – and also uploaded photos and a short video review. I tried to avoid checking back to the website that had been set up for the competition having initially seen people posting critical comments and giving me minimal star ratings, balanced only by feedback from friends and family. To my surprise I received a call sometime after the closing date of the competition inviting me to attend a Lotus Champion event at the company's premises in Hethel, Norfolk. I had been chosen as one of 20 to go through to the next round and was delighted to accept. I was told that the day would include drives in both the Elise and the Evora S, tours of the facilities, and a passenger lap. We would be interviewed and would be assessed on our driving ability so that they could shortlist five people for a final interview before choosing the winner.

I already knew that Lotus offered these kinds of experiences to paying customers as part of their Lotus

Academy programme. It was something I had already considered doing as a chance to learn more about one of Britain's best-loved car manufacturers and to experience the legendary Elise on the recently redeveloped test track. The opportunity I was being offered as part of the Lotus Champion event seemed like a 'best of' from the Lotus Academy programme. Even if I didn't win an Evora S for a year I was now really pleased to have taken part in the competition and it was just a matter of making the most of the day.

Having stayed in Norfolk the night before the event I only had a 45 minute drive to Hethel to make the 10am start time. I later discovered that one guy had driven all the way down from Ayrshire that morning and would be making his way north again afterwards! Thankfully I was well-rested if a little nervous. As much as I knew it would be about having fun I also knew that I would be under the spotlight somewhat and also had no idea what my fellow competitors would be like. As it turned out it was a really good group of people. I can't say that I spoke with everyone as we were split into four sub-groups, but those I did speak to turned out to be friendly car enthusiasts that were as excited as I was about the day ahead.

The car park on the way in was an interesting sight. Unsurprisingly, considering the group was made up of *evo* readers, the focus seemed to be on drivers' cars. I spotted a couple of Lotus Elises, a Ferrari 360 Modena and a Nissan 350Z. However, my eye was immediately drawn to the numerous Evoras that were scattered around in different specification. As I parked up in the F355, the car that had been whizzing noisily around the track rolled by. It was a GT4 specification Evora which looked suitably aggressive with its extended bodywork and large rear spoiler.

After coffees, fruit juice, pastries and a welcome from the Lotus team and *evo*'s Feature Writer, Roger Green, we were taken off to start various bits of the programme. My group began with a tour of the factory. It included chassis assembly, body bonding, painting, and a wander around the room in which leather is cut and stitched. We were shown the different production lines and saw both Elises and Evoras in various stages of production. There were also a number of Tesla Roadsters lined up and going through quality checks - the electric car being manufactured by Lotus on the Elise/Exige platform for the Californian company, the powertrain coming from elsewhere. We were shown the limited edition Evora S GP Edition, which is designed to reflect the black and gold paint scheme of the Lotus Renault Formula 1 team racing livery, and a limited edition of the Exige painted simply in matte black. After a short Q&A session we were ushered back into the hospitality suite for more coffee and awaited the return of the other groups from their various activities, then it was on with safety helmets and off for our first driving experience in the Lotus Elise.

The 3.6km circuit can be split into two parts to enable dual activity sessions to be carried out. We were told that it had recently been FIA-homologated, meaning that Hethel would be allowed to host FIA GT Championship races and could be used for testing Formula 1 cars. My group would begin on the north circuit which had been set up with cones to form a staggered gate slalom course along the main straight. The rest of the circuit would be used to teach us the best racing line and appropriate braking discipline for track driving. Finally, there would be a brief introduction to lift-off oversteer on the dampened steering pad. Meanwhile another group would be driving the Evora S around the south circuit and we would swap over in due course.

I had been wanting to drive an Elise for years as it is the archetypal modern, lightweight sports car but now I would really be thrown in at the deep end. Clambering into a roofed Elise for the first time with a helmet on was not the easiest thing. I'm sure that there is some kind of bum-in-first technique but I seemed to pull-off the awkward-first-timer technique with much more success. I didn't have much time to assess the cabin but it was certainly basic and designed to focus the driver on the task in hand. The seats were not heavily padded but were still comfortable and it seemed pretty easy to find a good driving position, even if a helmet always leaves you feeling a bit blinkered if you're not used to it.

Some fifteen or twenty minutes later, I got out of the car feeling a little disappointed with my performance. That first session in the Elise wasn't great. I think that I'm a pretty decent driver on the road but I simply had no idea of how different the discipline of track driving is. The first challenge was to try and take on board the numerous directions being shouted over the buzzy little engine of the Elise by my instructor.

"Turn here." "Use all of the track." "Brake!" "On the gas." "Off the clutch."

It went on lap after lap to the point where I wasn't driving even as well as I would have been without any instruction at all. Not to say the things I was being told were wrong. Quite the contrary. I had no idea how late and hard you should brake on track for example, my mindset being one of smoothness and progression for road driving. Understanding where the apex of a corner really is and the timing between braking, turning, downshifts and acceleration left me reeling slightly. Over time, with the track to myself, I would have probably worked out these things for myself but this was intense. My instructor also insisted that I keep my hands in the quarter-to-three position as much as possible, meaning that my arms would cross over on tight turns but allowing me to accurately straighten the car without relinquishing control. It worked. It was particularly useful when I accidently provoked the car into oversteer on one of the corners, managing to keep on the power and to snap us back into line before we spun. I think it was the one moment that impressed my instructor on that first run. Overall I felt embarrassed with my performance and found myself apologising for how poorly I had driven. That said, I also walked away with respect and understanding for the simplicity and ability of the little Elise. It really is a serious drivers' car. The fact that it is efficient and relatively cheap to run means it is a perfect sports car for today.

Next up was the Evora S, this time on the south circuit and with much the same track set up. There was a slalom and a continued focus on improving speed and consistency through braking, choice of racing line and utilising the car's power. That power is much more substantial in the Evora S and, in many ways, it is a very different driving experience. It is slightly softer and certainly more cosseting in the cabin but the precision and feedback is still there. If anything, I found myself enjoying this more than the Elise, the experience not being quite as much of an assault on the senses and therefore allowing me to focus on doing as I was told and trying to build a rhythm.

We all convened for lunch in one of the mobile hospitality centres that are normally used at motorsport events, people comparing notes with each other and ducking outside to see and hear the GT4 car testing again. My group was then taken off to tour the motorsport factory to get a feel for the numerous racing and bespoke customer options that Lotus can provide. This included a look at the Evora S with GT4 modifications that British actor Tamer Hassan drove in the 2011 Gumball 3000.

It was the Classic Team Lotus tour that seemed to make the biggest impact on everyone. These are the workshops that look after classic Lotus racing cars, many now privately owned and raced in heritage events around the world. The mechanics know the cars and their histories inside out, some having worked directly with F1 legends such as Senna, Mansell and Clark. The detail, evolution and stories associated with these wonderful and much loved cars gave real insight into Lotus' past glories and the personalities involved. I think everyone in my group approved of the fact they are still being raced by their enthusiast owners today, no matter how rare and valuable they might be. After all, that is what they were made for.

Things came to a head in the middle of the afternoon as my group returned to the track for the second time. Despite his attempts to find another car, my instructor and I found ourselves clambering into an Elise Club Racer - an even more stripped-out version of the already focused and functional sports car. The issue for us would be less noise insulation and it soon became clear that the instructions would have to be shouted even louder and at least twice. Even so, this run was much better for me and I was really pleased to see that some of the details from the late morning run had sunk in, allowing me to drive with better speed and consistency. I would have liked more time to tie all the different components together but even the instructor was complimentary about my progress. It would have been great to drive well from the outset but I was happy to settle for notable improvement.

Then it was into the Evora S again, though this time it was strapped up with video equipment on both the inside and outside of the car. We hadn't been allowed to take our own cameras in but the organisers were making a solid effort to compile material for their websites. There would only be time for a few laps and these would be assessed as the culmination of the day's tuition. It went by in a blur but I recall immediately being more aggressive than I had before, though the subsequent passenger lap with my instructor on the full circuit showed just how far I had to go to really make the most of car and track.

It was a superb day out. If my brief experiences at the Nürburgring and Spa-Francorchamps had given me a taste for track driving, then the sessions with professional drivers here had really shown me that there is significant scope for development in my driving, something that could never really be achieved safely on the road. I might not have impressed enough to be given an Evora S for a year but I came away with some great memories and a burning desire to buy a Lotus.

Racing the Orient Express

Coffee with Russ Malkin

Sometimes you meet someone who is exactly the kind of person you expected and sometimes that can be a very good thing. That was certainly the case with Russ Malkin. I had imagined him to be friendly, open, dynamic and interesting, and he was. Russ was the man who I hoped would shed some light on the supercars versus Orient Express race which Lord Mexborough had mentioned to me earlier in the year.

Russ' hectic schedule and constant adventuring and documentary-making meant that it was a good few months before we were able to meet and by the time our planned meeting came around I was really excited to meet him. The more I had read about him the more it became clear that he was the kind of person that made his own rules. If there was something that he wanted to do then he would find a way of doing it. That was how he managed to forge a career around his passions. For me, as someone actively trying to follow a passion and having met so many people at the Autotweetup that were trying to marry their love for cars with their careers, I found reading about Russ' approach to life and work very inspiring. In one of the articles I read, Russ had made a comment about humans not being put on Earth to be miserable. Instead he felt that we should strive to make a living from whatever it is that we love. I quiz him on this once we've hung scarves and coats on the back of chairs and sat down with our coffees in a noisy cafe by Clapham Junction station.

"People think it's all about problems but it's not is it? It's supposed to be about enjoying yourself. We're not supposed to be miserable, finding issues with everything and worrying about what people think about us. The object is just to be happy. Not that I'm the guru of this by the way. "

He might not be a guru but he leads an exciting life that is based around this ethos and his passion for adventure. Adventure is inextricably linked to movement and it came as no surprise to learn that Russ grew up with a more localised passion for motoring before he was crossing continents. It is the motorbikes that he remembers first. His father was always working on bikes, pulling them apart and then putting them back together again, and soon Russ was getting his hands dirty as well. He vividly remembers the Kawasaki KH250 and Honda CB250 that they rebuilt together, as well as his first bike which he bought at the age of 14. It needed a lot of work, he tells me, and the gears would always seem to slip, but this was the beginning of an ongoing passion, something that was all about fun and the simple pleasures and freedoms Russ began to associate with whizzing around on a bike.

It wasn't just bikes though. Visits to Brands Hatch with his brother and parents from the age of five or six years-old had a big impact on Russ. He looks back fondly to events like the Race of Champions where he got to see legendary racing drivers such as Denny Hulme, Jody Scheckter and Joachim Rindt. He also vividly remembers seeing his favourite Formula 1 car of all time on one of these visits - the Yardley BRM - and watching Dave Brody racing his mk1 Ford Escort and Gerry Marshall in his Vauxhall Firenza.

As he got older, Russ began racing motorbikes but decided to abandon any hopes of making a career of it in a moment of clarity back at Brands Hatch.

"I was going along the long straight, whizzing along with my fingers on the clutch," he tells me. "It gives you time to think that straight, which isn't good. I began thinking, 'What am I doing? What if the bike seizes up and I fall off at these speeds?'. Somebody had died the day before and I realised that I could kill myself doing this and I'm not even that good at it. So I changed to karting and four wheels. But on my first race, in my brand new kart, I found myself hanging upside down in my kart and it suddenly didn't seem much safer than the bikes!"

Even so, Russ found karting to be really exciting and very competitive. He was quickly recognised as being a very competent driver. In the early 90s – by then no stranger to organising high profile events – Russ used his experience and connections to set three karting world records. The first of these was an indoor endurance re-cord which Russ took on alongside his brother and friends David Coulthard and David Brabham. They were some of the first people to be sponsored by Red Bull, who sup-ported the team by donating £5,000 and a pallet of the then recently-launched energy drink - something which would come in handy during their challenge. The four drivers took it in turns to complete a constant lap of a Clapham bus depot, flat out at around 40mph for 24 hours. After a few hours of going around in circles Russ' neck muscles gave in and he was forced to continue driving with his head to one side and a bad case of double vision. He knew that the right-hand image was the more accurate so he focused his efforts on aiming for that apex. There was also a small bump in the circuit which, over a prolonged period of time at high speed, caused painful ligament damage down one side of each of the drivers' torsos. David Coulthard apparently still berates Russ for talking him into this horribly painful record breaking challenge a day before he was due to go for a seat fitting for his racing car.

"We were in tears," says Russ, with a rueful smile. "I couldn't get out of bed properly for three months afterwards but we set the indoor karting world record and were in the Guinness Book of Records."

As a result of this success Russ set about setting the outdoor karting world record, this time at Brooklands with Neighbours star Stefan Dennis replacing David Coulthard. Finally, Russ was approached by a German company who invited him to set the electric karting record in their new electric kart and Santa Pod was chosen as the venue. The drivers took it in turns again, with quick changeovers designed to ensure almost continual progress and to work around fatigue. At around 4am Russ was due to take his turn again and approached the kart bleary eyed only to discover that it was being put away by the technical team. It turned out that they had gone through three clutches which gave the driver the ability to modulate the power to the wheels and, having run out of spares, the technical team was ready to throw in the towel. After some explanations and a few probing questions from Russ, it was decided to connect the battery directly to the engine which would mean full power would be delivered to the wheels instantly, a big red button acting as an on/off switch.

"I sat in the kart and hit the button and there was instant power to the back wheels and the kart was all over the place," Russ explains. "Because it was raining it was slipping but eventually it bit and I took it straight up the drag strip at about 55mph, turned the power off, coasted around the bend, hit it again and back on the power and down the straight."

This technique meant they could complete the record attempt and it is a record that I'm told still stands today. "So if anyone wants to break it, there's a challenge for you," Russ tells me.

So what about the Orient Express race? Russ had been approached with the idea of an event in which one car would race the Orient Express to Venice. But record-breaking Russ felt that there was scope to take the concept to the next level to make this event the biggest and most glamorous it could be. In this case it meant trying to race ten or twelve supercars against the train and inviting celebrities to take part. It was sponsored by Orient Express and was such a success that it ran in both 1990 and 1991 before Russ pulled the plug. The second event even saw some high profile people coming forward to request a place in the starting line up having heard how good it was the previous year. In most cases the amateur and celebrity participants were paired with experienced racing drivers, the cars either being owned by the participant or sourced by Russ, all cars that he loved and wanted to have involved. Lord Mexborough drove his

Porsche 959 with Derek Bell. Simon Le Bon drove a Lamborghini Countach with Paul Stewart, Jackie's son. There were Maseratis, Ferraris, and even James Coburn in a Honda NSX.

The race began at Victoria, the train starting from a different platform than usual as to accommodate the cars, drivers and interested media. The cars were lined up her-ringbone fashion, the drivers all dressed in racing over-alls waiting for the flag to drop. As the train started mov-ing off, the drivers ran to their cars Le Mans style, started up and set off. Unlike Le Mans, as soon as they were moving they had to contend with London traffic un-til they passed the city and could make a good run for the coast and really start mounting a challenge against the train. Of course, as soon as the road opened up all the drivers upped the pace considerably and the Americans began undertaking slower traffic on the motorway.

Barely an hour into the 1991 event the group had been pulled over by the police. From Russ' perspective this was a nightmare start. The last thing he wanted was to lose some of the cars and drivers before they'd even made it over the Channel. Many of the drivers had got out of their cars, those who hadn't been pulled over ini-tially now joining the group to see what was happening. The policeman started to ascertain what was going on and was ready to start writing some speeding tickets when James Coburn unfolded himself from the NSX, a huge cigar sticking out of his mouth. An imposing man, he approached the policeman passing by his co-drivers and puffing out a huge cloud of smoke, by this stage an unmissable presence even amongst the other stars in the group. The policeman recognised him instantly.

"Officer," began James in his gravely American tone, "is there anything that you can do to help smooth our way through this situation?"

The policeman, a little gobsmacked, scanned the row of eager and hopeful faces and then looked back at James Coburn. It turned out that he was a big fan of The Magnificent Seven, in which James had starred, and he ended up letting them off in exchange for an autograph and a promise to stay within the speed limit whilst they were on British soil, which is exactly what they did.

There was a chosen route through France, Switzerland and Italy. This meant that the race could be filmed along the way and that any cars that broke down or ran out of fuel could be helped out by a sweeper truck that followed at the back of the pack. Even so, with a bunch of excited drivers in the world's most desirable supercars it was no surprise that some of them went *off piste*. One such example was Damon Hill who was driving a De Tomaso Pantera. It turned out to be a particularly fuel-thirsty vehicle and Damon found himself in a dark, mysterious forest somewhere in Switzerland in the hope of finding a petrol station that was open in the middle of the night. Detached from the rest of the group and completely off course, it was at this moment that one of the conrods failed, breaking through the crankcase and showering the tiny rear window with oil. Not only were Damon and his co-driver out of the race but they were now stranded in the middle of nowhere, dressed in racing suits.

These races were emotional at times. Everyone really wanted to make it to Venice first, to beat the train, but a number of cars broke down on the way. Thankfully there were no accidents and no one was hurt. Even so, those that didn't complete the race were missing from the black tie event that was held at the Cipriani and were missed like fallen comrades.

The races were a huge success and increasingly high profile, the 1991 event even being covered by Robin Leach on *Lifestyles of the Rich and Famous*. But Russ was worried about it getting out of hand. Some of the drivers were pushing very hard to win the race and that meant reaching very high speeds on public roads. The last thing Russ wanted was for his event to become dangerous or disrespectful to the communities which the drivers would be passing through. He had hoped that it would be more of a classic racing challenge, something more civilised and less about outright speed. In essence, he didn't want this challenge to turn into something like today's Gumball 3000. Even so, he enjoyed it while it lasted, telling me that they were "heady days".

The following year Russ organised a very different event. The Riviera Challenge was focused on the past, present and future of motoring. It was a three-day event, this time less about high speed driving on public roads, with on-track challenges part of the programme instead. There were three teams, each with an old car, a current car and a car of the future. It included things like a 1932 Le Mans winning Jaguar, a Venturi Atlantique and the three-wheeled Grinall Scorpian and again culminated with a black tie event, this time in Monaco.

"At that time I wanted to do big audacious events," Russ tells me when I try to understand how he made the shift from enthusiast to event organiser to documentary film maker. "After the Orient Express race I organised the world's largest aerobic event, so it was literally whatever came into my head and inspired me. On that occasion we had 17,000 people working out and I've still got that world record. In the case of the Orient Express race, I love cars, I love the idea of speed and I love trains, so it was about putting those things together."

Russ had organised for a film crew to get involved on the Orient Express race in the hope of producing a documentary or, at the least, having strong material to distribute to news channels. He was let down at the last minute and though he managed to sort out something else at short notice he was unimpressed with the quality of the work. This was a big turning point for Russ. He realised then that he could only guarantee work would be up to the standard he expected if he was to take ownership of all aspects of his events. Today that means the TV production, DVD production, sponsorship work and book production is all managed by Russ' team.

It is the documentary work that Russ is perhaps best known for today and he is probably assumed by many *just* to be a filmmaker rather than an event organiser, adventurer and businessman. In practice it is difficult to pigeonhole him with the application of job titles because Russ is simply doing what he loves and that means crossing boundaries, both geographic and in terms of the diverse roles he undertakes. All of this stems from a passion to see more of the world and to engage with it, not just during holidays but as often as possible. One of the first TV shows that he had commissioned allowed him to visit every motorcycle manufacturer in the world. In short, television allows Russ to live his dreams and also gives others a chance to learn more about the world through the adventures he organises and captures on film.

Russ and I chatted for a while longer, pausing only for him to take a call from Charley Boorman, presumably about the film editing work for their most recent adventure or perhaps planning their next trip. I was genuinely inspired to learn what Russ had accomplished simply by being true to his passions. In some ways it felt like vindication for my own journey and the risks I had taken with my career. I was a good communications strategist but would cars one day come to be a central feature of my life as they had for many of the other enthusiasts I had met? Russ had managed to construct his career around his many interests and doing the same was undoubtedly appealing. What would I do with cars though? Perhaps organise events or make documentaries like Russ? I really had no idea. It was something I would have to think about properly once I had completed the European road trip.

Club Med

A Bentley, a car park and a party

The prospect of driving up through France and back to the UK wasn't nearly as appealing as the journey that took me there. For one thing, going home is never as exciting as heading off into the unknown. It somehow feels devoid of opportunity, like some kind of dull descent into normality.

Looking at the map and the potential routes available was an uninspiring process. The journey that had taken me to Vence had been so focused and so filled with excitement whereas the return leg would be little more than a delivery exercise to get my car back to London. I had contacted a number of French race circuits but none had responded to my requests for information and my eagerness to set up some track experiences on the way home. I had attempted to line-up a visit to the Bugatti factory but had received an unequivocal "non" in response. There were no motorsport events taking place that would tie-in with my dates and some of the potential sections of road that might tempt were simply not going to fit into the three or four day itinerary very easily.

It was going to be very different from what I had experienced with Ned and Spencer but I would make the most of the situation. For my part I was happy to simply fall into the character of driving tourist, taking in a few towns that I had never visited before and enjoying the simple pleasure of travelling from one place to another. The concept of the driving holiday is certainly not a new one and, in many ways, hails back to the grand touring that became popular with the upper classes from the 17th century, a sort of cultural and social rite of passage for young wealthy men at the time. Of course things have moved on and rather than milling around with bewigged men in horse-drawn carriages I would follow in the footsteps of the thousands of British holiday makers that travel through France by road each year.

The plan was to head across to Grasse and then over the Route Napoleon – the N85 – to Grenoble. The next day would take us up to Dijon, ever a popular stopping place for those driving to the Cote d'Azur from the UK. The final stop-over would be in Reims – a cathedral town in Champagne country – and then back to the UK. The journey would be easily do-able in one or two days but that wouldn't be any fun. Besides, I'd convinced my friend Jelley to take a week off from work to join me and it would only be fair to make an adventure out of it. I felt that I had let him down by pulling out of the banger rally to Prague which we had agreed to take on together. I hoped that three or four days at the wheel of a Ferrari might appeal as a good alternative. It did. Jelley is a pretty laid-back guy and he was happy for a bit of adventure and perhaps a little partying, no matter what the circumstances. Thankfully the fun was to start immediately. We had been invited to a friend's birthday party in St Tropez and were expected for dinner in Juan les Pins the very evening Jelley arrived. To make things more interesting I had been offered a chance to take out the Bentley Continental GTC again as the owners hadn't been able to give it a decent run for a while. Dealing with the traffic of the coastal roads wouldn't be nearly as fun as my drive on the Col de Vence earlier in the year but I was happy to oblige, even if that meant limiting myself to one beer when everyone else was intent on starting a weekend of serious partying.

The Bentley Continental GT, in both coupe and convertible forms, is a car that people have very mixed feelings about. Its two tonne weight is simply too excessive for those who seek a pure driving experience above all else and its design and badge will always be too conservative for some. Even so, it's a very impressive machine on paper and ticks an awful lot of boxes should you be looking for a near-200mph, two door, four seat, luxury car. The convertible at my disposal for the evening was the ideal prospect for cruising around the Riviera, looking particularly tasteful in silver paint with contrasting navy roof and navy leather interior. The interior is sumptuous and everything feels well made, solid. Once you've fiddled with the buttons that can adjust your seat in every way imaginable you turn the key, watch the lights flash up on the dashboard, place your foot on the brake and then press the start/stop button. The noise from the twin-turbo W12 engine (essentially two V6s bolted together), is quite unique. The sound of the starter motor is sharp and metallic leading you to expect a huge explosion of sound from the exhaust pipes when it catches. Instead the noise is very restrained; a low, smooth and bassy rumble that fits perfectly with the image of the car as a luxury continent-crusher rather than out-and-out racer. It's a feeling that continues as you pull off, the automatic gearbox shifting gears imperceptibly as you waft along and attempt to get a feel for the dimensions of the car.

It doesn't take too long before you're at ease; it's that kind of car. You might find yourself tensing up when passing traffic on smaller roads but at really slow speeds the parking sensors at all four corners let you know how much trouble you're in. When the feeling takes you there is an abundance of power, the flexing of your right ankle resulting in a jet engine-like whooshing sound that is compounded by the hardening of the exhaust note and a feeling of being pushed back into your seat. Drive through a tunnel or past high walls with the roof down and the sound is amplified further, immediately reminding you how potent the Continental GT is even if the laws of physics aren't on its side. It is something that becomes a little bit addictive once you've experienced it. To really make the most of the sporting credentials of the car you need to put it in sport mode at the very least or, ideally, take control of the gearshifts yourself using the large paddles that sit behind the steering wheel. Start throwing the car into the corners and you might be surprised by how hard it can take them, the four wheel drive system and huge tyres helping to ensure that there is plenty of grip available.

Once you've driven one it becomes clear why these cars are so popular. There aren't many cars that can seat four people in such considerable comfort and make such devastating progress, all the while hinting at whatever connotations of personal taste or financial success Bentley ownership might imply.

The drive down to Juan les Pins, which sits on the coast next to Cap d'Antibes, was uneventful. We got stuck in traffic on the Promenade des Anglais coming out of Nice and then managed to escape to the motorway. Here it was surprisingly quiet and we were able to press on quickly, even if the sights didn't quite match those of the coastal road. We wormed our way onwards through Antibes, the sat nav once again proving a useful tool, before pulling up at a lovely modern villa that sat right at the water's edge. Hugs, kisses, handshakes and my one and only beer of the evening all attended to and it was off to dinner.

Once Spencer and our friend James had clambered into the back of the Bentley – both in town for the party the following day – we set off in pursuit of the others, our hostess having shot off a moment earlier in a packed Renault Espace. Jelley and I took the opportunity to quiz the boys as to who was who in the group, us having forgotten names already. A few minutes later we slowed down in front of the entrance to an underground car park, to my considerable dismay.

"No, no, no, no, no," is all I could manage, though in retrospect there might have been some swearing involved as well. The boys stopped their chattering to look at me.

"What's the problem?" asked Jelley calmly.

"It's these bloody French underground car parks. They're an absolute nightmare."

"You'll be alright mate. Just take it slowly."

I edged forwards to sounds of approval from the back seat, before creeping over the lip of the ramp that plunged downwards and spiralled into the bowels of the town. Immediately the parking sensors fired up, all of them beeping one after the other. It's a pretty standard system; the more regular the beeping, the closer you are to the wall. If you're about to make contact it will make a flat-line noise that implies you would be better off dead than manoeuvring a

Bentley in a French car park. Everyone leant out of their respective corners and shouted instructions at me, helping progress but not my heart rate. We reached the first floor but it was for residents only. Shit. Next floor down and we were blocked by a barrier that implied it was for permit holders only. Balls. Third floor down appeared to be more welcoming, though the sweat dripping into my eyes was not. By that point I had developed an audience. Everyone that I had met only half an hour earlier was standing watching as the prat in the ostentatious car attempted to park it before they could go and enjoy their dinner. I managed it, got out, took a deep breath and tried to compose myself before joining the others.

A few hours later – after a violent storm had forced everyone inside from the tables on the beach and a flash flood had invaded the restaurant via the stairs that led from street level – it was time to get the Bentley out of the garage again. Needless to say it wasn't something that I was looking forward to but with my crew watching each corner of the car we made it out unscathed and I was able to return the car in the same condition in which I received it. One thing's for sure, the prospect of Bentley ownership in the south of France was no longer so appealing to me. The Continental GT is a formidable companion on the open road but it is much less well-suited to the small towns and smaller car parks that line the Riviera. That's probably why you see so many battered Renault Twingos and Clios around instead.

The next day was to be one of the highlights of the summer but, I warn you now, it had absolutely nothing to do with cars.

After the getting-to-know-each other dinner the previous night, Jelley and I didn't have much time the following morning before it was time to head back to the coast for the birthday party proper. We got a lift down to meet the others on Cap d'Antibes and were immediately transferred over into one of two minibuses that had been organised to carry us down to Pampalone beach beyond St Tropez. It was the last Saturday of the summer holidays and the sun was already shining intensely despite it being quite early in the morning. If you have ever travelled to St Tropez by road you will realise that this didn't bode well, the small town attracting much more traffic than it can handle and causing tailbacks for miles. Some of the group were optimistic but the veterans amongst us knew that we were looking at a three-hour journey, at the least.

I say veteran but the truth was that I had only visited St Tropez a handful of times before and had never been to the season closing party at Voile Rouge. It was one of the many beach clubs that lines Pampalone beach and the one that had come to be recognised as the place where the party really kicks off. We were expecting loud music, champagne spraying and general mayhem amongst the great and the glamorous. Only weeks before an unbelievably crass song had suddenly appeared on the music channels called *Welcome to St Tropez*. If its video – filled with bikini-clad women, supercars and politically incorrect lyrics – was anything to go by, we were in for a seriously good time.

My last visit to the beach here had taken place a few years earlier when Spencer, Ross and I had come for a slightly more reserved lunch at Club 55 ("cinquante-cinq"), the original St Tropez beach club. Cinquante-cinq came into being when Brigitte Bardot and her director-husband Roger Vadim came to this near deserted stretch of beach outside St Tropez to film *And God Created Woman*. It was 1955 and a local family supported the production by serving the crew food and drink from their beachfront property, something that has continued ever since as more and more people have flooded to this now iconic spot on the French Riviera.

It must have been idyllic back then. Visit now during peak season and you will see how commercialised it has become. People come from all over to visit, the open spaces between the numerous beach clubs being taken up by bronzed families sprawling over colourful beach towels. Emerging from the car parks and gridlocked roads that come to an end behind the beach, you are greeted by a bay filled with luxury yachts, tenders delivering their wealthy owners to their favourite beach clubs, tables most likely booked well in advance or last minute with sufficient palm-greasing. Walk along the shoreline and you will find yourself dodging bat-and-ball players and evading crumbling sandcastles as children try to rescue their fragile constructions from the ravages of the tide. Every now and again a helicopter will touch down behind the beach, off-loading the serious high-rollers.

As I sipped on my first beer of the day and looked around, feeling the swelling beat of the sound-systems somewhere nearby, I had no doubt that this was the place to be and to be seen.

Having been huddled around the bar getting a feel for things our sizeable group was shown to a table that could just about fit us all around. Over the next hour or so numerous jeroboams of rosé wine came and went. Platters of food were delivered and grazed on lightly by most. The sensible ones amongst us tucked in heartily so as to hold on to the fading remnants of sobriety for a few moments longer. Conversations began to flow more freely, well-known businessmen and celebrities were pointed out, and the music got louder and louder. We spotted crates of champagne being unloaded onto nearby tables and the next thing I knew a very jovial Swiss guy was spraying champagne in my face. Then everything really went wild.

It would be impossible to describe the exact moments of transition from seated dining to dancing on tables, swigging wine and being showered by champagne. It was a bit surreal and we quickly lost all sense of time. I have a blurred memory of Jelley being told off for taking champagne bottles from one of our neighbours for spraying purposes and also of hearing *Welcome to St Tropez* being played repeatedly at high volume. Then the party seemed to come to an abrupt end, and it wasn't even dark yet. There is often a tidal feeling about beach clubs like this; the way that people seep in slowly and then disappear again leaving you to question if it was ever as busy as you thought. It is the same at Voile Rouge.

The rest of the night remains a blur. We ended up on a huge yacht, drank more, socialised, sang and danced. The amount of fun that we had that day must only have been countered by the experiences of our driver on the way back to Antibes, where we all ended up staying for the night. He had to deal with chauffeuring a bunch of very drunk guys who were intent on listening to 'gangsta rap' at high volume despite struggling to maintain consciousness.

He was probably hoping that we would pay for it with killer hangovers. All I will say is that building two days recovery time into our itinerary for returning to the UK was a stroke of genius on my part.

In Napoleon's Footsteps

Vence-Route Napoleon-Grenoble

I had resigned myself to the fact that the journey back up through France wasn't going to be as exciting as the journey that had taken me there. Even so, I had missed the Ferrari during my time back in the UK and I couldn't wait to get onto a decent driving road once more. It had become addictive during the trip through Belgium, Germany, Switzerland and Italy. Every morning I was excited at the prospect of firing up the V8 engine and setting off into the unknown. By the time Spencer and I reached Vence in the south of France I was still raring to go. I would have happily set off the next day, maybe headed towards northern Spain instead of flying back to London. Months had passed since then but I was ready to pick up where I left off.

As I hadn't managed to organise any motoring activities or experiences, the focus would be on delivering my car safely back to London and enjoying the journey. That would mean exploring a few unfamiliar towns, eating some good French food and drinking the odd glass of wine during the overnight stops. Of course, we would make the most of any decent driving roads along the way and I knew there would be some good opportunities to experience the F355 at full throttle once more. Jelley isn't much of a car guy, though I knew he enjoyed taking the occasional road trip. He was looking forward to the adventure of a few days driving through France in a Ferrari and seemed happy to go along with whatever itinerary I put in front of him.

"We must do the Route Napoleon," I told him when we were discussing which way to go, though the blank look on his face showed me that I might have to sell the idea a little. "It's supposed to be an epic driving road. You'll love it!"

There was no reason for Jelley to have heard of it. The N85, to give it its official name, runs from Golfe-Juan on the Riviera, to Grenoble at the foot of the French Alps. It is the route that Napoleon took in 1815 on his return from exile on Elba, a route that was chosen to avoid unnecessary run-ins with those loyal to Louis XVIII and to give him the best opportunity to return to Paris and regain his position as Emperor. I must confess that it was not through knowledge of European history that I was aware of this road; rather it was the numerous references to it in *evo* magazine. I had read so many exciting stories in which the magazine's journalists brought together the world's best performance cars and pitted them against each other along this stretch of tarmac. These were the kinds of articles that had brought me to this point on my own personal journey and I was adamant that the N85 would form part of our journey north, even if I had no idea what Grenoble would be like at the other end.

We set off mid-morning and made our way patiently along the tight, winding road that runs from Vence to Grasse, the Ferrari ever the centre of attention as we passed through sleepy towns and villages. Typically, both Jelley and I had fallen victim to mild food poisoning from our dinner the night before. The car had been filled with antacid tablets, water and toilet roll, the latter hopefully just for peace of mind. I was at the wheel for the first section and Jelley had decided that we would use the map rather than sat nav, at least until we needed to find our hotel within the cities in which we planned to stay. At these points we felt sure the map's lack of detail would let us down, potentially compounded by our questionable navigation skills. It wasn't long before we approached Grasse and the first real challenge to Jelley's map reading abilities.

"Do we need to turn right at this round-about?" I enquired, very aware that we had very little time to decide, particularly with all the traffic that had appeared with the proximity to the town ahead.

"Wait a moment," replied Jelley. He started flicking through pages and tried to discover where we were.

"Too late. I'm taking the turning." I swung the wheel and we jinked sharp right and uphill. I knew that we needed to head inland at some point so this seemed as good a time as any.

"Yes," said Jelley a moment later.

"Yes what?"

"Yes. We do need to take the turning."

"That's a relief," I replied, with slightly more sarcasm than I had intended. "Are there any other turns coming up that we need to be aware of?"

It turned out that there weren't. Instead we were immediately thrown onto the kind of road that I had been hoping for. After a few tight corners the road unfurled in front of us, dragging us toward the hills that seemed to be propping up the clear blue sky above. For some time we pressed on and I once again enjoyed pushing the car hard and hearing the sound of the engine bouncing off the rocks that lined the side of the road. Each time the car turned through another hairpin the view over the Cote d'Azur would open up, the deep blue of the sea melting into that of the sky on the horizon.

I was really enjoying being back on the road again, soaking up the first couple of miles of a road I had wanted to drive for years, in a Ferrari of all things. I wasn't pushing too hard but was still surprised to look in the rear-view mirror and see a Fiat 500 Abarth right on my tail. Anyone who has ever driven in southern Europe will be used to the spectre of the small car driver that seems intent on embarrassing you. It's never clear whether they know the road intimately or that you're driving too slowly. Either way, it never fails to push you to drive that bit harder, particularly when you're in the much more powerful car.

It's always easier to follow than to lead and I was getting a little frustrated at the little Fiat making up ground on the twistier sections of the road, even if I managed to eke out a little distance on the straights. I just didn't know what the corners would be doing ahead and had no chance of getting any rhythm going. Inevitably I soon found myself taking a corner quicker than was comfortable, flinching slightly as it continued to turn almost back on itself. As I braked on the lead-in to the corner I had a brief moment to admire the unconvincing barriers standing in the way of the cliff edge that lined the apex of the corner. Even in the heat of the moment I found myself reflecting on the moment when the brakes locked up when Spencer and I were in the Alps. I held the wheel steady and pushed the throttle gently, enough to maintain our momentum without unsettling the rear of the car or causing us to lose the inside line and be forced to shift over to the other side of the road. We made it around without problem but I still felt like a fool for having pushed harder than was really necessary on an unsighted bend on a public road. I had made it clear to Jelley that he should only drive within his comfort zone and I should have been heeding my own advice. The last thing I wanted to do was give him the impression that it was ok to drive like a maniac. Besides, I wasn't even sure how competent a driver he was yet having only spent ten minutes with him behind the wheel the day before and me being a notoriously edgy passenger. We pulled over into a lay-by to change over. The little Fiat, now a little way behind, had a chance at enjoying the open road without opposition.

It was Jelley's first real drive in the Ferrari and, local Fiat drivers aside, it was the perfect place to get a feel for it. The roads were long, wide, well-surfaced and lightly-trafficked. Visibility was generally good, even on the sections which were made up of back-to-back turns.

Jelley had lost my second pair of sunglasses in St Tropez so I was forced to part with the ones I had been wearing while he drove. Thankfully the sun was almost directly overhead meaning that squinting was rarely required. Soon the views began to change once again as we pressed onwards into the hills and away from the coast. Sporadic patches of blue would light up the landscape as the sun glinted off lakes and reservoirs. Jelley proved to be an excellent driver and was soon revelling in the experience. We weren't the only ones enjoying this stretch of tarmac either. An old Porsche 911 sat on the side of the road parked up behind a vintage car of some sort, the drivers milling around chatting, presumably comparing notes on the experience of the Route Napoleon up until that point. They must have heard us coming and waved furiously as we passed by, me leaning out of the window and waving back. The camaraderie of car enthusiasts is something I had now come to love and will never tire of.

We soon pulled over to fill up on petrol and then Jelley had one of the best drives of the entire trip; a period of unimpeded progress that led us upwards into the hills and down fast flowing valley roads. I sat back and played the role of DJ, attempting to pick out appropriate tracks from the thousands on my iPod while soaking up the amazing views. There were times when the rock-faces protruded out over the road and lorries were forced to halt progress as they edged out against oncoming traffic to take a corner unscathed. At other times the road ploughed straight through the rock, cave-like holes barely big enough for one car slowing the pace of the traffic. We passed a number of caravans going the other direction and how they fitted through these gaps in the rock I will never know. On one particularly challenging section we found ourselves behind a local recovery van, the driver obviously knowing the road intimately. For half an hour we followed him closely before the road straightened in front of us and we passed him, blasting off towards the horizon once again.

The day continued like this, with Jelley and I switching positions and taking turns at the wheel to make the most of this epic road. We would get held up here and there, find ourselves taking the wrong turn in a town, or get caught behind a lorry on one of the steep sections of road. But it didn't matter. The sun never stopped shining and even a very average sandwich for lunch couldn't dampen our appetite for progressing deeper into the ever more Alpine scenery which lay on the other side of the windscreen. Of course it had to come to an end sooner or later and we found ourselves rolling into Grenoble in late afternoon, some six hours since we had left the coast, the sat nav once again hooked up and directing us to the hotel that I had booked online some time in advance of this trip. The criteria hadn't changed – secure parking, relatively central location and good price – and this meant that we found ourselves checking in to an anonymous hotel in a section of town that left me questioning whether it had been a good idea to come to Grenoble for the night.

As we turned down a side street – only minutes from our hotel if the sat nav was to be believed – I heard some shouting from behind the car. Looking in the mirrors I saw two scooters that were carrying three people between them and closing in on us quickly. They looked pretty incited by something and the shouting continued. I ran through the past five minutes in my mind and tried to work out whether it was possible that I had cut someone up at a junction or run over an old lady's toes as she waited to cross the road. It was possible that these young guys were just protecting their neighbourhood from brash Brits flaunting their ostentatious supercars. Finally, as one of the scooters pulled alongside and began to make some vague hand gestures to accompany the shouting, it dawned on us that they just wanted to see and hear the F355 at full acceleration in much the same way as people had in Italy. In a moment of uncertainty I had perceived the encouraging calls of a group of petrolheads for the aggressive calls of irate locals. I quickly tried to make amends and gave the throttle pedal a prod, causing us to lurch forwards suddenly. The only problem was that the street seemed to be infested with speed bumps so there was little chance of building any momentum and giving our new friends the show they wanted. Still, it was a sudden reminder of how cars like the F355 really are a rare sight and seeing one had clearly been a great pleasure for this band of Ferrari fans.

Car parked, coffees drunk and showers taken, we chatted with the concierge about our options for the evening ahead. Like many of these hotels after a certain time of day, it appeared to be a bit of a one-man-against-the-world situation; the concierge trebling up as check-in attendant and barman. He can add 'tour guide' to his list of responsibilities because he soon had us in a cab and heading toward the old town of Grenoble and then deposited next to a large decorative fountain and plenty of bars. We jumped out of the taxi and skipped over the tram tracks in the direction of the nearest bar for some beers, as is the English way. As our drinks were set down in front of us, Jelley began chatting to our waiter.

Sometime after finishing university Jelley took himself off to France with the intention of learning French. Rather than going to classes, he decided to take a job working in the kitchen of a restaurant, giving himself no option but to learn the language fast. It was something that I really respect him for doing.

"What was all that about?" I asked him after he had finished speaking with the young waiter. My French is nowhere near as good as Jelley's and the conversation completely passed me by.

"He says that I'm allowed to smoke but it is forbidden for him to provide an ashtray." We put this down to the intricacies of French smoking laws, it being the one and only time this happened in the course of the trip.

Ashtrays aside, Cafe le Centenaire was a typically French street cafe. The seats and tables fanned outwards onto the cobbled Place Notre Dame and allowed us to engage in a little people watching as we reflected on the drive we had just experienced. It really was one of the best roads I had ever driven and it exceeded my expectations. Somewhat depressingly, it would be all downhill from here. We would be able to find a few nice country roads but it would more or less be motorways. I had already driven all the roads that I had wanted to in this part of Europe and had failed to find anything of interest to fit in with our itinerary from here on in. On the positive side, I had two more days of driving through France with a good friend and I was sure there would be plenty of laughs alongside the opportunity of seeing some new places, even if we would have minimal time to really explore any of the towns. After all, the pleasures of driving relate as much to feelings of freedom and adventure as they do to attacking a great road in a fast car.

Grenoble was a complete unknown to us both. As we wandered around the pedestrianised streets and stopped in for another drink at what appeared to be a Communist-themed bar, it became clear that there were a lot of young people around. As the evening progressed we could only assume that it was the first night of the new semester and the city's university and college students were out in force. It was nice. There was a buzz to the town but it was never hectic. It seemed as though these French students were slightly more laidback than their British counterparts, the focus seemingly on conversation and relaxed drinking as opposed to drunken mayhem, noise and debauchery. I guess there's a time and place for both approaches but on this occasion Jelley and I were happy with what we found.

Despite having pre-booked all the hotels I hadn't planned any restaurants. At each stop we were reliant upon the good taste of our hotel staff or simply upon seeing what caught our eye. On this occasion we were fending for ourselves and Restaurant la Ferme a Dédé on Rue Barnave seemed much more tempting than the numerous Indian, Mexican and steak restaurants we had seen. Being at the foot of the Alps it seemed appropriate to order a fondue, Jelley ordering a platter of cured meats and salad to keep our wine company while we waited. The waitress was clearly having a hard time stopping herself from laughing at the look of dismay on Jelley's face when she set down a second platter of cured meats and salad which came as a standard accompaniment to the fondue. A heads-up at the ordering stage would have been preferred to amusement later but thankfully it was a good fondue. They also offered a great little tasting option for dessert which included espresso, chocolate fondant, a profiterole and some other little bits. Feeling satisfied, we had a couple of drinks among the students in another historic square and then retreated to the hotel for the night.

In the hotel that night I lay awake, thinking about my experiences of the year so far. In particular I questioned whether I could have done more, made a greater effort to engage with the world of motoring. The answer was probably "yes". In fact the more that I experienced, the more that I wanted to experience. I wanted to do more road trips, buy more cars and drive on track again. I was also still desperate for adventure on the road and thought about my long-held dream of driving Route 66, something I was close to arranging on more than one occasion in the course of the year but had somehow talked myself out of.

The problem was that really embracing a passion for cars is both expensive and time-consuming. I think that's why some of the most committed car enthusiasts I met were those whose careers were built around their love for cars, as well as those that were trying to open doors for themselves through blogging or providing services based upon their knowledge and passion. And what of those motoring journalists that had played such a role in inspiring my own adventures? Being a motoring journalist might never allow you to become a millionaire but it can provide an opportunity to engage with cars on a day-to-day basis, take part in epic trips and road tests, and be invited to take part in events that would be prohibitively expensive for most people to even consider. In that sense it can be seen as an experiential profession built around a passion and it is for that reason that it is such a desirable path for many petrolheads. It is much the same if you do public relations work for a leading tyre manufacturer or motorsport organisation, or organise budget car rallies, or run a supercar club. There are numerous interpretations of people trying to make their passions work for them, much as Gildo Pastor implied was a necessity. For these people cars are not simply an interest but are a central focus within their lives.

It occurred to me that my friends and family would probably now regard me in similar terms and for some strange reason that meant something to me. The question remained as to whether it would prove important enough for me to try to make a living out of the passion or whether I would fall back to the position of more passive hobbyist. All I knew at that point, lying in a hotel in Grenoble, was that I wasn't satisfied yet.

Nudity and Confessions in Champagne Country

Grenoble-Dijon-Reims-Calais-London

The air felt much cooler the next morning as a result of our position at the edge of the Alps but the sun was immediately warming on the skin whenever you stepped into its rays. It looked like we would have another great day of weather for the drive to Dijon.

Once out of Grenoble we turned to the roadmap once again, me starting out as navigator and Jelley at the wheel. I'd read somewhere that it was best to avoid Lyon due to traffic and so we planned to head cross country towards Bourg-en-Brasse to start with and only jump on the motorway if the back roads were taking too long.

The scenery was less dramatic now as we moved away from the mountains, settling quickly into rolling, green agricultural land. The road flowed and writhed around the landscape, cutting through pretty towns and then opening up again. Jelley was having a great time. He was now very comfortable with the car and found himself driving roads that allowed for smooth, high speed progress. I leant back and watched indistinct towns pass by, checking the map sporadically to ensure we were going the right way. One of the larger towns must have been preparing for a local festival as metallic-looking bunting hung across the main road for at least a mile, zig-zagging from roof to roof and glittering in the bright sunshine. With the window down you could even hear it rustling as the wind caught it, the sound like a thousand sheets of aluminium foil in hushed conversation.

As pleasant as it was, the drive through the countryside was slowing us down. As I took the wheel I elected to head west and join the motorway at Macon meaning we could head north past Chalon-sur-Saône and directly into Dijon. By now the sun had done its work and the air temperature had risen significantly. Coming into any traffic meant that the car was not receiving the fresh air that filters through the side vents to cool the throbbing engine behind us. In turn the dials would react, the engine temperature shown to be rising almost immediately. On the motorway there was no such problem and the engine temperature would drop just as quickly, after a little while the oil temperature dropping slightly too. The F355 thrived in these high speed cruising scenarios, making relentless progress with zero fuss and being far more refined than you might imagine.

After a quick sandwich at a roadside service area we pressed onwards for the final section of motorway so that we could get into Dijon and enjoy what was left of the afternoon sunshine. The outskirts of the city centre seemed to be clogged up with road works. No matter where we went during the home leg of the journey there appeared to be works and renovations taking place. So we crawled along in the dense traffic, the sat nav once again dusted off to help guide us to the hotel. I took a look at the temperature gauge again and saw that the car was not happy, the engine temperature having rocketed. We had gone from a high speed run to being almost stationary, no cool air flowing into the engine and the air temperature in the high 20s. I told Jelley but there was little that either of us could do. We weren't far from the hotel and I reasoned that we would be better stopping for the day rather than stopping and starting in an effort to let temperatures drop. Besides, it wasn't only the car that was overheating. Jelley and I had turned off the air conditioning in an effort to alleviate the energy requirements on the car and we just wanted to get to the hotel to relax.

As we got closer to Place Darcy and the hotel where we would be spending the night, things got worse. The needle was now dangerously close to the red line that sits at the upper reaches of the engine temperature gauge. I may not have had the manual handy but I was pretty sure that wasn't good. We crawled over the broken surfaces of Place Darcy which seemed to be the centre point for the city's roadworks. Neither of us could spot the hotel and the entrance to the public underground car park looked far too steep. The last thing that I wanted was to be reversing out of the entrance ramp and into traffic so we settled for 'pay and display' parking a little further on. I turned off the engine as soon as I could, assuming that this was the best thing to do. As I stepped out of the car I heard the unmistakable sound of liquid gushing out of a small hole at high pressure. Peeking under the car I could see steaming hot liquid trickling out from beneath the engine. As it flowed out from under the car the green tinge of the coolant fluid became obvious. It was a sickening moment. Ever since I had bought the car I had been more on edge than I would have liked, always half expecting something to go wrong. I had read that Ferraris were much more reliable these days but I was also ingrained with the view that 90s Italian supercars were trouble.

The fact is, most cars are trouble at some point; some are just more expensive to deal with. If the radiator needed replacing... well, the cost simply didn't bear thinking about.

Jelley directed us to the nearest hotel and we planted ourselves in their garden with coffees and sparkling water while I made some phone calls. I'm not much of a smoker but I'm sure it came as no surprise to Jelley when I leant over and helped myself to one of his cigarettes in an attempt to calm down. I was a bit upset and mildly shell-shocked at the potential implications of what had just happened but I pressed on with making the required phone calls, occasionally apologising to Jelley for having to ignore him. I spoke to Ferrari's *With You* roadside assistance scheme which would, theoretically, transport my car to the nearest authorised repairer. It turned out that it was managed by a local breakdown organisation in each country and I had the pleasure of speaking to a guy back in the UK who had never heard of the scheme before. Eventually he discovered some details of the programme on his corporate intranet system but then couldn't find any record of my having signed up for it. I got frustrated and decided to try the AA with whom I had European breakdown cover and who seemed much more helpful. Finally, I tried to speak to someone at Foskers, where I had bought my car, to see if they could ascertain the seriousness of the issue if I explained what had happened.

Jeff Fosker himself called back some ten minutes later and, based upon my overview of events, felt that it was possible the car had simply expelled the hot fluid rather than anything having burst. I was to let it cool down properly, get some water to replace the coolant and then call him back and he would talk me through what to do. If all went to plan we would be able to drive the car back home ourselves rather than putting it on the back of a lorry. Things were looking up.

In the meantime Jelley and I had a chance to collect our bags from the wounded Ferrari and check into our own hotel, which Jelley had located while I was on the phone. It was another average hotel but perfectly pleasant, well-priced and in a great location. A trip to the shops, two phone calls, five litres of water, some fiddling with the air conditioning and we were back on the move again. It transpired that keeping the air conditioning system on might help to fan the engine if one of the sensors had failed, as it had appeared had happened. So our decision to switch it off earlier had done no good whatsoever. When everything seemed ok, Jeff advised us to go for a short drive to see if it would run without overheating.

"Avoid any traffic," he insisted. "And if it starts overheating pull over immediately, wherever you are."

Typically we found ourselves rolling forwards into rush hour traffic. I rolled along slowly, watching the temperature gauge like a hawk and giving Jelley a running commentary on any slight fluctuations. Thankfully it showed no sign of overheating despite a 45 minute drive in traffic. Very much relieved, I parked and we went and freshened up before heading out for a well-earned drink and some dinner.

Of all the towns that we visited on this homeward journey through France, Dijon came as the biggest surprise to me. I had envisaged a faceless town made up of cheap hotels and industry. Instead we discovered the picturesque old town with its cathedrals and pedestrianised streets. Here the buildings seemed to lean in above us and shops cast their light onto dark streets like something out of a Dickensian fantasy. We walked around for a while, the only other interest in this historic part of town coming from a handful of tourists, the locals sticking to the more modern streets and shops a few moments away.

We found ourselves on Rue Quentin, a street lined with restaurants that overlooked what looked to be a fruit market, long since closed for the day. You could walk right around the market and take your pick of the dining options on offer, though none really jumped out at us. We selected one anyway though it dawned on me we might have chosen poorly when Jelley was handed a squeezy bottle of Carrefour Dijon mustard as opposed to a local brand like Maille, this one presumably bought at the supermarket 15 metres behind the restaurant. To be fair, it was probably a sign that we were both tired if we were getting upset about such things and so soon made our way back to the hotel for an early night. Besides, I had a feeling the following night might be a heavy one.

The journey north to Reims the next day was uneventful and far from memorable. This was probably a good thing with regard to the car but it more or less signalled the end of any real driving on this European road trip. Instead it would be motorway driving from here to London and the only excitement came from knowing that our night in Reims, the final stop of the journey, would be very good fun. The main reason for this was that my friend Tom – whose parents I had stayed with in Yorkshire on the way to meeting Lord Mexborough – had decided to head out from London on his motorbike, just for one night, just to party with us. That pretty much sums Tom up and I was looking forward to seeing him. Not that Jelley and I were sick of each other; it was only our third day on the road after all. In fact this was the longest time we had ever spent together and we were getting along famously, partly due to a shared love of quality music – both of us had presented specialist music radio shows at university – and silly banter. Jelley was quickly becoming a massive fan of the F355 as well, something else we had in common.

Arriving in Reims, confused by the one-way streets, we ended up doing a few circuits of the area in which our hotel was to be found and caught a glimpse of the hugely impressive cathedral. This massive building, parts of which are 800 years-old, sat at the bottom of Rue Libergier like an ancient creature holding court over the entire town. By contrast, Campanile Reims Centre – our hotel for the night – was anything but grand. Thankfully it was well-placed near the main roads and just a stone's throw from the bars and restaurants of the town centre.

Inside everything was in disarray. Unsurprisingly, as far as Jelley and I were concerned, they were undertaking renovations and contrary to the reassurance of the very friendly receptionist our rooms were clearly not ready yet. Maids were milling around and reacted with a degree of confusion at our presence. Jelley even discovered someone else's stuff in his room. We elected to hold onto our bags for the time being and went downstairs for a beer to wait for Tom. Before long the three of us were heading off in search of somewhere to enjoy the late afternoon sun and catch up.

The rest of the night is a bit of a blur, the tipping point probably being the bottle of Pol Roger we ordered in recognition of being in the Champagne region just before we were due to go for dinner. Despite being in good spirits by the time we reached the restaurant, La Vigneraie on Rue Thillois was a disappointment to us all as it seemed to be completely devoid of atmosphere, somehow sucking the energy out of our own conversation. It had been strongly recommended to us at the hotel and the food was actually ok. It just happened to be the least fun meal I've had in recent memory, something which had nothing to do with the company. We paid up and moved on to Place Drouet d'Erlon, a predominantly pedestrian street lined with bars and restaurants that we had discovered earlier in the day.

True to form, Tom immediately decided that it was time to raise the bar and a shot of Jaegermeister and a very strong beer were soon thrust at me. Like Grenoble, Reims seemed to be a popular student town and there were plenty of young people sipping beers, smoking cigarettes and chatting throughout the rows of tables outside each bar. Jelley and Tom struck up a conversation with a nearby group of students, one of whom was very excited to be showing off her English skills. I made the mistake of trying to chat to some of the others and was soon caught up in a strange conversation with a slightly edgy-looking guy.

"Where are you from?" he asked.

"London."

"Do you support a football team?"

"Yes. Chelsea," I replied.

He nodded knowingly before asking, in a manner

that implied he recognised a kindred spirit, "Are you a football hooligan?"

"No!"

"I am," he asserted smugly before showing me that he was wearing Lonsdale boxer shorts, clearly a signifier of hooligan status in Reims.

Slightly lost for words I simply nodded sagely and started to move away. It was time for us to move on.

The next bar was far more popular but still the same student clientele. I made some excuses about needing to get a decent night's sleep before the drive to Calais the following morning and the subsequent journey into London. As I suspected, this didn't go down well with the others and my attempts at leaving somehow landed me in a karaoke bar singing along to Dire Straights until the owners ran out of tequila and asked us to leave. My last memory is of Tom stripping off and streaking through the deserted streets. It is a memory that disturbs me to this day.

I managed to react to one of my alarms and dragged myself out of bed the next morning but it was tough. I went to Tom's room and woke him up, him making confident assertions that he would be ready soon. I went to Jelley's room and knocked, discovering the door was actually open already. He had somehow neglected to close the door properly before he went to bed.

"Morning mate," I ventured. "Can I come in?"

"Urrghh..." I took that to mean "yes" and edged in, astounded at the amount of mess he had managed to make in less than 24 hours.

"Dude, it's time to get up. We need to leave in 45 minutes."

"Ok."

I could see this wasn't going to be much of a conversation.

"It's insanely messy in here," I said, looking around in a bit more detail before spotting a used condom wrapper by the spare pillow on Jelley's bed.

Naturally I jumped to some conclusions based upon the fact that I knew he had returned to the hotel alone but there is no obvious social etiquette to deal with such a situation.

"I like your style," I said coolly, pointing at the subject matter.

Jelley's eyes hovered for a moment as they began to focus and he realised what it was.

"That's not mine!"

"No judgement mate."

"Seriously, that's not mine!"

The shock and disgust painted on his still-drunk face told it to be true and it transpired that there were still some other belongings of the previous guests of this room left there as well. Clearly the cleaners hadn't bothered to do more than make the bed, failing to remove evidence of whatever had gone on the previous night. Jelley was right to be disgusted, although this would probably be amplified in his vulnerable hungover state. Even so, he didn't get out of bed and I had to wake him and Tom up twice more each before we left.

We loaded up the car and Tom's bike under blue skies and sunshine. I really didn't envy Tom. At least Jelley and I had a stereo and conversation to carry us through our hangovers along the boring motorway to Calais. For Tom it would be periods of intense focus between frequently required stops.

Almost immediately the Ferrari became the centre of attention once more as we were pulled over at the first *péage* leaving Reims. Thankfully it appeared to be customs officials rather than the *gendarme*. Tom wasn't stopped but pulled himself into the fray as a show of solidarity and, presumably, as something to break the monotony. The usual questions ensued. Whose car is this? Where have you been? Where are you going? We explained through the window what we were up to but the officer obviously hadn't finished.

"Tell me," he began, as casually as he could manage, "do you have more than €10,000 on you?"

"Um, no." I managed to stop myself from smiling at the idea. "I'm not sure we even have €10 on us."

At which point I was requested to get out of the car and to open the boot. I knew we had nothing to hide but I was fairly sure we smelt as though we had just fallen out of a nightclub.

"Perhaps you have something special on you?" We both shook our heads. "Maybe some drugs?" More head shaking. "Have you ever taken drugs?"

"No," I replied sternly. The truth didn't really seem relevant at this point in time.

"Well..." came a voice from inside the car. "I did try marijuana at university once."

My mouth must have visibly dropped open at Jelley's eagerness to confess his past sins to the customs officer without any need whatsoever. Thankfully the officer made a face to imply he thought Jelley an idiot and we were sent on our way.

For the last time on this dream European road trip we ploughed on along the fast lane of the motorway, quickly closing in on Calais, the train under the Channel and London. French drivers would politely pull over when they saw us approaching behind them but the increasing number of British drivers seemed eager to sit at low speeds in the overtaking lane; a taste of what we would be returning to. We waved at another Ferrari driver, lost Tom briefly as he was forced to slow down to conserve fuel, and revved the engine for a kid that had been inspecting the car with interest at a service station. Now we just wanted to get home, park the car and relax for a while. In truth, I would have turned around and gone south again if I could but we were soon driving through the familiar streets of London and the trip was truly over.

Going Green

Driving the Tesla Roadster

I didn't find myself as emotionally flat on my return to London as I had after the first leg of my European adventure. I had enjoyed some great experiences over the preceding four or five months and felt some satisfaction in having finally embraced the petrolhead within. Unexpectedly, I had also found great pleasure in engaging with other car enthusiasts, from high profile people like Gildo Pastor and Charles Morgan to those I had met at the Autotweetup event and classic car rally. But I hadn't yet experienced any of the new technologies that I had been reading so much about.

An invitation to drive the latest version of the Tesla Roadster would change that, providing me with a chance to get behind the wheel of an electric car for the first time. If technological developments such as the shift to electric-power had the potential to change motoring forever, I wanted to get a feel for how corrupted the traditional driving experience might become.

Over the past couple of years electric and hybrid cars seem to have moved further into the mainstream but it doesn't seem as though many of us are actually buying them. In 2011 almost 2 million new cars were registered in the UK but only 1,082 of those were electric. Part of the problem is that people are put off by the limited range of electric vehicles, even if many of us only occasionally take journeys of a hundred miles or more. The other issue is that manufacturers have been focusing their attention on developing more efficient petrol and diesel engines and moving into hybrid technology rather than developing compelling electric alternatives. There are a handful of electric cars available for the environmentally-aware consumer but nothing that is designed to appeal to someone looking for an exciting and dynamically accomplished electric car.

That's likely to change with all-electric cars like the Tesla Model S saloon. It is a competitively-priced, technology-laden luxury car with good looks and strong performance credentials. The fact that it is a purely electric car means that the batteries – the heaviest components – can be built into the chassis. This results in an incredibly low centre of gravity and superb weight distribution. Electric motors can also be designed to be small enough to fit between the driven wheels meaning that there is no loss of power. It is exactly the kind of electric car that many motoring enthusiasts have been waiting for and is set to transform perceptions towards zero emissions motoring.

Tesla has been undoing stereotypes since it launched the Roadster in 2008. It was this two-seater sports car that demonstrated that electric vehicles needn't be frumpy and boring. For the first time there was an electric car that was fast and exciting; an electric car designed to appeal to the performance-minded motoring enthusiast. People were drawn to its looks and its straight-line performance and were also encouraged by Lotus' involvement in developing the chassis. Only around 6% of its components are actually shared with the

Lotus Elise but potential customers approved of the tie-in with one of the most revered sports cars of recent times.

Visiting the company's modest UK headquarters just outside of London, I learnt that the Roadster has actually been little more than a marketing exercise for Tesla, a way of showing what the technology is capable of. Of the 2,500 Roadsters produced, almost all had found homes by the time of my visit. By contrast, Tesla is expecting to build between 20,000 and 40,000 units of the new Model S saloon each year. This is the first step to making the technology more accessible, with prices starting around 40% less than the Roadster.

It won't stop with the Model S. The company plans to build on the new platform over the coming years with SUV and GT derivatives a strong possibility. More certain are plans for the Generation 3 - or 'Bluestar' - a car that will rival the BMW 3-series and Audi A4 and bring Tesla further into the mainstream. Apparently there are no plans for the company to develop a city car, though strategic partnerships are already in place for Tesla technology to be used by the likes of Toyota and Daimler. This ensures that Tesla's influence goes beyond its own models.

I was impressed to hear about Tesla's ambitious plans for the future but it was the Roadster that I was really interested in. At a cost of £85,000, was it really good enough to entice drivers away from their Porsches and Aston Martins? Reviews in magazines had been positive and the performance figures were certainly impressive but I still had my doubts.

As strange as it is to have a sports car approaching you in complete silence, my first impressions of the Tesla

Roadster were overwhelmingly positive, even if the Lightening Green paint wouldn't have been my first choice. You don't see many of them around and that rarity value will appeal to some buyers. It is a striking car and very much its own design. Once you've squeezed yourself between the roof and the large door sill and down into the sculpted, leather-trimmed seats, you find yourself in a smart and functional cabin. It's exactly the kind of thing you would expect in any modern sports car but look closer and you'll spot some differences. Where you would normally see a gearstick there are simply four buttons – P, R, N and D. Simply turn the key, put your foot on the brake, press the D button and you're ready to go.

It's hard to know what to expect as you lift your foot off the brake but the car creeps forwards slowly and without drama, much as it would if you were driving any modern automatic. Give the throttle pedal a prod and things get interesting. The electric engine gives you instant power, meaning that you have all 295lbs/ft of torque and 288 horsepower available from standstill. In this Roadster 2.5 Sport, the latest version of the car, that equates to 0-60mph in 3.7 seconds and a top speed of around 120mph. It certainly feels that fast. Whenever you find a bit of space the car lurches forwards and continues to accelerate until you run out of road. It is a different sensation from driving a manual sports car, in which there is a pause every time you change gear, but it is quite similar to some of today's dual-clutch supercars which also manage to build speed relentlessly.

It is not completely silent from the driver's seat even if it appears to be from the outside. There is a little road and wind noise once you get moving but most prominent is the jet-like whirring sound that comes from the engine behind you. It is particularly evident when you are travelling at speed. It might not be as intoxicating as the sound of a V8 or V12 petrol engine but there is a certain appeal once you come to associate it with the significant performance of the car, particularly if you are impressed with its zero emissions credentials.

Lack of engine noise and eerily effortless acceleration aside, the Roadster handles as a sports car should do; it changes direction sharply and feels taut and responsive. It also feels remarkably analogue. Its unassisted steering is heavy at low speeds and requires a little bit of muscle when on the move but it is sharp and positive and certainly adds to this Tesla's credentials as a drivers' car. Body control is also impressive. The car feels incredibly stiff yet pulls off the trick of not being too firm over the bumps and broken surfaces that characterise the average British road, even if it doesn't feel quite as pliant as something like a Lotus Evora. It's a car that inspires confidence from the outset and allows you to throw it into corners knowing that it won't bite. The regenerative braking system means that the car slows as soon as you lift your foot of the throttle pedal, forcing you to recalibrate required braking distances. This is one thing that might take a little getting used to.

The Tesla Roadster is a remarkable car and an intriguing ownership proposition, particularly when you consider how efficient it is from a wear-and-tear perspective. I'm told that many owners use their cars for their daily commute and little else, but the Roadster is clearly much more at home on the open road. The claimed 211 miles per charge seems more than sufficient for most journeys and the growing network of HPC (High Power Wall Connector) outlets across the UK and Europe means that a well-planned road trip isn't out of the question.

These vehicles are hugely efficient in maintenance as well as energy terms. An electric motor can go for up to 800,000 miles without needing any attention, there is no clutch to replace, and regenerative braking means that the brakes last three to four times longer than in a petrol or diesel-powered car. One German owner has apparently clocked up 130,000kms in the course of just one year of ownership. With a fixed-price service of £500 per year - which Tesla will do on your driveway – the Roadster begins to look good value for a rare, high-tech, carbon fibre car that can hit 60mph in under four seconds. It also comes with the associated perks of being a zero emissions vehicle, such as being exempt from car tax in the UK.

I would never have imagined that an electric car could be as fun and desirable as a 90s Ferrari but the Roadster was just that. Perhaps the biggest compliment I can pay Tesla is that I would have happily taken that bright green car home to join my ageing Italian supercar. I loved the idea of having the ultimate motoring gadget. Many others will come to feel that desire as soon as more electric cars offer proper driving thrills, particularly in those parts of the world where consumers rush to have the latest technology.

There might be a number of threats to the simple pleasures of driving but perhaps emissions-orientated legislation isn't something to worry us petrolheads after all.

Epilogue

"The truthful travel book rarely works to a climax;
the climax is the point of disembarkation and everything beyond it an attempt to revive artificially, under the iron lung of rhythmic, day to day observation,
the revelation of first acquaintance." (Hugh Thomson,
Tequila Oil: Getting Lost in Mexico)

Rita and I arrived at the 7 Hotel Diner in Kent an
hour early and just in time to catch the end of the
Sunday breakfast menu. There had been talk of
snow but thankfully it hadn't arrived. Even so, I was glad
to have recently invested in an outdoor cover for the Ferrari on recommendation of Richard at Foskers. As the
service manager, Richard had become my go-to guy for
any queries about the car and he had seen it a few times
over the months to deal with various bits and pieces. It
was in great condition now but winter had arrived and I
was worried about leaving the car outside overnight in
case the freezing temperatures had a detrimental effect
on anything in the exposed engine bay. Sure enough, the
temperatures had dropped below zero overnight and I
was glad to have bought the cover once I spotted small
sections of frost lining the coarse waterproof material.
Much to my surprise the car started first time and we
were soon at the American-style roadside diner, Steve the
duty manager directing me to park the car right in front

of the building instead of in the car park, an arrangement previously made via Twitter.

It was because of Twitter that we were here at all, Rita having agreed to accompany me to the final Autotweetup event of the year as well as the Foskers Christmas dinner we had attended the previous evening. I hadn't quite known what to expect there but Rita wasn't phased, once again showing me that she was more than happy to embrace my interest in cars. It turned out to be good fun, not at all stuffy as I had feared. We were some of the youngest there but it was a great mix of people and everyone was very friendly. There was good food, good conversations and some inappropriate humour, which is always appropriate as far as I'm concerned. I liked the fact that all the Foskers guys were aware of my European road trip, almost all of them asking me what I was planning next during the course of the evening.

The Autotweetup event on the Sunday turned out to be a much mellower affair than the one I had attended earlier in the year, many potential attendees having gone to a much bigger meet-up over at Goodwood, and burgers and milkshakes being chosen over cocktails. It wasn't any less pleasant for it and we happily spent a couple of hours chatting with various car enthusiasts, some of whom I had met at the Covent Garden event. There were some pretty serious petrolheads here. All of them had stories to tell about their work with cars, the rallies that they took part in every year, the online forums that they ran, or the events they had taken part in alongside motorsport legends and in iconic cars. Their stories were based upon years of experience and a deep passion for cars and driving but I now had a few more stories of my own.

We made a bit of a scene when we left, me having to ask three different people – including Tim, the organiser of the event – to move their cars so that we could get out. The Ferrari seemed to go down well with some people and I was more than happy to talk about it. Had it behaved during my trip? Was it standard or had I fitted a custom exhaust? Did I have any more trips planned? These were the things that people wanted to know.

Since I had taken the plunge and bought my first Ferrari I had come to know it quite well, better understanding its intricacies. But as a 15 year-old car with almost 40,000 miles on the clock, I often wondered about its past. Who had owned it? How had they driven it? Was it for posing or for fun? Had the previous owners made the most of this wonderful car in the way that I had?

It was by complete chance, as I was checking out some car reviews online, that I discovered a video clip of Jeremy Clarkson raving about the Ferrari F355. It was from his 1996 video *Unleashed on Cars*, in which he claimed that the F355 was one of the greatest cars ever created. Naturally this meant some enthusiastic driving on a closed track, Clarkson showing off the abilities of the car and its composure at more than 160mph. As I watched him hooning around and talking excitedly, my eyes were drawn to the number plate which looked strangely familiar. I was flabbergasted when I realised that Clarkson was driving my actual car. The world's best-known car enthusiast had not only driven my car, hard, he had also proclaimed it to be the greatest driving machine of all time! I knew that the game had moved on since 1996 and no one would lavish the F355 with such praise anymore but it was still a strangely satisfying discovery, particularly when the car had come to mean so much to me personally. In many ways it had come to symbolise everything positive and exciting in my life, embodying the changes that had come since I left my job in Aberdeen. Sadly, my time as custodian of this wonderful car was coming to a close. I would stay true to my intention to sell it on reaching the first anniversary of ownership.

I definitely wanted to do some more road trips though. This wouldn't be the end of my love affair with cars and driving. I was already discussing various options with Spencer for the year ahead and it looked like another European adventure might be on the cards, even though I had no idea what I would be driving. I had a feeling that the loss of the Ferrari would leave me with a void that would need to be filled by an exciting yet much cheaper car. Running costs for the Ferrari had been a little higher than expected but I had kept it in tip-top condition and that would hopefully make it easier to sell when the time came. Plans for attending another Grand Prix had also started finding their way into pub conversation, my brother-in-law expressing his eagerness to visit one of the European circuits and me more than happy to get involved. If Ned had his way, there would be some more track driving on the cards too. My car-related activities had lessened as the year went on, particularly as my total expenditure had risen and the temperatures had fallen, but I was already looking forward to getting some motoring activities in the diary for the year ahead.

A year earlier, during my last days working in Aberdeen, I was filled with excitement at what lay ahead. In many ways that excitement was completely justified. It had been a year filled with highlights for me, both on the road and in my personal life. I had some incredible experiences and had met a variety of car enthusiasts along the way. The truth was that I had become one of them and I didn't know where this passion for cars and driving might take me next.

Despite my fears around the future of motoring it didn't appear as though dramatic change was just around the corner. The people that I had met gave me hope for a rich future of driving enjoyment. With one of my brothers just starting to take driving lessons, I saw that as a good thing. As long as there are car enthusiasts pushing their passions and sharing their interests, and as long as there are car designers and engineers that are sympathetic to the demand for vehicles that put the driver at the heart of the action, things will be fine. Perhaps I didn't have to rush to embark on my dream road trip in an old fashioned, petrol-burning supercar after all. But I'm glad I did. It's all too easy to put your interests to the side and tell yourself that you'll return to them another day, just as I had with my interest in cars until this point. Often you need to take the initiative to make things happen for yourself, as many of the most committed car enthusiasts I met on my travels had done. It was people such as these and the many petrolheads that I connected with on Twitter that showed me just how diverse the wide world of car culture is. In truth, I hadn't even scratched the surface.

Back in London Rita stood back and watched as I used the jet wash to blast off grit and grime picked up driving the Ferrari to Kent and back on winter roads. I knew it would be professionally cleaned two days later but I couldn't bring myself to leave it as it was. Rita and I both glanced back at the gleaming red car before we walked up the ramp and out of the car park.

Rita had been remarkably supportive over the course of the year, not once questioning my slightly obsessive motoring pursuits. I was expecting her to be less understanding, at least until I got to know her better and realised that she would support me no matter what.

"Would you like to do a trip somewhere in the spring?" I asked her as we emerged into the darkness, the sun seemingly having set in record time.

"I'd love to!"

"What about a track day? We can take the Clio."

"Sure," she replied nonchalantly, pausing a moment before looking at me with a serious expression on her face. "When are you getting me insured on the Ferrari?"

I knew that I would meet a diverse range of car enthusiasts during the course of the year but I would never have imagined that my girlfriend would start to develop a passion for cars as well. I think I might have found a new co-driver for my next adventure, perhaps Route 66 or another attempt at the Stelvio Pass.

References

Frankel, Andrew. "The Best Aston Martin for 40 Years (Motor Sport, June 23 1999)." Clark, R. M.

Aston Martin: Ultimate Portfolio. Brooklands Books, 2006.

Marsh, Peter and Collett, Peter. *Driving Passion: the psychology of the car*. Jonathan Cape, 1986.

Sach, Wolfgang. *For the love of the automobile*. University of California Press, 1992.

Thomson, Hugh. *Tequila Oil: Getting Lost in Mexico*. London: Weidenfield & Nicholson, 2009.

Lightning Source UK Ltd.
Milton Keynes UK
UKOW051819020812

196975UK00001B/5/P

9 780957 272125